Europe 1992
and
The New World
Power Game

EUROPE 1992
AND
THE NEW WORLD
POWER GAME

Michael Silva and
Bertil Sjögren

WILEY

JOHN WILEY & SONS

New York • Chichester • Brisbane • Toronto • Singapore

Library of Congress Cataloging-in-Publication Data

Silva, Michael A., 1951–
Europe 1992 and the new world power game / by Michael Silva and
Bertil Sjögren.
p.   cm.
Includes bibliographical references.
ISBN 0-471-51550-7
1. Europe 1992. 2. European Economic Community. 3. European
Economic Community countries—Economic conditions. 4. United
States—Economic conditions—1945- 5. Japan—Economic
conditions—1945- 6. Economic history—1945- I. Sjögren, Bertil.
II. Title.
HC241.2.S517 1990
337.1'42—dc20   90-33731
CIP

90 91 10 9 8 7 6 5 4 3 2 1

To
Karen and Aina
for their constant support

and
Senator Wallace F. Bennett and Mattey
for their contagious idealism.

PREFACE

There is a beautiful stretch of highway that links Switzerland with bordering Liechtenstein where progress has presented itself in the form of a posted speed limit. With the right car, cooperative weather and a disposition toward daring you can easily make the journey from Vaduz to the Zurich airport in less than two hours at 160 kilometers per hour (roughly 100 mph). At that speed distractions are deadly. Blinking alone consumes 25 feet. Professional baseball players, incredible examples of conditioning and reflex, strike out at pitches thrown slower than the speed travelled by Porsches and BMWs cruising in the left lane. The passing lane on the road to Zurich isn't the place to consult a map.

Business leaders and political policy makers are similarly speeding toward world change. The domino decline of communism in Eastern Europe is not only a statement against suppression but also a lesson in global velocity. It wasn't the directional adjustment that was so stunning, but rather the speed. A corporate or political blink could cost a dedicated leader his future.

We envision our effort in this book as a map to help to navigate in a changing global scene. It is written for those with serious responsibilities but a scarcity of time. Most important, it is directed toward a certain type of decision maker who worries less about specific street signs than about changes in the global neighborhood.

What will it be like in the new neighborhood?

The chairman of Heinz calls it "hand to hand combat." Larry Williams of Caterpillar predicts only the survival of the fittest. IBM dispatched Swiss-born marketing ace and vice-chairman Kap Kassani to deal with the changes, while Jack Welch, General Electric CEO and master strategist, warns that the next ten years will make the experience with our Japanese neighbors seem "like a cakewalk."

These American executives and thousands of their counterparts around the world are gearing up for the revolution of 1992, when Europe, for the first time in history, will begin to flex the full power of its united economic muscle. For Europeans, 1992 has been front page news for the last 36 months. For Americans, however, the European revolution was just beginning to make the headlines when it was suddenly eclipsed by the events in Eastern Europe, highlighted by the crumbling of the Berlin Wall. Once again, 1992 is back page news, placed symbolically next to the obituaries.

However, astute map readers are not fooled. They are careful to differentiate detours from more permanent developments, carefully separating spectacular effects from less known and appreciated causes.

It might appear heresy to brand the events in Eastern Europe as mere detours, especially considering the courage of their nucleus of decision makers. But the fall of communism, when finally put in perspective, is only a lane-change in the drive toward a united Europe.

In 1992, or more realistically January 1, 1993, twelve countries—Belgium, Denmark, France, the Federal Republic of Germany, Greece, Ireland, Italy, Luxembourg, The Netherlands, Portugal, Spain, and the United Kingdom—will unite to achieve one integrated economic market. Their motivation is pure survival.

The countries comprising the European Community, or EC, see themselves as pawns in a rapidly escalating trade war between the United States and Japan. Separately, each nation represents only a statistical blip in global accounting. But united as the EC they become an economic powerhouse that dwarfs Japan and directly challenges the heretofore unchallengeable economic output of the United States. While freedom in Eastern Europe is philosophically pleasing, the EC revolution is raw, real, and immediately affects the international power balance.

There are some who suggest that the detour presented by Eastern Europe may derail the development of the EC. They cite the unification of West and East Germany as the major pothole that will swallow up EC unification efforts. The argument links the participation of the Federal Republic of Germany (West Germany in its current form) directly with the success of the EC. That without German industry, central banking, and the powerful Deutschemark, the other members of the EC will be unable to reach the critical economic mass needed to compete head on with Japan and the United States. The *coup de grace* comes in the form of a pointed question. Does a united West and East Germany need the EC? A quick response is needed, and one is provided below.

From the perspective of the other EC members unification is essential, especially if West Germany fails to participate. Remember, unification is a move of self-defense against the trade prowess of Japan and the United States. A combined Germany would become the world's third ranked trade power and another threat to an already trade battered EC. The failure to unite, in light of West German delay or outright withdrawal from the EC, would insure individual EC members a prominent position on the list of trade impotent nations. Countries that would be important enough to be included in the global trade war, but not powerful enough to influence the outcome.

West German tactical focus is clearly on German unification, but its strategic gaze remains on its role in the EC. Consider two points. First, West Germany is acutely aware of its kingpin role in EC unification. The invitation to exert influence over what will be the single largest import-export economic zone in the world is just too tempting to pass up, particularly with other EC members pleading for West German participation. Second, there exists beyond the issues of German and European unification the lure of Soviet and East European economic development. Against competition from Japan and the United States would West Germany compete more effectively for these new markets alone and isolated, or as part of a pan-European competitive entity? In response, logic leans toward continued support of EC unification.

As a map, this book is less about Europe 1992 than about the Europe of the next century. The difference is significant. Today there is Western Europe, Eastern Europe, and EFTA Europe (Austria, Finland, Iceland, Norway, Sweden, and Switzerland which are not members of the EC). Mikhail Gorbachev is talking about a Europe that includes the Soviet Union; and the Vatican, facing a global cash crunch, sighs longingly about the economics of Catholic Europe. The year 1992 is the beginning, not the end, of a revolution that will reshape the geopolitical borders and the psychological boundaries that surround each country.

What emerges may be more powerful and influential than ever imagined by Jean Monnett and Robert Schuman, who are considered by most Europeans the founding fathers of the unification effort. It is an effort which traces back to 1957 when Monnett and Schuman (and many others) envisioned a united Europe which they translated to paper in the Treaty of Rome. Like the American actions in 1776, what results from European efforts between 1957 and 1992 may dramatically exceed the original objective. Revolutions have a historical habit of taking on their own momentum.

Of course, it might turn out that EC 1992 becomes nothing more than a conveniently located theme park where members periodically gather to escape global reality and play the import-export game with little risk to national objectives, a kind of Disneyland of European trade. Or the EC might become the new powerhouse of global affairs, encompassing all the Europes mentioned above, obscuring even Japan and creating another trade-driven bi-polar world with the United States and Europe positioned on top.

We have strong opinions about the outcome of the changes occurring in Europe and how they might influence other global neighbors. These we will save for later chapters. Regardless of how the outcomes ripple through the next century of the emerging global village, our book is a warning that the first stone will be cast by revolutionaries in Europe—in 1992.

Michael Silva
Bertil Sjögren

Salt Lake City, Utah
London, England

May, 1990

ACKNOWLEDGMENTS

Writing a book is similar to constructing a house. You can take credit for the design and the organization, but you did not actually produce the bricks.

In our case the bricks are the concepts, experience, and skill of many individuals who create change, rather than write about it. In the course of building this book we have tried to link individuals with their specific contributions, but some have given so much that they deserve special mention.

We first would like to thank those who so willingly granted interviews so that we could invade corporate privacy with pointed questions. From this group there are those who gave us hours and half-days rather than minutes. In particular Dr. Horst Avenarius, Belmiro de Azevedo, Percy Barnevik, Jan Carlzon, Oscar Fanjul, Sir Harvey Jones, Dr. Gian Morio Rossignolo, and Dr. Peter Wallenberg.

Since all books start with ideas, we are grateful to Mike Snell and John Mahaney for visualizing an end result from our mental meanderings.

Matthew Bradley deserves special mention for great research on issues and topics five thousand miles away from his library nook, and Tim Baird for his many snippets on significant, yet often overlooked, issues.

Two Marys, de Jong and Kowalcyk, are unsung heros who put forth long hours with little recognition, keeping the project on track, and Dixie Clark who invented the art of scheduling.

Special mention also must go to Tom Fries who traversed chasms of international complexity with a single story about titanium ice screws, and John Baird who so effectively kept the wolves at bay. Craig Hickman also merits deep appreciation for his role as a fellow student in the quest to write better books.

Our deepest appreciation to Ulf Hubendick, Jan Persson, Sven Soderberg, and Bengt Almgren who saw value in a very creative project and committed the resources and experience of Indevo to develop what we hope is a valuable literary map of Europe's emerging global borders.

Finally, we wish to acknowledge our children—Brandon, Kjrsten, Joshua, Jason, Kaile, Helena, Gabriel, and Christina—who are the motivation and purpose for all our endeavors, especially this book.

CONTENTS

Contents

Contents

Contents

EPILOGUE
283

PROLOGUE

Europe 1992:
A Consumer Revolution

*Then suddenly this new spirit arose in Europe
triggered by the Single European Act signed in 1986.
There was a new momentum for European integration,
for the borderless Europe.
Whatever comes out of all of this,
I think that the spirit has been important for Europe.
For however long it will last, you can call it Euphoria.*

PERCY BARNEVIK
CEO of Asea Brown Boveri

INSIGNIFICANT ISSUES AND HARD EVENTS

In November of 1989, while the Iron Curtain parted in Berlin, construction was completed on the world's largest McDonald's in Moscow. On Tiananmen Square, workers wiped away the blood of massacred students while the Wang family patiently stood in line to spend their hard-earned renmimbi on American fried chicken. Like the Moscow McDonald's, Beijing's Kentucky Fried Chicken outlet is the biggest in the world. In Washington, D.C., as the United States Department of Commerce plots trade war against Japan, the Federal Drug Administration makes food history when one of its directives frees Japan to export fugu, a member of the pufferfish family, to the United States. Fugu can be so potentially lethal that chefs in Japan must obtain a license to prepare it from the Japanese government. Small amounts of the poison found in the pufferfish's ovaries lead to a pleasant tingling of lips, fingers, and toes; larger doses can kill in minutes. To win FDA approval for this export, the Japanese government has assured that it will carefully monitor all fugu exports.

Admittedly, Big Macs, fried chicken, and sashimi provide an unexpected introduction to a book on the unification of Europe in 1992 (EC92 as it is called in Europe) and other global change. We have become accustomed to the glare of other sorts of headlines shrieking events that shape our lives and how we do business: THE BERLIN WALL CRUMBLES, U.S. INVADES PANAMA, SCIENTISTS CREATE NUCLEAR FUSION USING TEST TUBES AND CAR BATTERY. But underneath the world's headlines beats the pulse of another global life sign. The changes in what journalists and opinion leaders would label insignificant—a McDonald's in Moscow—often provide the most insight into where we are going, and, more important, why. The invasion of Beijing by the Colonel's secret herbs and spices says little about the demonstrations in Tiananmen Square, but a great deal about the future of Communist China. It is fascinating to see what did not make the front pages of the world's newspapers but may, in fact, be turning the pages of world history.

3

For example, in Moscow, the number of television sets owned by Soviet citizens has increased dramatically in the last ten years, but one in three apartment fires in Moscow in 1988 was caused by an exploding Russian-manufactured TV set. And while the world continues to applaud the Japanese work ethic, British labor silently bypassed the Japanese, with an average of 41.9 work hours per week against only 41.2 hours per week in Japan.

Ten years ago, who would have expected India to become a software exporter? An American math professor might have. For years, educators have noted the large numbers of Indian exchange students flooding graduate programs in engineering and mathematics. U.S. educated brainpower is now churning out millions of lines of computer code, a task that makes good sense for a country like India because it requires little capital investment or inventory.

In Belgium, major corporations are scrambling to establish "merger embassies." With over 450 mergers in 1988 compared to a scant 117 in 1983, the European Community (EC) is taking dramatic steps toward merger regulation that is prompting acquirers across Europe to set up political shop in the heart of Brussels, the headquarters of the European unification process.

During Kolhberg, Kravis and Robert's (KKR) landmark acquisition of R.J. Reynolds Nabisco for $25 billion, humble Bolivia, with a total gross national product less than the value of the takeover transaction, quietly left its mark on world finance. The Bolivian government agreed to protect 1.5 million hectares of primitive rain forest in exchange for forgiveness of a $650,000 debt by a U.S. lender. The bank, in turn, discounted the loan by 85 percent and sold it to a conservation group interested in preserving the rain forest because of its relationship to the threatened ozone layer. Bolivia shed a portion of its debt, the bank collected almost $100,000 of its uncollectible loan, and members of a national environmental group slept better knowing that they may have made at least a small dent in the greenhouse effect.

What makes these seemingly insignificant issues important is that they serve as pulsating beacons of global change. They are little things, emerging as pinpoints of light, warning us that jarring adjustments in the way we live are already upon us. Somewhere, lost in the blare of front-page headlines, are indications of a world being dragged kicking and screaming to a point of change that seems fuzzy on the horizon, but more focused if we look closer at the signals around us. Europe 1992, the uniting of 12 different and fiercely independent nations, is one of a surge of signals that the world is entering a new order.

Europe 1992 is a global signal worth investigating. But EC92 is only a single flash in an explosion of change that is sweeping across the world. Japan's struggle with dominance, American resurgence, technological growth, and the worldwide communist convulsion, all promise to play a key role in our future, equal with European unification in significance. For our purposes, EC92 serves as a point of reference, a tool providing order, so we can draw in diverse issues but not lose track that all this change is taking us somewhere. Above all, the changes in Europe give us a handle on three forces that are subtly sweeping the world.

THE CONSUMPTION EXPLOSION

The nuclear era actually began on May 29, 1919 when photographs of a solar eclipse, taken on the island of Príncipe off the coast of West Africa and at Sobral in Brazil, confirmed a new theory of the universe proposed by then 40-year-old Albert Einstein. However, the public generally did not acknowledge the nuclear era until 1959 when worried Americans began building backyard bomb shelters.

Insignificant issues give birth to eras. Startling change only serves to announce the era to an unsuspecting public. It takes years, even decades, however, for new thoughts, new inventions, and new habits to invade everyone's consciousness and make us fully aware that our lives have permanently changed.

5

Microwave ovens, portable music systems, alarm watches, pocket televisions, and smaller floats in our checking accounts combine to jar us to the realization that we live in an electronic era. Miniaturization has advanced to such a point that the size of our hands and the focus range of our eyes, rather than technology, limits further progress. We can now pack a personal computer into a box the size of a deck of cards, but its small monitor and tiny keyboard would render it virtually useless.

Little devices, such as optic fibers, fax machines, and computer telephone modems have heralded our entrance into the information era long before we felt even an inkling that the electronic era had begun to wind down. In 1960, consumers completed two million transatlantic calls between the United States and Europe. By 1987, the number of calls had boomed to 707 million. The new fiber optic cables replacing the old-fashioned ones that could only handle 20 calls at one time, can now simultaneously process over 40,000. The affordability of the fax machine has forever altered how we receive and respond to information. When Columbus discovered the New World, it took three months for word of his achievement to reach Queen Isabella. Headlines reporting the assassination of Abraham Lincoln crossed the Atlantic in 13 days. By fax, a full-page letter crosses 3,000 miles of ocean in just under 12 seconds. With a modem, that communication can occur seemingly instantly.

Like the electronic era, the information era has not begun to run its course, even as another era has begun pressing into our lives. Deep in the heart of the Amazon rain forest, a primitive hunter provides the family meal by killing and carrying from the forest a small pig. He shot the 30-pound animal with a poison tipped wooden arrow, then pursued the beast for three miles before the poison dropped it. Back at camp, the hunter's wife cleans and dresses the meat, then begins cooking the meal over an open fire, using five shiny Teflon-coated aluminum pots. Even the Amazon cannot escape the explosion of the consumption era.

Like the eras that precede it, the consumption era began with little things. In the summer of 1989, Beijing University students protested the lack of democracy, clad in Guess jeans. That same summer in California, Hmong refugees from Cambodia crammed entire families into $75-a-month, single room apartments with bathroom, bedroom, and kitchen divided by sheets hanging from the ceiling, but they drive to their minimum-wage jobs in turbo-charged Mustangs and Grand Prix. A tribal elder in Olisabebee, Africa, watching young elders dig a trench to bring water to the village using the same primitive tools of his forefathers, chides a young worker for taking a break to replace the batteries in his Walkman.

The consumption era is an explosion in the global quest for products, and it is quickly escalating into a worldwide economic shopping spree that spans the richest to the poorest nations. Clearly, the quest for possessions is hardly a new phenomenon. For centuries, humans have sought inventions, built industries, and waged wars in order to create, disseminate, and retain products. But it differs from historical consumption in scope and focus.

The new consumption is truly global. Almost all countries, regardless of their current levels of development, have fully plunged into buying and selling. Historically, only the richest nations consumed. The poorer countries simply provided raw materials. However, a close look at South Korea reveals a reversal of the old "rich get richer" theme. In 1979, the United States manufactured millions of microwave ovens each week, compared to barely a few dozen being made in South Korea. Today, when a U.S. consumer buys a microwave oven, one-third of the time it bears the stamp, "Made in Korea." Not surprisingly, then, the American press has begun to compare Korea with Japan. The analogy, however, does not hold up. While Japan has been an industrialized country since the turn of the century, as recently as 1960, South Korea was considered a less-developed country.

In addition, the consumption quest centers on wants rather than needs. Teflon pots in the Amazon rain forest, Walkmen in the African bush, and turbo-charged Mustangs in Hmong households reflect more how we want to live, not how we need to

7

live. For centuries, the drive for products centered around gathering food, keeping warm, and staying healthy. Nowadays, it hinges more on style, whim, and personal preference, and it produces an interesting blend of products and services. Bangkok boasts a Pizza Hut restaurant a scant 20 miles from farms still using human fertilizer, and in ultratechnical Japan over half the households are not connected to a municipal sewage system.

But the recent consumption explosion is not only different from previous historical quests for products, it also differs from the industrial, nuclear, electronic, and information eras that preceded it. Three differences are worth attention.

First, the consumption era propels itself with remarkable speed. The industrial era, commencing in the mid-1880s required a full 100 years to restructure 4,000 years of dependence on agriculture and hunting to a society based on industry and cities. But the nuclear era, beginning in 1945, took only 20 years to create a world dominated by just two powers, the United States and the Soviet Union. In the last ten years similarly the electronic era has increased computer productivity by a factor of 1,000,000, while the machines themselves have plunged in size and price by a factor of 1,000. The speed with which the information era is changing our lives is symbolized by a 1988 multinational Mount Everest climbing expedition which loaded their Sherpas with traditional tents, ropes, and pitons, but also included two items not found in previous Everest assaults: a cellular telephone and a portable fax machine. Taiwan, South Korea, Malaysia, and a clique of oil-rich Middle East countries illustrate how quickly nations can transform from third world underdeveloped outposts to ultramodern consuming machines in less than two decades. We should expect this rate of change to continue through the consumption era.

Second, for perhaps the first time in history, a number of earthshaking eras overlap each other. In the 100-year transformation to an industrial world from agriculture, not all parts of the transformation went at the same rate. Even today, we can witness telltale remnants of eras past. In fact, we actually strive to pursue living models of pre-industrial life by spending millions of dollars to protect primitive cultures from change. However, we would not dream of doing that with our own high-tech culture. In fact, ever since World War II, we have done our best to force quicker transitions from one era to the next. The electronic era currently lies sandwiched between the nuclear and information eras, with not one of them having come close to running its course. Each still generates even broader, deeper dimensions of change. Such advances as superconductivity, pinhead microscopic chips with storage capacity of 500 pages of text, and optic fibers capable of transmitting an entire encyclopedia in 1.5 seconds continue to happen every day. The consumption era overlaps and embraces all these events, and it will constantly be buffeted by all the innovations produced by its sister eras, with virtually no end in sight.

Third, and most unique, the consumption era reflects a basic creed with implications far beyond those of a mere product-delivery system. While the nuclear, electronic, and information eras borrow their names from delivery systems, few people have centered their lives around a nuclear, electronic, or information religion. We want the progress or power these eras represent, but we view them more or less as simple means for accomplishing that progress or power. The consumption era is different. Consumption has become an end in itself, a driving creed that alters existing political and social institutions and positions them to serve as more efficient consumption devices. In a mere five years, the eastern block of European communist nations has radically changed government policy to join the flow of world consumption, and *perestroika* signals an era where politics serves a population bent on buying more consumer, not military, hardware.

Buying and selling have come to so thoroughly dominate all of our activities, that entire governments have begun restructuring themselves in order to gear up for a war of consumption where victory will be won with products rather than warheads.

9

American children sit transfixed for an average of seven hours each day before a machine whose programming owes its very existence to buying and selling. Mothers in the African bush mix contaminated drinking water with powdered baby formula in a confused attempt to live up to the advertising that reaches even to the very edges of our consuming civilization.

THE SOFTWARE OF CONSUMPTION

Every era includes a delivery system, which transports change to a waiting world. Since World War II, three major delivery systems, (nuclear, electronic, and information) have provided the hardware to shape our lives into the eras that bear their names. In contrast, the consumption era, rather than introducing new and technologically superior hardware, has created a sort of sociological software, which can direct and integrate the hardware of its sister eras. The economic superiority of Japan, for example, comes about at least partially as a by-product of the electronic era. In the Soviet Union, change occurs because the state can no longer protect its citizens from product information. A recent Pepsi commercial humorously suggests that the soft drink propelled *glasnost* and *perestroika.* To the entrenched Communist leader, the consumer revolution in their country is no laughing matter.

Three major forces drive the software of consumption: consumers, capitalism, and consortia. Obviously, we could not embark on a consumption era without consumers. But while consumers have, of course, existed for thousands of years, until quite recently, basic survival absorbed most of their consumption energy.

In the 40 years since World War II, however, relative prosperity has shifted for most of the world's citizens from survival to luxury consumption. A Chinese worker, relatively well fed and clothed and sheltered, will save the equivalent of six months income to buy a portable black and white television. The definition of luxury varies, from person to person, but Teflon-coated aluminum pots in the Amazon rain forest suggest a shift in focus from obtaining enough to eat to the niceties of eating in style. The shift by no means limits itself to the Amazon. Three hundred twenty-five million travelers will venture outside their national borders in 1989, while only 25 million did so in 1960. Over 2.4 billion of the world population enjoy life spans 11 to 13 years longer than their grandparents. Roughly 10 percent of college-age Brazilians, Indians, and Turks sign up for higher education, only slightly fewer than did so in England, Italy, and Japan in 1965. In some regions, the increase is overwhelming. Thailand and South Korea send 26 percent of their college-age kids on to higher education, up from less than 2 percent 20 years ago.

Living longer, in better conditions and with more education helps push consumption concerns past the necessities and on to the luxuries. Sales of BMWs in Japan increased 28 percent in 1988, while farming families in Mainland China save for their first color TV set. In the United Kingdom over 100 available channels of television, available by satellite, has triggered a British satellite war with Sky Television and British Satellite Broadcasting slugging it out for the attention of some 90,000 satellite dish owners. So intense is the competition that British Satellite Broadcasting is considering giving satellite dishes to potential subscribers.

The pressures of increased consumption have begun to strain the world's manufacturing and product-delivery systems. The demand for more goods and services at higher levels of quality will, in all probability, weed out inefficient methods of production and select with Darwinian objectivity the best way to make and sell the world's goods. In this way, capitalism has become, without challenge, the preferred method for producing and delivering products. One by one, the nations of the world, even the Soviet Union and communist China, have adopted capitalistic methods. Illogical? By no means. The Communists just finally saw capitalism's true colors as a methodology rather than an ideology. So we cannot view the changes as an ideological victory over communism; rather, we must see them as the natural result of a new ideology—consumerism.

As a result of the global acceptance of a consumer ideology, communism has virtually self-destructed as its two primary exponents struggle to make up for lost time. Capitalism, they feel, offers the best engineering choice for doing so. The battle between capitalism and communism, originally fought on high moral ground, has gradually given way to the ticker tape.

Communist countries with roughly 33 percent of the world's population account for only 10 percent of global exports, a scant 3 percent of technological innovations, and under 1 percent of nonmilitary economic assistance dished out to developing countries. In 1985, lowly Singapore exported more machinery than all of communist Eastern Europe combined. Consumption, as measured by automobile ownership, suggests the same failure of the communist method to produce: 1983 statistics reveal one car per 1.8 Americans, 2.5 Germans, and 4.4 Japanese, compared to 14.2 Soviets. Oppressed Blacks in South Africa own more cars per capita than do citizens in the Soviet Union.

Just as consumerism drives capitalism, so has capitalism given rise to the new international consortia, the alliances and partnerships assembled to create product and service corporations that cross beyond national boundaries. Originally, consortia usually operated as behind-the-scenes manipulators of world events, and for years, fiction writers and filmmakers have painted vivid portraits of fabulously wealthy and powerful tycoons silently directing the political and economic affairs of whole nations. Nowadays, they have come out of the smoke-filled rooms, boldly, but not really menacingly, gripping the reins of international change. For example, in 1981, semiconductor giant Texas Instruments pursued legal action against Japan's Hitachi for patent infringement. Pent up protectionist emotions in the United States ran high as Hitachi seemed poised to pay the price of technological piracy. But in 1986 before the trial even began, TI and Hitachi announced to a shocked world the beginning of a joint venture to pursue the advancement of semiconductor technology, and not coincidently, drive all other competitors out of business. The landmark alliance arose not so much as a function of premeditated manipulation as from the realization that joining forces created a greater competitive advantage than a prolonged legal battle ever could.

Such consortia emphasize globalism over nationalism. Until recently, nationally based companies who functioned overseas left no doubt about whether General Motors was American or Mercedes was German. Now, however, the pressure of consumption has admitted some doubt. Who owns Doubleday, the publishing house that bears the name of the founder of America's so-called national pastime? A German firm called Bertelsmann, AG. IBM's non-U.S. sales accounted for 78 percent of pretax earnings in 1988. Over 41 percent of 3M's work force live outside of the United States, and roughly half of American chemical workers get their paychecks from non-U.S. owners. In 1987, British Petroleum, Unilever, and Hoeschst, all European companies, occupied three of the seven top spots on *Fortune's* ranking of U.S. Deals of the Year.

The rise of international consumer power and the capitalist method for producing and delivering goods and services has already placed competition beyond the reach of the purely national company. Until recently, the personal computer business of American bastion AT&T was run by an executive on loan from Italian corporate power, Olivetti. And the cost of a mortgage in Iowa and state taxes in Georgia depend, oddly enough, on the activities of money centers in Tokyo, Bonn, and London. Even Mikhail Gorbachev acknowledges that "not one state in the world today can regard itself as isolated from others in the economic respect."

For companies as well as countries, the rise of consortia generates some justified worries about misuse or abuse of power, but it also creates unprecedented opportunities. U.S. politicians and policymakers may grapple with the question of what makes a company American, but the question itself may have already become rhetorical. Americans have been so absorbed in questions of their own competitiveness in the global economy that they have overlooked the fact that most consumers really do not *care* who makes the products they buy. Do American car buyers inquire whether their Honda was manufactured in Osaka or Georgia? Not as long as it is a Honda. By the same token, Alka Seltzer does not lose any of its "plop-plop, fizz-fizz" just because it is owned by West German Bayer AG. For business people interested in competing overseas, consumer "origin blindness" issues an open invitation to greater market share and profitability. And it has helped evolve the early alliances, joint ventures, and outright mergers that signaled the beginning of this trend into sprawling international networks with products manufactured in Taiwan, assembled in Korea, distributed through Mexico, marketed by Japan, and financed in West Germany, with their owners legally headquartered in the United States. Thus has General Motors underwritten a car that will be designed in West Germany, engineered in Ireland, built in South Korea, and sold in the United States.

EUROPE 1992, THE PIVOT EVENT

EC92 is a pivot point, marking the end of our century and paving the way toward a new order in the year 2000 and beyond. This is a heady assumption that can be argued in two ways. We can research it to death and look for every quantitative indicator, or we can look at the flow of world events somewhere between the trivia of fast food and the trauma of toppling governments. We prefer the latter method and follow this approach religiously throughout the book. The world is changing faster than the intelligentsia can revise their predictions and jump on the bandwagon. As a result, the executives and policymakers in the trenches are having to face the future with common sense and grass roots observation, two analytical tools that are scoffed at by political theorists, economists, and academics. Our analysis of EC92 and other world changes is not offered as a prediction, but only as a direction that overpressured and underread decision-makers may want to be aware.

In line with common sense, the unification of Europe is a pivot event of our century because it touches so many other changes occurring in the world. To Japan and the United States, the EC is an instant and relatively equal competitor, just add water (in the form of legislation). Look now and you see separated and bickering countries. Look again and you still see bickering, but this time in the form of a colossus. For Japan, not buying Spanish oranges might mean not selling Japanese cars anywhere in Europe. To the United States, it might mean being invited to stay a NATO member rather than determining membership. And while we stand in awe of the domino decline of communist governments, we should not overlook the fact that Western Europe and Eastern Europe share the same last name. Finally, Mikhail Gorbachev eats with a fork, not chopsticks, bear hugs rather than bows, and prefers potatoes to rice. Although bordering on Asia, the Soviet Union has a history of breaking bread with the West, and Europe has not declined the invitation to join in the building of the Soviet economy. Ironically, this occurs while American communist-watchers debate whether the United States should let the Soviet Union crumble, as if there were no other power on earth capable of coming to the rescue.

These mental meanderings alone should perk up some attention on EC92 as a global, rather than a regional, event. If not, the numbers—population, gross national product, trade volumes—can be convincing.

By means of a mere 300 directives, 12 independent and richly diverse nations with a 1,500-year history of conflict and tension will come together as a united economic power. The move to do so did not spring from the charisma of one brilliant political leader, nor from the prompting of a single country. Europe does not march to the beat of a messianic drum, but rather rides the widening waves caused by the spontaneous explosion of world consumerism. Europe faces two choices: remain the offshore battleground of consumer superpowers Japan and the United States, or forge a single consuming and production entity that can offer the world a third alternative to U.S. and Japanese product domination. The answer: 12 European nations hammered into one formidable power called the European Community, or, more simply, the EC.

Headquartered in Brussels, the EC faces a formidable task as it issues directives designed to break down centuries of physical and cultural barriers. These obstacles to geopolitical unity by 1992 come in two forms, hard and soft. But smart observers will not let those labels mislead them.

Hard obstacles include the different and, at times, conflicting laws, procedures, and administrative practices that dominate each individual country. To break down these sorts of obstacles, Brussels issues directives to be ratified by the member nations. The soft obstacles encompass the cultural and social methods, morals, and mores that have kept Europe a patchwork of separate states since the decline of the Roman Empire. Interestingly, the EC finds the soft issues the hardest to address.

The hard side of Europe 1992 involves three central issues: tariffs, taxes and currency. These issues sit at the heart of the 300 directives which mainly try to establish some common ground for 12 nations that have in the past maintained vastly different financial and fiscal perspectives. Not surprisingly, the member nations have ratified only 70 of them by the beginning of 1990.

Tariffs. These are the costs countries tack on to goods that cross the national boundaries. For instance, because of tariffs, a BMW priced at $17,000 in West Germany retails for over $50,000 in

Athens. Obviously, the Greek government wants to limit the number of BMWs its citizens buy. For the most part, tariffs aim at protecting indigenous industries from cheaper or more attractive foreign competitors. However, because of the close geographical proximity of EC members, tariffs excite terrific emotions.

The landmass isolation of the North American continent tends to make Americans less sensitive to border issues. To better appreciate them, an American can imagine being able to buy products from 12 different nations within a three-hour plane ride, an 18-hour train trip, or a leisurely three-day drive that would encompass an area roughly from Chicago to New York City. Without tariffs, consumers would naturally search out the best price, not from competing stores, but from competing countries. This type of cutthroat competition would devastate certain local industries that could not match prices. Thus, the EC members find themselves in something of a Mexican standoff: They want to unite, but until they standardize tariffs or dispose of them, they cannot fully accomplish their goal.

The struggle for standardization causes both tears and laughter. West German mortgages and insurance policies funded by the more stable Deutschmark will almost certainly dominate the competition for financial services if allowed to cross national borders unimpeded by tariffs. Untaxed, the German financial machine could wreak havoc on the financial infrastructures of other EC members. On the lighter side, importer Rewe Zentral took the German government all the way to the European Court on the importation of the black currant liqueur Cassis de Dijon. To meet certain import-export agreements, the German government had claimed the liqueur to be essentially nonalcoholic. France balked, Zentral sued, and the European Court ruled that Germany must recognize France's domestic drink regulations, which clearly classify Cassis de Dijon as alcoholic.

Value Added Tax. VAT poses an even thornier technical barrier than tariffs. Whereas relaxing or eliminating tariffs could shut down some industries, standardizing the VAT could derail whole governments.

Europeans add the VAT to the cost of a product prior to purchase by the consumer. Unlike sales taxes in the United States, which applies a percentage set by state governments across the board to all designated products, VATs apply product by product and flow into federal coffers. The added cost, in the absence of tariffs that would prevent a flow of products across borders, significantly affects consumer decision-making. A video recorder in France carries a hefty 28 percent VAT, while the same machine bears only a 14 percent surcharge in West Germany. Assuming no tariffs, consumers will obviously purchase their VCRs in Germany rather than France. On the other hand, if France reduces the VAT on VCRs to allow French machines to compete more effectively, the government would lose sorely needed revenue.

VAT rates vary widely among EC members. Denmark and Ireland maintain the highest standard rates and, not unexpectedly, resist EC efforts at standardization that could lower their VAT revenues. The Commission originally proposed to abolish all existing national rates, replacing them with two bands of 4–9 percent and 14–20 percent, within which member states could set their rates as they chose. The two bands represented a compromise attempt to narrow the differential between nations, while still allowing EC members to decide the trade-offs between higher taxes or more competitively priced goods. When the United Kingdom, led by free market proponent Margaret Thatcher, opposed the two-band system as too competitively confining, the Commission again compromised, setting a 17 percent minimum VAT on luxury items and permitting the EC states to set their own VATs within the lower 4 to 9 percent band.

Currency.   This clearly stands as the kingpin issue of the three hard obstacles to unification. This key issue has attracted the most scrutiny and debate among Europe's leaders, as it may very well hold the key for Europe's competitive future vis-à-vis Japan and the United States.

In 1972, Europe unified its currency via the "snake." The snake was a tracking formula that tied EC currencies to a narrow trading range based on the U.S. dollar. However, intense speculation on the dollar during the late 1970s made the snake's currency parities more and more difficult to maintain. Therefore, in 1979, the European Monetary System (EMS) replaced the snake.

Instead of basing currency stability on the dollar—which can fluctuate with the changing fortunes of a U.S. economy under assault from Japan—the EMS devised its own currency, the European Currency Unit (ECU). The ECU represents a mixed basket of fixed amounts of 10 of the 12 Community currencies (Spain and Portugal excluded), broadly reflecting each member's gross national product and share of EC trade. For example, the Deutschmark exerts a 34.9 percent weighted influence on the ECU, while the Luxembourg franc exerts a mere 0.3 percent influence on the value of the ECU. The EMS's Exchange Rate Mechanism (ERM) stabilizes member currencies by requiring each government to maintain its currency within a band of 2.25 percent on either side of its fixed ECU value. Member countries must also assist in stabilizing a currency that moves outside of the allowed band.

Most recently, the EC has weighed the concept of a common currency, a single "Eurodollar" that would become the legal tender of all participating nations. Most EC members agree that a single European currency would be stronger against the dollar and the yen and would thus stimulate lower interest rates and sustain stronger international competitiveness. West Germany, however, fears that other countries, notably the socialist-run ones, will lack the internal willpower to maintain a conservative economic policy and thus lower the value of a potential Eurodollar. Furthermore, Margaret Thatcher strongly opposes replacing the pound with a currency under central bank control, which would most likely involve strong West German influence, if not direct control. Survival of the EC clearly depends on overcoming such biases. The Organization of Petroleum Exporting Countries in the early 1970s and Japan in the 1980s made capital an international commodity by trafficking in two major currencies, the yen and the dollar. EC leaders know full well that 1992 must offer the world a third option, a true Europe-dollar backed by one Europe rather than a muddle of currencies from 12 jousting nations.

While the hard issues confronting Europe's unification continue to tax the Commission, the soft ones pose even greater difficulties. Within the borders of the 12 EC member countries and their non-EC neighbors seethe hundreds of years of social, cultural, and moral differences. Some, such as language, are profound; others, such as ritual lunch hours, can be downright funny.

Geographically, two countries, the United Kingdom and Greece, do not even touch any other EC member's borders, although the UK will soon connect with France via the Channel Tunnel. Two non-member countries, Austria and Switzerland, drive a geographical wedge into the EC between Germany to the north and Italy to the south. The 12 countries speak 8 languages, though they would claim 13. The United Kingdom and Ireland, alone among the EC states, drive on the left-hand side of the road. Work habits also differ sharply. The Germans arrive early, break for lunch at noon, and leave the office at 4:00. The Greek government, on the other hand, recently rescinded the age-old practice of taking three-hour lunch breaks. Put it all together, and you have a bubbling stew that would make turn-of-the-century New York City look like one smooth cultural pudding.

Overshadowing the many soft issues attending unification are the deep emotions that still linger in the aftermath of World War II. The differences in raw numbers make it difficult particularly for Americans to grasp the continued impact of a conflict that ended over 40 years ago. While no one may ever calculate the exact numbers, some 40 million soldiers and civilians died in a few scant years in Europe and the Soviet Union. This compares to fewer than 1 million *total* American soldiers killed in all foreign wars fought since and including the Revolutionary War of 1776. The number of German casualties suffered during a single air raid on Dresden on February 13–14, 1945 was equal to one-third of all U.S. soldiers killed during World War II. On the night of Shrove Tuesday, countless children died wearing gay carnival costumes. Another German city, Hamburg, lost 214,350 homes, 4,301 factories and 37.65 percent of its population in just one night of bombing. The city of Cologne, with a prewar population of 750,000, had just 30,000 inhabitants when the war ended. The population fled the city when subjected to seemingly endless bombardment.

The differences in perspective between the United States and Europe did not end with the war itself but continued well into the post-war years as the recovery began. Compare the 3,350 average daily calories consumed by an American in 1951 to a European's daily average of only 1,115 that same year.

The war in Europe, like the Great Depression to American grandparents, never recedes far from any decision or opinion. The vast European population now between the ages of 55 and 65 were old enough in the 1940s to remember virtually every detail of a conflict that raged for five years, not overseas, but in their factories, schools, and backyards. Amazingly, however, the current surge of consumerism and the international competition to meet the demand has been doing more than anything else to soften those memories.

Language poses a slightly less emotional barrier. Along with taxes, currency, and borders, language does the most to preserve national unity. Their speakers take considerable national pride in their native tongues, which do so much to market geographical areas through which one could drive in less time than it would take to get from Denver to Los Angeles. Despite all the pride, however, Europeans have clearly moved toward accepting English as the common language.

The movement gained momentum without sponsor or organized effort. Ironically, it springs less from the influence of the United Kingdom, where English is the national language, than from the fact that Europe's two economic rivals, Japan and the United States, do business almost exclusively in English. For this reason alone, English has become the most widely taught foreign language in Europe and the world.

The impact of soft issues such as World War II and language often affect government regulation and activities. Directly and indirectly they guide consumer preferences and help to determine industry structure. Take advertising, for example. In the United Kingdom, television advertising pools messages in short bursts for maximum effect, timing them to coincide with natural breaks in programming. Advertisements occur relatively infrequently at the beginning of long programs so that the story can involve the viewer, then they become more frequent as the film progresses. In Germany, by contrast, television ads pool their messages into relatively infrequent 10- to 12-minute breaks. This predictable length of time invites viewers to leave their sets and perform various household chores before programming resumes.

BRAVE NEW WORLD

No one who drives a car, snaps a picture, uses a calculator, or switches on a computer doubts the impact of the Japanese economic explosion on our lives. But, remarkably, our lifestyles remain untouched by the Japanese cultural influence. Although hard commodities such as video cameras and Walkmen and a few soft services such as sushi bars and Japan Airlines have traveled easily to our shores, the customs, mores, and social institutions of Japan have not exported well at all. This will not be the case with Europe 1992. Europeans have been exporting culture to America ever since the first immigrants landed at Jamestown. European unification represents the beginning of a veritable lifestyle revolution in the United States and the world. Underneath the fierce competition to supply consumer products and services seethes an even fiercer underground current of social change. Paradoxically, to best grasp this change, we must think of technological growth.

While contemporary technology can basically change every 18 months, our social patterns and institutions can only absorb new technology at a much slower pace, perhaps as long as five to seven years. As a result, natural social resistance somewhat stems the tide of technological innovation. The human race really does exercise a little caution when planning for the full integration of new technology into its daily life. For instance, we have possessed the means to create a cashless society since the mid-1970s. Computer-based electronic banking, Automated Teller Machines, and satellites could have rendered coins and bills obsolete. But our human side resisted that technology. In 1975, the United States selected Hawaii as the best test site for a cashless society, and offered Automated Teller Machines at malls, airports, apartment lobbies, and sports complexes. Consumers could pay their bills simply by picking up the telephone and punching in digital instructions, thus completely bypassing human assistance. A consumer could even pay for groceries by simply inserting a bank card at the register and automatically transferring payment to the store. All this happened almost two decades before 1992, but it never did result in the obsolescence of pieces of paper and metal coins stamped with the visages of dead presidents.

On the other hand, Europe 1992 comes at a time when we have learned some lessons and sit below a poised avalanche of technology about to crash into our daily lives. Now, technology can advance in two significant new ways.

First, we have gotten to the point where we realize that we can let technology attack our routines, without robbing us of our souls. The advance of technological change in the 1970s and early to mid-1980s struck quickly and coldly at the heart of our lives.

On the horizon loomed a cashless society, depersonalized video conferences, nameless nutrients and officeless companies where executives worked from home via modem and fax. The priests of high technology, however, out-of-step with the needs and dreams of flesh-and-blood people, failed to appreciate how our souls depend on the low-tech dynamic of touch. We like the feel of cash, the close interaction of seven people stuffed in a conference room, food that appeals to all our senses, and the comfort of working in the office each day. If change promises a bucket of gold at the end of its silicon rainbow, maybe we just do not want to be that rich. Still, we do willingly accept change, almost without reservation, in areas that do not matter to our hearts and souls. Consequently, change in the 1990s will fairly easily alter our routines and daily humdrum, leaving us time to explore deeper lifestyle values in a more leisurely fashion.

Second, the future will involve much more integration than innovation. In 1988 scientists broke through barriers of conductivity that will revolutionize the semiconductor industry, but the world yawned. Our threshold of excitement over innovation has risen dramatically, as on an almost daily basis we have come to expect earthshaking technological advancements. That was life in the 1980s, newer this and smaller that. But we have yet to achieve effective integration. When we do, we may sit up and take notice. When a computer, fax machine, telephone, cellular telephone, copy machine, and entertainment system all come packaged in a single portable machine, that will be real progress.

The current lack of integration is obvious. We constantly read of computer-operated households where heat, lights, alarms, ovens, water usage, and even electric blankets are controlled centrally by a microcomputer. The technology is present and even affordable. But, the penetration of personal computers into America's households is proceeding at a slower pace than futurists expected, despite dropping price tags on once cost-prohibitive personal computers. The reality is that producers of high technology are still relying on the consumer to make the integration connection. Each is marketing its own little contribution to a higher tech lifestyle, but so far, no major competitors are packaging our technological advances into turn-key applications that a consumer can buy and simply plug in. This snag in high tech marketing has slowed the pace of penetration into our lives; but not for long.

The unification of Europe will greatly affect, if not dominate, the impact of integrated technology on our lives. How we let technology govern our routines comes about as a function of culture, and how we integrate technology occurs as an outcome of design. Culture and design: in these two areas Europe has always greatly, if not masterfully, influenced the American lifestyle.

Culture. Rather the lack of it, may be the single greatest failure of the Japanese marketing system. No one will accuse the Japanese of poor service or product quality. But in the last 20 years the world, and particularly the United States, has not incorporated Japanese outlooks, attitudes, and beliefs nearly as fast as Japanese products. We have, however, swallowed European perspectives hook, line, and sinker. With the exception of the rather recent trend of Hispanic influence on the American coasts, Europe continues to provide the United States with its richest source of offshore cultural integration. From Mercedes, Porsches, and BMWs to MonteBlancs, Adidas, and Evian, European products have come to mean more about how we feel about ourselves than what we feel about the products. While the owners of Hondas do not think of themselves as part of a breed of Honda owners, Mercedes owners feel like part of an elite family. Those who would disagree by citing the huge price gap between a Mercedes and Honda need only recall that even the lowly Volkswagen Bug claimed a breed of buyer different from the herd. We go to Cannes for films, Paris and Rome for art, Athens for history, London for language and literature, and West Berlin for a jolting reminder of how close we came to losing it all. We go to Tokyo strictly to do business.

Europe 1992 adds economic muscle to cultural influence. Our natural affinity for things European, particularly in high-end status products, will now receive the attention of 12 unified suppliers. Just as American prosperity in the 1950s and 1960s and Japanese prosperity in the 1970s and 1980s pushed American and Japanese products across the oceans, so will European prosperity propel European goods and services throughout the world.

Design. The rounded torso and sloping front ends of almost every top-of-the-line American and Japanese car suggest not only a deep genetic debt to the Mercedes 190 but also a tribute to dominance of European design. Germany and Italy shape our cars, Scandinavia our furniture, and France our clothes. Even Switzerland has turned something as common as a bank account into something with a touch of mystique and class. European design may represent the world's most successful non-value-added industry, second only to American leveraged buyouts.

The technological advances of the last 15 years have already overcome production and price barriers, placing many new products within the reach of most Japanese, American, and European consumers and not far beyond the grasp of a growing number of Eastern European, Soviet, and Communist Chinese consumers. The only major hurdle now is design, which can seductively fit technology into our lives in ways that make us feel good about both the machines and ourselves.

Swedish furniture and Saabs say something about the owner. American recliners and Pontiacs also send a message, but quite a different one. Both sets of products provide the same functional service. Only design differentiates them. In the world of high technology, we have just begun the process of design differentiation, and ultimately, design will culminate in an integration of technology into our lives not only as a cost-benefit decision, but also as a status one. A 1984 Apple computer commercial

26

symbolized this aspect of technology when it depicted an auditorium filled with emotionless, drab drones, all dressed in regulation business grey, challenged by a beautiful female wearing a colorful aerobics suit and athletic shoes. The message? A certain kind of business person chooses IBM, another opts for Apple. Which would you rather be?

A REALIGNED WORLD

Military technology, specifically nuclear military technology, has provided the impetus for geopolitical rankings since the end of World War II. The ability to devastate the planet created a unique club of two: the United States and the Soviet Union. But while military prowess still commands the world's attention, new measurements have arisen for assessing the who's who of global power.

The consumption era shifts superiority to those nations or regions that can produce and consume products and services. Equal emphasis on production and consumption is important. As Japan attempts to play the role of provider, all the while shirking its responsibility as a consumer, the imbalance stimulates protective U. S. actions.

The production–consumption balance in tandem with the 1992 unification of Europe creates a new consuming triad consisting of North America, the Pacific Rim, and Europe. Specifically, the United States, Japan, and a united Europe will compete as spheres of simultaneous production and consumption. These spheres will span the planet, overlapping and influencing each other every minute of the production and consumption day. As their fortunes ebb and flow, the real war will occur not with ICBMs and MIRVs, but with VCRs, computers, books, movies, rice, beans, and wheat.

As the spheres interact, natural affinities will occur. Japan clearly enjoys the early lead in financing the growth of the Pacific Rim. As a prime investor and joint venture partner with the Four

Tigers (South Korea, Taiwan, Singapore, and Hong Kong), Japan exerts a staggering influence on all that goes on in the region. The United States, with its natural resources and free trade agreements with Canada, will almost certainly dominate North and South America. Then along comes Eastern and Western Europe, providing a dominant force over some half a billion people.

The addition of a united Europe to the international economic battle marks the beginning of the end of Japan's economic dominance and the initiation of a more balanced and evenly competitive world market. Already facing aggressive U.S. demands to open domestic markets, Japan can now expect to hear a united Europe's insistence on access to Japanese consumers. Whereas Japan currently negotiates its reciprocal European trade agreements country by country, in the future it may be forced to open its gates to all of Europe simultaneously. In order to bank in France, Japan may have to allow Spanish oranges into Osaka. If Japan refuses, the EC can deny Tokyo access to its 320 million share of European consumers, a move Tokyo could not afford.

The pressure to prompt Japan from world provider to world consumer will seriously affect Japan's exporting prowess, which it won at a high domestic price. Over one-half of Japan's households remain unconnected to a municipal sewage system, and the roads outside of high-tech Tokyo cry out for repair. However, the Japanese have traditionally sacrificed domestic spending in order to promote exporting activities. If they increased domestic spending, that would reduce the amount of yen dedicated to capturing U.S. and European market shares. Further, the prospect of increased consumption will force a decline in Japan's chief asset, its per-capita savings rate. Yen committed to Japanese banks for fueling international expansion will, as domestic Japanese consumption rises, transfer to U.S. and European banks and, in turn, fuel the battle against Japan.

These changes will not result in a devastated Japan begging the world's forgiveness for unfair international trade advantage with its domestic savings rate. Instead, they will conspire to create a more balanced world chess board with no one of the Big Three possessing a significant competitive advantage over the others. Even so, the balance of production and consumption power among the United States, Japan, and Europe will not last forever and probably not long past the turn of the century. By then three additional power players will have swept into the game: the Soviet Union, Communist China, and Eastern Europe.

In the past, these countries' internal ideology and the rest of the world's revulsion to communism have forced them into closed economic systems, essentially consuming their own production with little in the way of imports and even less in the way of exports. Now, however, consumerism has begun to overwhelm the ideology of communism at a pace that has taken the free world by surprise. Soviet leader Mikhail Gorbachev makes radical moves to revise the Soviet outlook on politics, arms, and domestic economics, while American network television crews film the realities of rioting Chinese students, who, though many died in the confrontation with hard-liners, represented a tidal wave that will eventually sweep China into the 21st century. But nothing has matched the drama of East European governments dropping like dominos in the face of a new global economic reality.

In the emerging communist-turn-capitalist nations, the initial phase of production, encouraged by legions of Western corporations eager for a position in a relatively virgin market, will give way to a phase of consumption as the flow of foreign capital gradually nudges the domestic standards of living upward. In short order, an additional one and one half billion producers and consumers, almost double the combined populations of the United States, Japan, and Europe, will be playing the game. Imagine an American, European, or Asian company doubling its global market penetration by initializing agreements with only a handful of governments!

A quick way to sense the impact that Soviet, East European, and mainland Chinese consumers will have on the world market is to measure the market penetration of two very common consumer products: cars and telephones. Compared to 540 autos per thousand in the United States and 228 per thousand in Japan, there are only 36 cars per thousand Soviet citizens. Assuming that Soviet car ownership approaches the levels found in the United States, an additional 200 million cars will have to be produced to meet the demand.

The same geometrical production growth is expected with telephones. There are roughly 80 telephones per hundred people in the United States as compared with 53.5 telephones per hundred people in Japan. There are only 10 telephones per hundred in the Soviet Union. Bringing the Soviet Union on-line could almost double world telephone production. Soviet consumption of just two basic products that industrialized nations take for granted could radically alter the entire auto and communications industries. This is not taking into account the 1.2 billion consumers that mainland China and Eastern Europe would add.

Arithmetic aside, the world is waking up to the inevitable impact of consumers seething behind an ideological curtain that has restricted their access to the world supermarket. But the curtain is rapidly rising and the game of consumer catch-up is likely to result in an economic shake-up as nations and consumption spheres jockey for position.

A WORLD MORE TRAVELED

Advances in information and communication technology have shrunk the world into an ever smaller and more accessible marketplace. With buyers and sellers from all countries clamoring for their share of worldwide production and consumption, momentum has gathered for another radical transformation every bit as momentous as the Industrial Revolution. Only the consumption revolution will not take 100 years. The 40-year Japanese and German recoveries and the 20-year history of OPEC illustrates how technology, information, and money can combine to transform even beaten and subsistence nations into ultra high-tech competitors.

The pressure for products is blurring ideological loyalties. Young men discussing political issues at Moscow University glance at female comrades wearing jeans copied from U.S. designs, manufactured in Singapore, and hawked in Hong Kong. Detroit has given up on trying to make the nation "Buy American" and focuses instead on buying stock in their up-and-coming Japanese and Korean competitors. In these and countless other situations, consumer choices are upstaging our traditional outlooks on politics, business, and national loyalties. World peace through the next 20 years may have more to do with microwave ovens than military superiority; and the quest for world revolution may finally come to pass, not with ideological principles but with products. In this book we hope to sketch the central role Europe 1992 will play in this startling drama.

Chapters 1, 2, and 3 will investigate the three forces that are dragging the world kicking and screaming to a true global market. Capitalism, consumers, and consortia provide the powerful current that flows just beneath the surface of seething world change.

The actual mechanics of unification and the economic and cultural barriers that threaten to block the reality of a united Europe appear in Chapters 4 and 5. The impossible part of the impossible dream of 12 united European states rivaling the trade power of Japan and the United States is also reviewed.

Three sister changes—the decline of Japan, the revitalization of the United States, and the explosion of technology—combine with Europe 1992 to usher in the 21st century—the focus of Chapters 6, 7, and 8. While Europe 1992 represents a political and economic revolution, it will ultimately affect the day-to-day lives of all the world's citizens. Advances in technology, communications, food, and banking especially promise to restructure how we spend our time and our money. These issues receive close attention, helping us track world change from high-level negotiating tables to the dining room tables of the 600 million consumers who live in Earth's most industrialized nations.

Finally, Chapter 9 returns to the political, economic, and business issues of world realignment. New directions in the relationships between Japan, Europe, and the United States with a cautious eye toward the rapid consumerization of Eastern Europe, the Soviet Union, and Communist China are explored.

In all this, Europe serves as the pivot point as it embarks on a desperate and determined attempt to shed old structures and traditions and become a geopolitical superpower in the next century.

CHAPTER ONE

Consumers: The New International Power

Because of man's innate drive to improve his condition the world has never stood still.

PAUL KENNEDY
Author of *The Rise and Fall of the Great Powers*

BALLISTICS, BANANAS, AND A
BIGGER BITE OF LIFE

Just two-and-a-half miles south of the East German border, the 50,000 West German residents of Hof have always lived with risk. When the Cold War turned hot, Hof would cease to be a city and become the first casualty in a shooting war that neither side, capitalist nor communist, could or would ultimately win. On Saturday, November 11, 1989, Hof was invaded by over 60,000 East Germans. But these were shoppers, not soldiers, and their objectives were bananas and Big Macs, not battlefields.

Egon Brinkmann, manager of the local Kaufhof, an all-purpose department store chain in West Germany, sold ten tons of ripe bananas before the amazed East Germans began buying the green ones. When the day ended, the Kaufhof and every other store in Hof were bananaless. Brinkman was astounded that many of the East Germans had never seen, much less eaten, a banana.

Just down the street, Klaus Rader, the manager of the local McDonald's, spent the weekend scrambling for emergency shipments of hamburger patties and french fries. Since the Berlin Wall fell on November 10, Rader's volume of burgers, fries, and drinks increased 300 percent.

For 40 years, the world was so predictable, so reliably divided, so partisan. True to form, the United States and the Soviet Union have sparred toe-to-toe in a bipolar nuclear bout that could have resulted, at any moment, in world annihilation should either partner unleash its most devastating punch. And like ringside spectators, the rest of the world gazed at the combatants as if hypnotized by all the jabs and parries of Cold War diplomacy. But by the end of the 1980s, the enormous cost of sustaining worldwide military superiority had caused both superpowers to reassess the very nature of the Cold War contest. While the ultimate outcome remains unclear, both the United States and the Soviet Union have embarked along a path toward lessening nuclear tensions. The rest of the world looks on in wonder, and perceptions begin to change. In West Germany, only 8 percent of the population view the Soviet Union as a threat to world peace compared to an overwhelming 80 percent a mere ten years ago. In this climate of more relaxed nuclear tensions, the world's tourists flock to Moscow and Beijing, as well as to Washington, D.C. While the continued existence of thermonuclear weapons reminds us that all-out war could still break out, our attention has turned, at least momentarily, to a new arena, where economic rather than military muscle struggle in a battle of international consumption.

International consumption, the rate at which goods and services move among nations, has become the new contest in which nations can attain superiority. The rankings of the power–players look dramatically different in a war where the weapons have shifted from ballistics to bananas. Now a handful of former spectators have entered the throng to challenge the superiority of the United States and the Soviet Union. Certainly Japan and West Germany have handled themselves handsomely in the early bouts of the global trade war, and a number of so-called Asian Tigers— South Korea, Singapore, Taiwan, and Hong Kong—have scored impressive victories in the lightweight divisions that worry even their role model, Japan. Now, joining the ranks of Japan, West Germany, and the Asian Tigers, come the likes of Switzerland and Great Britain in the vanguard of a new European attack for a share of the goods and services traded in the world market.

From the point of view of offensive tactics, the more goods and services a nation exports the greater imbalance of trade it can create with its trading partners. Japan, which maintains trade surpluses with everyone, perfectly illustrates the point. From a defensive standpoint, restricting an aggressor trading nation's access to your national market can stifle the aggressor's potential for future economic growth. Japan, for instance, shipped 37 percent of its exports to the United States in 1988. West Germany, in contrast, shipped only 14 percent to France, its largest export partner that year. While we might envy Japan's export volume to the United States, we need also point out their vulnerability. In the six-year period between 1983 and 1988, 91 million American households bought 62 million microwave ovens, 57 million washers and dryers, 88 million cars and light trucks, 105 million color television sets, 46 million refrigerators and freezers, 63 million VCRs, 31 million cordless telephones, and 30 million telephone answering machines. The power of American consumers to purchase $700 billion in manufactured goods over five years represents a serious potential threat to Japan's future if that power becomes off limits to Japanese goods and services. The same vulnerability does not exist for West Germany, which has spread out its exports over multiple partners. This is important because balancing offensive and defensive trading tactics is escalating into a primary government and business issue, the resolution of which will require a shift in thinking from military to consumer strategy.

A nation's consumer strategy hinges first on wealth. Without money to buy, consumption is a spectator sport. But for nations with money to burn, like the United States, Japan, and members of the EC, access becomes the hot issue. Access is the means by which nations control the exportation and importation of goods and services. In the battle for access, each country takes a slightly different approach. For example, the United States hesitates to impose harsh quotas because it adheres quite strongly to its historic *laissez-faire* economic ideology. Instead, the United States relies on voluntary quotas established through considerable arm twisting of such trading partners as Japan. The French prefer a subtler approach, demanding that all Japanese electrical goods arrive through a single customs house in Poitiers, which has remained mysteriously understaffed for the last ten years. For their part, the Japanese spend millions persuading the world that the undermining of its domestic rice industry by cheaper foreign imports would strike an unacceptable blow to the very "soul" of Japan. Still, while consumer strategy varies from country to country, one overriding goal transcends all national boundaries and languages: the creation of a trade advantage for oneself and a corresponding trade disadvantage for one's trading partners.

Consumer strategy has evolved into an art form in Japan. With only 3 percent of the world's population living on .03 percent of the country's habitable land, Japan can survive only as a trading nation. It imports 99 percent of its oil, 92 percent of its iron, and 100 percent of its copper. With virtually all of its raw materials coming from abroad, Japan must export mightily in order to maintain any sort of positive trade balance with the world. Consequently, Japan directs the whole nation's strength toward international trade. The best and the brightest of Japan's executives have dedicated themselves, in one way or another, to the business of importing and exporting with the clear goal of creating the greatest favorable balance possible.

But Japan does not stand alone in trading prowess. The changes on Europe's agenda draw attention to countries like Switzerland and Sweden, which also must trade to survive. Both countries have less total population than the city of Tokyo and neither is particularly resource rich, unless unsurpassed natural beauty is counted as a resource. Yet headquartered in these countries are just a few of the most competitive companies in the world: Nestle, Asea Brown Boveri, SAAB, Electrolux, and SAS. With less than 17 million Swiss and Swedish consumers, these companies are acutely aware that their future flows on the whims of access.

Unlike Switzerland, Sweden, and Japan, for the United States and much of Western Europe, international trade represents only one element in the vast array of issues that merit national attention. Given competition in those countries between military and social welfare priorities, consumer strategy, and access in particular, has not received the emphasis that made it an art form in Japan. For example, up until the late 1980s, the United States attempted to export to Japan household appliances that did not physically fit into the average Japanese home and automobiles with steering mechanisms on the wrong side of the vehicle. Europe has fared even worse than the United States, with the 12 largest Western European countries accounting for only 6 percent of imports to Japan (1988) against the admittedly dismal 20 percent share posted by the United States. The assumption that Japan would alter its consumption habits and standards to accommodate American and European products, and the almost total lack of cooperation from Tokyo to remedy the situation, symbolize the combined lack of skill when it comes to consumer strategy.

On the other hand, Japan's skill at consumer strategy is symbolized by the balance of private and public sector involvement. Competitive advantage, left exclusively to the private sector, often lacks focus and can deteriorate during petty territorial squabbles. By the same token, too much government involvement can infect competitors with the same bureaucratic lethargy that plagues government. Japan's Ministry for International Trade and Industry (MITI), while far from perfect, does strike productive balances between industry and government that elude most other countries. Although trade clashes with Japan and other countries over the last 20 years have made the United States and Europe wiser and more skilled in the craft of international consumption, the Japanese trade machine continues to leave most everyone in its wake.

NATIONAL SECURITY AND INTERNATIONAL CONSUMPTION

Paul Kennedy in his book *The Rise and Fall of the Great Powers* observes that the continued costs of maintaining world military superiority can virtually bankrupt currently dominant nations and send them reeling to second- or third-rate status. His point so captivated thoughtful readers that two of Kennedy's less sensational theses all but escaped attention. One of them points out that, excluding police actions, when wars have erupted between great powers the side with the most material resources has always won. So why wouldn't such powerful nations as the United States and the Soviet Union continue to dominate the world stage with their tremendous natural and military resources? That brings us to Kennedy's other neglected observation; that all major shifts in the balance of power among nations have been *preceded* by changes in the productive ranking of nations.

Only two countries, the United States and the Soviet Union, possess the material capability to achieve total thermonuclear annihilation. This fact alone has kept the two powers dominant on the world stage. But in the absence of war, a number of other nations have propelled themselves up the productive rankings; a fact that, if Kennedy's axiom holds true, could change the current balance of power among nations. According to Kennedy's second thesis, a period of prolonged peace could boost nations with little military might into positions as kingpins in the game of world economics. Relying on this very logic, Japan has adopted a policy of ZENHOI HEIWA GAIKO, or omnidirectional peaceful diplomacy. Clearly, Japan's continued economic prosperity depends heavily on continued world peace. In the absence of peace, Japan would be forced to take sides in the conflict and thus find itself restricting exports and redirecting energy and capital from its trade machine to military expenditures. In a perverse sense, the world's preoccupation with military war and its consequent price tag in defense spending have given Japan a distinct competitive advantage. But the advantage may be short lived, based on changes in Europe.

The domino decline of communist governments in Eastern Europe is creating a double benefit for Western Europe. Not only can the reduced threat of communist domination eventually translate to lower defense expenditures, but also the economic rubble of Eastern Europe is immediately becoming one of the most significant investment opportunities of the century. Right in Europe's backyard. Everyone wants to participate in the rebuilding, but as will be demonstrated in a later chapter, Europe clearly has the inside track on rebuilding Europe.

Kennedy's logic bears down hard on the prevailing super-powers for whom the moment-to-moment potential for war and peace has created a double burden. The United States and the Soviet Union must, in addition to military superiority, maintain some form of economic superiority. To lag behind economically would eventually downgrade their power rankings. Withdrawal from Vietnam and Afghanistan, coupled with the willingness to reduce nuclear arms gradually on a bilateral basis, signal the realization by both countries that economic growth and peace go hand and hand. Brush wars and unnecessary nuclear weaponry soak up tremendous sums of money that might otherwise fuel consumerism. Yet the transition of focus from military to trade competition will not happen quickly.

Neither superpower is prepared to totally bury the hatchet, though both sides are admitting, reluctantly perhaps, that ten nuclear hatchets are enough. But the dilemma persists. If either the United States or the Soviet Union prematurely transfers its focus of resources from military to economic strength, it may be vulnerable to a sudden resurgence of the Cold War. If it takes too long in the transition, trading competitors like Japan and a rapidly changing Europe will end up eating their trade lunch. Timing is crucial.

To complicate matters, the superpowers are coming to realize how much they depend on partners to create and maintain economic growth. As the economic gains expand from smokestacks and manufactured goods to include information systems and technical services, no nation can sustain economic growth without participating in world trade. No nation, including the United States, can fuel its growth behind a policy of isolationism.

Two commodities bind nations to international trade, technology and capital, and dependency on them has begun to affect the supernations. The Soviet Union cannot keep pace with the rate of technological change, which the Aspen Institute speculates makes some technology obsolete every 18 months. None of the Soviets' internal development efforts have enabled them to keep up with the rate of change, nor have KGB efforts to steal technology from others. Consequently, the Soviet Union finds itself with no choice but to acquire sorely needed technology on the world market. The same problem exists for each satellite in Eastern Europe in the quest for economic transformation. In both cases, Western European countries are running at full stride to break down the legal and political barriers that restrict the flow of technology to former adversaries.

However, lacking the hard currency necessary for direct transactions, the Soviet Union and Eastern Europe must open their domestic markets to foreign companies in exchange for that technology. Of course, opening their society to the outside world initiates another set of pressures and demands, one that some countries, like China, would rather avoid.

For its part, Beijing's quest for technology requires significant economic reforms. These involve the influx of foreign investment and personnel to Beijing, the creation of special economic zones on the coast, and the outflow of Chinese citizens, mostly students, to other countries. These changes place the government in a precarious position, as they encourage students to demonstrate for even more reforms. To give in to such demands would reduce the power of the Communist Party, but to reject the demands would discourage further foreign investment and the arrival of desperately needed technology. So the government crushed the student demonstrations with violence and bloodshed, but scrambled quickly to persuade trading partners not to reduce their participation in China's economic progress.

In contrast, the United States depends not on technology but on imported capital. In a relatively short period of time, the United States has gone from being the world's leading net creditor nation to being its largest borrower. Personal, corporate, and government debt exceeds eight trillion dollars. That is a hard number to grasp, especially when you consider that a million dollars is to a trillion dollars what one dollar is to a million dollars.

The total debt of the United States, which has quadrupled since the mid-1970s, now stands at double the nation's yearly output of goods and services. In 1985, for the first time since the turn of the century, the United States owed more to the rest of the world than the world owed it. By 1986, foreigners had invested over $1 trillion in the United States, some $170 billion more than the total of U.S. investments abroad. Yet as recently as 1982, American holdings abroad exceeded foreign assets in the United States by nearly $200 billion.

The United States attracts cash from around the world by being the leading marketplace for capital investment. How does another nation stockpile money to invest in the United States? It creates a trading surplus that it can convert to dollars. Without that surplus, a country must spend its wealth paying for imports. Thus, it comes as no surprise that Japan leads the list of countries that specialize in capital as a commodity and boasts seven of the world's top ten banks. As an already open society, the United States does not have the same risks for change as do the Soviet Union, Eastern Europe, and China. The United States does, however, face a different and equally enormous set of consequences. More American income must be set aside to service the debt. This means that a dollar that could be invested on factory equipment, research and development or improved education—all of which should bring future returns—instead is used as an interest payment. The danger is that the United States needs an ever-increasing dose of investment if it is to regain its competitive advantage in the form of trade surpluses.

In the absence of global military war, consumption has quickly become the new battleground for national superiority and security. How well a nation fares in the trade battle will determine how much it can afford to spend on defending its world position. This makes every country a player in the world power game. It also poses the risk that a major country will play poorly and, in desperation or perhaps because of pride, resort to the old game of military power and make the notion of consumerism, not to mention the human race, obsolete.

INFORMATION
AND THE WORLD CONSUMER

While the quest for national security has been pulling nations into international trade, another force has been pushing governments from the grass-roots level: the masses of consumers.

Traditionally, governments have represented the largest percentage of consumption in the world, as they bought and sold outlandishly expensive military hardware and natural resources. While this type of trade will certainly continue, its share of the consumption pie will be steadily reduced by the flow of goods and services with the sole function of making individuals capable, comfortable, and happy. The appetite for more personal goods and services gets whetted by the expanding information technology that knits the world more closely together every day.

Macy's Department Store or Saks Fifth Avenue places an ad in the *New York Times*, which on Sunday, November 13, 1987, weighed a record-breaking 12 pounds and contained an astonishing 1,612 pages and approximately 12 million words. Each year the *Times* uses enough paper to print a copy of this "book" for every man, woman, and child living in the United States, Japan, and Europe. And every one of those men, women, and children see that inviting ad for new clothes, appliances, and entertainment that will make their lives more comfortable.

Alvin Toffler in his book *Future Shock* observes that we are "creating and using up ideas and images at a faster and faster pace." These images get soaked up primarily by consumers around the world. Each twenty minutes of television in the United States contains roughly ten minutes of commercials, while the average edition of *The New York Times* dedicates almost 55 percent of its space to consumer advertising. In one year, the typical American will read 3,000 notices and forms, 100 newspapers, and 36 magazines, watch 2,463 hours of television, listen to 730 hours of radio, buy 20 records or tapes, talk on the telephone 61 hours, and read 3 books. Human beings literally swim in an ocean of information that makes it impossible not to compare lifestyles, clothes, automobiles, VCRs, and fast food franchises.

For decades, the closed nature of communist society allowed Communist Party leaders to spread the yarn that people in the Soviet Union and Eastern Europe lived fundamentally better than people elsewhere. While this propaganda might have held true to some degree for those party leaders with access to special privileges, it promoted an outright lie in terms of the ordinary citizenry. When the Eastern European governments fell, the lie became evident in cruelly comical episodes. While Romanian accountant, Drago Casanuo, was being interviewed by a western reporter, he spotted a bag of oranges in the reporter's car. "I do not mean to beg," he said, "but may I?" Casanuo then immediately ate four oranges, peels and all. He had not seen, except on television, or eaten an orange in eight years. East Germans, after briefly tasting life in West Berlin, critically compare their domestic-manufactured Trabants with BMWs and Porsches. The comparison spawned the joke, "How can you immediately double the financial value of your Trabant?" The answer, "Fill it with gas."

The gap between the standard of living in Communist Europe and that of the West, particularly the United States, became acutely evident when increased information technology made it more difficult for communist authorities to stem the influx of information about the West. In Romania, one week after the execution of its long-standing despot Nicolae Ceausescu, newly liberalized television stations did not celebrate freedom with Dan Rather or broadcasts of the Mormon Tabernacle Choir, but with *Gone With the Wind*, "Max Headroom," and Tom and Jerry cartoons. The heightened awareness of the gap of things both significant and trivial brought with it an intensified demand for consumer goods which an industry geared to military and heavy industry production could not begin to fulfill. In fact, Soviet senior officials conceded in *Trud* (a Soviet news weekly) on March

13, 1988, that "the demand for consumer goods is rising rapidly and we are unable to fully meet it today." The United States, Japan, and Western Europe would love to wrestle with that problem in their respective countries.

Television, radio, computers, fax machines, satellite dishes, and improved overseas telephone service combine with travel beyond national borders to raise the awareness of life outside one's "motherland." Country by country, consumers are clamoring to their governments for greater access to the goods and services that the information invasion has brought into their offices and living rooms. Television messages in particular, drawn down from the skies with relatively inexpensive satellite dishes, paint a vivid picture for even the poorest bushman in Africa. Squatting in the dust under the shade of gnarled Combretum tree, two dozen Ju/wa bushman with bows and arrows converse in a language consisting mostly of gentle clicks. Scattered on the ground lie empty Winston cigarette packages and smashed Coca-Cola cans attesting to the fact that you might be able to run from the flow of information, but you will never be able to hide.

CONSUMER POWER

The information invasion shaping the desires of the international consumer has simultaneously created a new political power. In the past, governments did not need to pay close attention to any constituents besides the elite classes, those with sufficient money or land to make a difference in the fate of nations. But in the game of world consumption, a nation not only depends on its ability to sell goods and services, but also on its ability and appetite to buy goods and services. Trade jargon calls this phenomenon reciprocity. Simply stated, reciprocity suggests that a country, in exchange for the privilege of exporting goods to another country, must allow the importing country to ship goods back to the exporting country. In an ideal and perfectly fair world, a country would buy and sell on the world market in fairly equal amounts. But the world is not perfect, and the issue of trade imbalance sparks fierce debates, with the Japanese most vocally challenging the concept and the very word itself. The mere mention of reciprocity in Tokyo elicits a combination of confusion and fear. That is hardly surprising considering the fact that the world all but ignored reciprocity for 20 years, allowing Japan to export freely while rigidly restricting imports. The fear comes with the realization that one-way trade will eventually go the way of the dinosaur, as only time protects Japan's domestic market from a flood of imported goods and services. If Japan continues to resist reciprocity, angry trading partners will retaliate with restrictions of their own, starting with Europe.

The American conceptual commitment to free trade requires that Washington speak in hushed tones about reciprocity. After all, free trade may not be all that equitable. But the EC has no such philosophical restrictions. In fact, they have already given Tokyo notice that reciprocity is the new rule of trade, and they are starting with banking. Under the old rules, the Japanese must allow London banks in Tokyo if Dai-Ichi Kongyo and Industrial Bank of Japan expect to do business in Britain. But under the new rules, Britain and Belgium (and all other EC members) are considered one trade zone and banks from each of these countries must all have banking privileges in Japan. The negotiations between Japan and Europe are already heated and the temperature is rising. At stake is not just banking, but eventually cars, electronics, and computers.

Europe's commitment to reciprocity and Japan's increasing vulnerability to this demand will be examined in Chapter 6, but for now the basic challenge that reciprocity creates for competing countries should at least be identified. First, the relationship between a nation's domestic provider of goods and services and its consumers must be alive and growing; second, a nation's consumers must be willing to participate in spending patterns that support government policies. The need for consumer cooperation in both these areas affords consumers, particularly those in developed countries, a great deal of political clout.

The impressive Japanese attack on the American auto industry, waged in the early 1970s, illustrates how the relationship between domestic providers and consumers can affect the competition for world consumption. In 1968, *Business Week* suggested that "with over 50 foreign cars already on sale here [in the United States], the Japanese auto industry isn't likely to carve out a big slice of the U.S. market." That shortsighted view was echoed in the actions of the American auto industry, which ignored the growing tensions surrounding Middle East oil and the concurrent development of fuel-efficient Japanese imports. In 1973, the sharp rise in imported oil prices sent gas prices soaring and consumers scrambling away from overpriced, underbuilt gas-guzzling American cars to less expensive, quality-built gas-conserving Toyotas and Datsuns (later changed to Nissans). Detroit immediately flooded Washington, D.C. with millions of dollars in lobbying efforts aimed at restricting the number of imported Japanese automobiles. The government complied and arm-twisted Tokyo into voluntary restraining exports while Detroit tried to improve its relationship with American consumers.

In order for reciprocity to work, a country's domestic products must compete effectively with foreign alternatives. The market relationship between the domestic manufacturer or provider of services and the domestic consumer must be sufficiently strong to make the wave of imports a constructive rather than destructive factor. In the 1970s, the American automotive industry so lost touch with American consumers, that unrestricted Japanese imports seriously threatened the entire industry. Some 18 years later, Detroit may have improved to the point where unrestricted imports would not destroy the industry but would merely provide more of a competitive environment to the benefit of consumers.

The same condition affects Europe. Italy allows less than 5,000 Japanese imports per year. To lift this restriction would do grave damage to Italy's domestic auto industry. West Germany, on the other hand, allows the unrestricted import of Japanese autos for two reasons. First, the domestic German auto industry can compete effectively enough with Japan that German consumers have not abandoned their Volkswagens, BMWs, and Mercedes for Toyotas, Nissans, and Hondas. Second, German cars account for 75 percent of foreign cars purchased by Japanese consumers. The potential market share lost to Japanese cars in West Germany is offset by gained market share of German cars in Japan.

The automotive experiences of the United States, Italy, and West Germany demonstrate that consumers considerably influence the international consumption policies of governments. If domestic providers do not cultivate and satisfy domestic consumers, then the government must either restrict imports to save domestic industries, running the risk that trading partners will retaliate with import restrictions of their own, or governments can allow unimpeded imports, which would mangle domestic industries and create a long-term decline in profitable industries capable of competing on an international scale. Regardless of the response, consumers make the final decision with their pocketbooks.

Reciprocity also hinges on consumer support for domestic trade policy, though lately consumers across the globe have become increasingly independent in their choices and less inclined to follow the purchasing directions of their governments. In Tokyo, the Ministry for International Trade and Industry has mounted a campaign to get every Japanese family to purchase $500 worth of American-manufactured goods annually. Under pressure from Washington, D.C., the Japanese government made this token attempt to increase the amount of imported American goods in Japan as a preliminary move toward reciprocity. But Japanese consumers, although traditionally obedient to government suggestion, rebelled, citing the lower quality of American alternatives. With the exception of IBM and Apple computers, selected pharmaceuticals and specialty food products such as

Coke and Mrs. Fields Cookies, Japanese consumers shy away from American offerings, regardless of government pressure. Japan's consumer resistance was surprisingly deep. The formal barriers restricting imports to Japan may be falling, but if consumers balk at buying American products, those informal barriers will court serious repercussions from the United States. At the end of his late 1989 public relations visit to Japan, former U.S. President Ronald Reagan ended an otherwise upbeat trip on a sour note, warning the Japanese of American anger over the tremendous trade imbalance between the two countries.

In other episodes, consumers in South Korea, a country on trade probation with the United States, have embarrassed their government by boycotting American grapefruit because they fear supposed cancer-causing sprays used on the fruit, and consumers in Europe refuse to purchase American beef treated with artificial hormones to stimulate growth. American farmers do use hormones to restore normal growth to castrated cattle. Castration makes the animals more manageable and their beef better textured, but it also retards growth and thus reduces the quantity of saleable meat. Hormones, implanted in the ear, can decrease the effect. Italy leads the battle against American hormone-treated beef, citing the relationship of the growth hormone DES to birth defects in Italian children. In light of this connection, consumers pressured the European Parliament to ban hormone-raised beef, which prompted the United States to slap 100 percent duties on tinned tomatoes and special hams exported by Europe to the United States.

This particular instance of consumer pressure comes at a most inconvenient time for Europe, because some observers have predicted the rise of Fortress Europe in the wake of 1992, and because consumer revolts against American beef play right into the scenario of a united Europe gone protectionist. Regardless of the outcome of the hormone-fed beef issue, however, consumers clearly yield the power to affect government policy and the international competitiveness of businesses. Even if Europe formally suspends the import ban on hormone-fed beef, an informal consumer boycott of the product would still threaten reciprocity between the United States and Europe.

EC92: A CONSUMPTION WARNING

The importance of international consumption and consumers to the domestic and international well being of a country poses a very thorny problem. Government needs its consumer base to strike a delicate balance between domestic and international spending. Too much domestic support, however, can cause trading partners to restrict imports of that country's products. Too much international spending, on the other hand, can cause the domestic industry to wither, leaving the country in a vulnerable position as an importer of foreign investment.

The more complete unification of Europe in 1992 adds another dimension to the flow of international consumption, the dimension of sheer numbers. With so much attention directed to Japan, the fact that a combined Europe would account for 20 percent of the world's exports, against 15 percent for the United States and Japan's 9 percent, has been overlooked. The impact of EC92 on reciprocity means trading as separate nations and then suddenly combining into one big trading and consumption machine. The offensive and defensive potential of this unification would alter the international scene.

As part of the 1992 unification, European consumers also become a potent power every global trader both inside and outside Europe must respect. In the traditional trade game, each country in Europe has viewed itself and has been viewed by the rest of the world as a distinct entity, a fact that greatly limited the potential of European consumer power. Now, in view of the plan for unification, Europe's previously disjointed consumers will combine to form a 320-million-person trading consumption machine that will fire up, both offensively and defensively, to achieve the international consumption goals of a combined Europe. Outnumbering the populations of the United States or Japan, Europe's consumers will add an interesting and powerful variable in the battle for reciprocity and international consumption. This variable, more than any other, has driven the private sector to seek its own solutions in the form of consortia.

CHAPTER TWO

Consortia:
The Evolution of
Multinational Traders

*The new electronic interdependence
recreates the world
in the image of a global village.*

MARSHALL MCLUHAN

GOING GLOBAL

After exhaustive analysis, Italian auto giant Fiat decided to suspend operations at its auto assembly plant in Poughkeepsie, New York, a decision that spilled hundreds of local workers into unemployment lines. Citing increased competition from Ford's new assembly plant, Fiat packed up its once prospering American operation and retreated unceremoniously to Italy. The year was 1918, and the competition that sent Fiat packing came not from Ford, the company, but Henry Ford, the auto assembler.

The Fiat experience in 1918 suggests that the problems encountered by multinational traders have existed ever since trading across borders began. In fact, so many foreign companies were operating in the United States in the late 1800s that Colorado Congressman James B. Belford complained that U.S. resources and consumers courted the dishonorable fate of becoming the "servile and supple tools of foreign capitalists." Belford was particularly incensed about the four million acres of cattle ranches in the Western United States owned and operated by British companies Prairie Cattle and Powder River. Besides cattle ranches and land companies, European investors had also bought into grain elevators, stockyards, cotton farms, breweries, and mines.

One hundred years later, many U.S. congressional representatives have revived Belford's worry about the level of control foreign corporations exercise over American goods and services. Their political pressure is aimed particularly at the Japanese, who have been swept up in an American assets-buying binge financed by the global sale of Japanese products. In Washington, D.C., elected officials appear on national television smashing Japanese manufactured products with sledgehammers as a not-so-subtle signal to trade-focused Tokyo that Americans are frustrated and angry. Japan counters with the argument that U.S. deficit-spending and American corporate decline, rather than Japanese goods and services, lie at the heart of the current trade imbalance.

While the political debate rages about Japanese ownership of American business assets, subtle signals from the private sector suggest that politicians have failed to detect a significant shift in global thinking on the part of the world's CEOs and directors. This shift renders the political debate obsolete and warns that those concerned about world trade should focus on Europe and not Japan. In *Fortune's* 1986 listing of U.S. companies boasting the highest return to investors, relatively unknown Jefferson Smurfit Corporation ranked number one. Jefferson Smurfit is a St. Louis-based subsidiary of an Irish multinational company known mainly for manufacturing cardboard boxes. In another little-publicized case, the 1989 merger of Warner Communications and Time Inc. brought to light the little-known fact that Warner Records represents the last remaining American-owned record company of significance, the majority having been bought by European interests. Phillips of the Netherlands owns Polygram, West Germany's Bertelsmann owns RCA Records, Britain's Thorn EMI owns Capital Records, and Sony recently bought CBS Records.

The world's multinational corporations are evolving into new global competitors best described as *consortia*: parent companies without national loyalty that own and coordinate business assets in multiple countries. In Europe the evolution has progressed so far that the global deck of multinationals has already been shuffled and the dominant hands have changed. In this particular area of international poker the Japanese hold a pair of deuces, while the Europeans and Americans hold full houses. Sam Kusumoto, CEO of the American subsidiary of Minolta Camera, comments that "Japan is still 15 to 25 years behind in terms of consortia." This aspect of the quest for global dominance has been largely overlooked. For example, in 1988 Smick-Medley polled Americans to find out which countries they thought invested most in American companies. Seventy-three percent of those polled assumed that Japan accounted for the majority investment, 10 percent cited oil-rich Arab countries, while only 3 percent knew that Europe had taken the lead. Ninety-seven percent of Americans would be surprised by the fact that in the period from 1980 through

1987, EC members placed over $92.2 billion in direct investment in American-operating companies. In contrast, the Japanese directly invested only $15.8 billion during the same period. Europe clearly leads the pack in developing consortia, a fact also evidenced by the number of American workers employed in U.S. operations owned by European companies. Economist Ned Hownestine, writing for the U.S. Department of Commerce, calculates that the EC accounts for almost two million American workers, or almost double the U.S. workers employed by the rest of the world combined. British consortia alone employ over 800,000 U.S. workers. Japan, on the other hand, provides paychecks for only 250,000.

At the center of the evolution to consortia lie the capitalistic attitudes of the world's CEOs and directors who doubt the ability of government and political systems to develop an effective solution to global trading problems. Consequently they have built consortia as their strategy for gaining competitive advantage in the global arena.

SUBTLE DIFFERENCES

On the surface, the definition of consortia does not differ markedly from that of the traditional multinational corporation, a term coined by David E. Lilienthal, Chairman of the Development and Resources Corporation, in a 1963 *Business Week* article. At that time the designation applied almost exclusively to American companies. According to a 1959 issue of *Fortune*, all but six of the 50 largest multinational companies in the world originated in American soil. Those large American multinationals, such as Ford, ITT, AT&T, and IBM, grew into giants in their domestic markets, then gradually turned their attention to offshore opportunities.

Having reached a critical mass with large chunks of domestic consumer loyalty, these companies saw that continued dramatic growth rested on their abilities to exploit relatively untouched foreign markets that placed a high premium on American goods and services. The resulting overseas expansion of the American multinational racked up profits, which, though impressive, never exceeded the profits earned in the domestic U.S. market, if certain sleight-of-hand accounting adjustments are set aside. In a sense, the American multinational of the 1960s functioned as a large corporation with manufacturing and marketing "colonies" conveniently scattered around the globe. The policies, goals, and management techniques of the various offshore operations looked distinctly American and could have taken place as easily in Cincinnati as in Caracas.

However, in the late 1970s and early 1980s, while corporate America focused its attention on Japan, the traditional multinationals began to change subtly in three crucial areas: domestic markets, subsidiary management, and national loyalty. As the changes gathered momentum, the traditional multinationals began their quick evolution into contemporary consortia.

Domestic Markets. Swiss-based Nestle is the largest food company in the world, and its acquisition of American-owned Carnation in 1986 for just under $3 billion emphasizes that Nestle intends to stay on top. Obviously, the population of Switzerland, a mere six and one-half million people, could scarcely drive even 20 percent of Nestle's sales. In contrast to the American model of the multinational, however, Nestle does not expand internationally on the strength of its domestic market share. Rather, the minute size of Switzerland and its lack of natural resources has forced Nestle and other Swiss giants such as Ciba-Geigy and Hoffman-La Roche to venture beyond the Alps for 85 percent of their market share. The fact that these companies call Switzerland home relates very little to their ability to generate revenue, as the Asea Brown Boveri merger illustrates.

On August 10, 1987, the largest cross-border merger in the world was announced, not in the United States or Japan with relatively large domestic populations, but in Switzerland. Sweden's Asea and Switzerland's Brown-Boveri would combine to form ABB, the largest electrotechnical company in Europe, headquartered in Zurich. By January 1990, over 1,000 companies spread over 100 nations were under the ABB leadership of CEO Percy Barnevik. The astounding fact is that no one country claims more than 15 percent of ABB's 220,000 employees. Barnevik, who once managed a U.S. operation and studied at Stanford University, likens the consortia evolution to a "ketchup bottle . . . first comes nothing, then comes everything."

Eliminating the old multinational dependency on a large domestic market base greatly expands the number of potential consortia that can compete for world trade. The traditional requirement that overseas expansion must stand on the shoulders of a large domestic market share limited multinationals to bases in developed countries with large populations. The new consortia observe no such limits. For example, Hyundai, a South Korean conglomerate, introduced a line of automobiles to the United States in 1982 that broke the existing record for sales of an imported car during its first year. Amazingly, Hyundai sold more cars during its first year in the United States than did Toyota and Nissan combined during their first full five years of U.S. operations. Hyundai's achievement, given the relatively small 25 million population of South Korea, vividly demonstrates that the new multinational trader can compete quite well without a large domestic market.

Subsidiary Management. Britain's Imperial Chemical Industries (ICI), like Switzerland's Nestle, derives over three-quarters of its revenue from foreign sales. In order to generate those sales, ICI employs some 180,000 workers, with three-quarters of its chemical sales outside the United Kingdom. The larger volume of offshore subsidiary sales compared to the parent organization raises the question of who really holds the upper hand. The domestic component of the traditional American multinational always held the dominant position in size and most other measures of strength. In most cases, all offshore operations combined could not begin to rival the power of the parent company operating in the United States. In contrast, the consortia model does not subscribe to the concept that the parent must be bigger or produce more revenue than the subsidiary. Unilever, for example, employs over 350,000 people in 78 nations, while Germany's Hoechst rivals ICI with a majority of its slightly more than 190,000 employees living outside of West Germany.

The definition of a subsidiary in the consortia model poses quite a bold leadership challenge. The traditional multinational managed its overseas operations using the same policies, style, and strategies that guided domestic operations. Their attitude essentially mimicked the colonial approach perfected by the British East India Company in the 1700s, duplicated by American multinationals in the 1960s, and continued by the Japanese in the 1980s. That attitude, however, falls by the wayside when it comes to consortia who assume more of a coordinating role vis-a-vis their subsidiaries. Those who lead the consortia, recognizing the multiplicity of needs and styles in a timely global market, strive to remain sensitive to the subtle nuances among rules, mores, and behavior that differ from one country to the next.

Were the leaders of consortia to impose, by mere virtue of ownership, one set of management practices on businesses operated in other countries, they would clearly court confusion, resentment, and even rebellion. No one is more sensitive to this issue than ABB's Barnevik. The lanky Swede manages the consortia like a federation of companies. "There is no parent around the traditional form; all operating companies are sisters. I sit in Zurich presiding over a hundred person headquarters. It will not get larger than this. It is a new concept of a truly European company we are creating. Some people say that we have no home country—the truth is we have many home countries."

Ironically, Japan, with its superior economic clout, consistently fails to convert local employees and management of its overseas operations to the Japanese management method, no matter how hard they try. Japanese-owned auto plants in the United States, once touted as the wave of the future, now face union drives by disgruntled American employees who have grown weary of company songs and mandated calisthenics. For all their trade muscle, Japanese multinationals fall victim to the outdated thinking of the old colonial order. Of the 50 largest multinationals listed by *Fortune* in 1988, only eight operated outside Japan. This number clearly runs counter to the economic and trade clout commanded by the Japanese, and it underscores the fact that Tokyo has moved slowly to accommodate the concept of consortia. Successful consortia take a hands-off coordinating stance with respect to their subsidiaries. B.A.T., an old-guard British multinational, nicely illustrates the evolution to consortia by managing a worldwide operation of 300,000 employees with a London staff of just 100 executives. B.A.T.'s so-called American subsidiaries include Hardee's (the fast food chain), People's Drug Store, and Farmers Insurance. Although any one of these companies could justify a headquarters staff of over 100, the consortia approach frees parent executives from meddling in efficiently run operations and allows them to concentrate on the broader concern of coordinating world trade. Hanson Trust, another British consortia, holds a wide range of manufacturing subsidiaries in the United States, including building products, chemicals, hand tools, food services, and textiles. Sir Gordon White, who runs Hanson's U.S. operations, has reportedly not visited one of his American plants in the last decade and has never set foot in Hanson's U.S. headquarters in New Jersey.

National Loyalty. While consortia can fairly easily solve the problems of domestic market share and subsidiary management, they face a much more difficult time with the emotional questions of national loyalty. The colonial approach of American multinationals in the 1960s and Japanese multinationals in the 1980s leaves no doubt as to the question of national loyalty. The involement of the International Telephone and Telegraph (ITT) with the Central Intelligence Agency in the overthrow of Salvador Allende's government in Chile proved ITT's loyalty to the red, white, and blue. Now, however, the global network of international trade makes such an approach obsolete in the 1990s.

For example, IBM CEO John Akers predicts that his company's growth will crest the $100 billion mark by the early 1990s. In 1988, 58 percent of IBM's revenue and 75 percent of its profit originated outside U.S. borders, with the firm's overseas growth continuing in double digits in 1989. If IBM realizes its growth objective of $100 billion, almost $75 billion of that must come from non-U.S. markets. When the question then arises, "What makes IBM an American company?" three responses come to mind: ownership, legal jurisdiction, and company headquarters.

American investors, both personal and institutional, hold the vast majority of IBM stock. In the sense of stock ownership, IBM is clearly an American company. However, since the total volume of stock traded on the Tokyo and London exchanges already exceeds that of the New York Stock exchange, current restrictions that limit the sale of stock across national borders will most likely dissolve in the future, thus providing the potential for a more internationally balanced ownership of IBM stock.

As a corporation, IBM adheres to American legal guidelines set both by the federal government in Washington, D.C. and by the state in which IBM is incorporated. Of course, IBM's overseas operations must also respect the various legal systems of the host countries. To understand how this works, consider Thomson, the French electronics company, which owns the RCA television manufacturing operation in the United States. Despite its French ownership, RCA operates under the jurisdiction of U.S. law. Turning back to IBM, if 58 percent of IBM's 1988 revenue came from abroad, that income was generated under the jurisdiction of laws other than those of the United States. From the point of view of legal jurisdiction, IBM would seem to be primarily a foreign company.

Finally, the corporate headquarters of IBM occupy real estate in Armonk, New York. However, given IBM's consortia approach to subsidiary management, that plays a smaller role in the internal operations of overseas companies. A steady shrinkage of the home office staff is in the works. The decentralized company of the 1990s will most likely view headquarters as the coach of a team comprised of a multiplicity of nationalities.

The issues of ownership, legality, and the location of headquarters raise but three obvious challenges to the balance, need, or even wisdom of national loyalty in the future of global economic change. Japanese author and consultant, Kenichi Ohmae projects a corporate world without borders and even suggests that "national borders are now irrelevant to most companies and consumers." The statement becomes more than hollow rhetoric when it is realized that Ohmae, the managing partner of McKinsey and Company's Japanese operation, reportedly contributes more than one-third of McKinsey's overall revenue.

RECIPROCITY AND THE COST OF TECHNOLOGY

The twin engines of reciprocity and market share drive the evolution of consortia. At this moment in history, reciprocity ignites intense debate. The concept itself looks on the surface to be overwhelmingly simple and fair, but politicians and trade policymakers have managed to make it amazingly complex. Three practical interpretations of reciprocity should be considered.

Overall Reciprocity. According to this view, all countries open up a little in different ways, but without matching each other sector for sector. When practicing this form of reciprocity, nations attempt to reach mutually comfortable trade levels not necessarily balanced in specific product areas. For example, overall reciprocity would allow Japanese dominance of electronic exports

63

to the United States, provided that, in exchange, Japan allowed importation of American rice. A certain imbalance would still exist among the two products, but that would not greatly bother the trading partners because they had agreed to the overall fairness of the situation.

Trade-Level Reciprocity. This sounds much like overall reciprocity except that it ignores specific products in favor of actual trade volume as a measure of fairness. Here, trade among partners must balance dollar for dollar. Simply speaking, one dollar of West German exports to South Korea must be offset by one dollar of South Korean exports to West Germany, without any exceptions.

National-Treatment Reciprocity. This approach to reciprocity specifically addresses the treatment of domestic companies owned by foreign firms. Under this approach, Japan must treat IBM's Japanese operations just as it would a domestic Japanese company, and the United States must treat Honda's Ohio-based auto manufacturing facility as a domestic U.S. company.

As international consumption gains momentum, each country favors a different interpretation of reciprocity. The European community currently favors overall reciprocity. Rather than tediously monitoring trade product by product, Brussels prefers mutually agreed upon trade volumes among partners. This approach buys Europe precious time before and after 1992 to protect its fragile industries from foreign competition without overly restricting the amount of European exports. In essence, it serves as a compromise between the desire for free trade on the world market and the reality that many of Europe's industries would not survive direct and unfettered competition.

The United States, even in light of current imbalances with Japan and other trading partners, favors national-treatment reciprocity. The strong American commitment to free trade defuses the fear that some industries might fail, especially given the fact that in a really fair system of reciprocity, the same chances for success or failure would befall all participating parties. The American position logically extends the current U.S. practice of treating all companies doing business in the United States under the same law and conditions, regardless of ownership. The United States expects tit for tat, especially from Japan.

The Japanese position understandably differs. With a population of 120 million and a national economy that pays the piper for Japan's exporting strength with high domestic prices, almost any version of reciprocity that lowers import barriers causes fear and anxiety. Since the end of World War II, Japan has enjoyed the luxury of unrestricted exports while stubbornly limiting its own imports. Under the guise of rebuilding from the near total devastation of war, it has cowed the United States and other countries into tolerating this position, but not for long.

Some form of reciprocity will eventually guide the world's trade volume. How long it will take the politicians and policy-makers to implement reciprocity in some form or another, no one knows. But one thing is certain: companies that live or die by the sword of international consumption cannot afford to leave their destinies in the hands of government.

For example, assume that, in the near future, the fears of "Fortress Europe" do materialize, causing trading partners such as the United States to erect trade barriers in retaliation. Restricted trade would have a devastating effect on companies like Nestle, which depend so heavily on international trade for survival. That very possibility prompted Nestle to buy a hedge against disaster in the form of Carnation, its American food subsidiary that could continue to sell to the U.S. domestic market even though, legally, Swiss-based Nestle could not.

Reciprocity appeals to consortia not because companies possess a finely honed sense of fair play, but because they understand the role it plays in allowing them to spread the fixed and developmental costs associated with technological change across broader consumer bases. The mathematics do not require an advanced degree.

If you make a successful product, would you rather sell it to a domestic market of 200 million or a world market of three times that number, excluding the Soviet Union, Communist China, and Third World countries? This simple equation has drawn many domestic companies into the world of multinational operations and evolving consortia. Until the 1980s the transition from domestic to multinational company was largely a matter of voluntary choice. However, the tremendous cost of developing new technology and the need for speedy product distribution make the move to consortia status mandatory for any firm bent on long-term survival.

The rate and range of technological change, which will be looked at more closely in Chapter 8, places heavy financial burdens on consortia desiring to keep pace with competitors. To succeed, they must offset the high cost of research and development with a high volume of consumer sales. Clearly, the larger the volume of potential sales, the greater investment a player can sustain. A consortium with a market of 700 million global consumers will be able to win a greater competitive technological edge over a company that can spread its costs across a domestic market of only 120 million consumers. The math has not escaped the attention of executives in Japan, the United States, and Europe.

Japan has long realized that its domestic population of 120 million alone cannot support the costs associated with the international technology game. In order to maintain an edge on quality and emerging technology, Japan and other world traders must not only dominate present market, but future ones as well. For example, C. Itoh, a *sogo shosha* (Japanese trading company) recently assigned the manager of its new products department to head the New Delhi office covering India, Bangladesh, Sri-Lanka, Nepal, and Bhutan. If C. Itoh tradition holds true, Shigeo Kojima will spend the next five to seven years developing a presence in India, not for current, but for future profit.

Executives in the United States are slowly awakening to the fact that while national opinion focuses on containing Japanese

66

economic expansion in the United States, the Japanese are effectively outtrading American companies in every other country around the world. Wisely, the American consortia have begun to look beyond the current condition and imagine what trading alliances may create the most profits in the future. The imagination naturally drifts toward Europe.

In the late 1970s and early 1980s American multinationals concentrated effort and resources on securing toeholds in trade-restricted Japan. Blocked at almost every turn, the American strategy now concentrates on leapfrogging over markets currently dominated by Japan to grasp markets where Japan still struggles. Like the World War II strategy of skipping over entire chains of islands held by Japanese soldiers, the American consortia strategy concentrates on cornering the future consumers that Japan needs to fuel its continued growth. Many of those consumers live in France, Italy, Germany, and Great Britain.

Corning closed ranks with Swiss giant Ciba-Geigy to form Ciba-Corning Diagnostics, which will develop medical equipment. General Electric and unrelated, but similarly named British competitor GEC, merged their European operations and are concentrating on the consumer products, medical equipment, and electrical equipment markets. Sara Lee, which already rings up just under $4 billion in European sales, is attacking the coffee market with the acquisition of a Dutch company, and International Paper is headed straight for Europe with its purchase of a major French paper manufacturer.

For their part, European business leaders who have also begun to realize the value of spreading costs over large consumer bases need only look in their own backyards. What now function as 12 segmented and relatively impotent trading nations (compared to supertraders Japan and the United States) will, in 1992, become a force of 320 million consumers over which the cost of technological and other product development and distribution can be spread before exporting to rich overseas markets.

67

JOINT VENTURES, MERGERS, ACQUISITIONS, AND DIRECT INVESTMENT

The new consortia have grown more horizontally than vertically as they spread across national boundaries, slowly establishing themselves in as many countries as possible. They have done so for two reasons: first, to get firmly entrenched in a host country so as to not be excluded during any future trade wars over reciprocity; and second, to participate in an additional market that will lessen the burden of technological and fixed costs. Four primary means accomplish this horizontal movement: joint ventures, mergers, acquisitions, and direct investment.

Joint Ventures. In 1881 Thomas Edison formed a "cooperative relationship" with German brothers Werner, Carl and Friedrich Siemens to manufacture filament lamps or light bulbs for European markets. Today, Siemens, one of the world's largest electronic companies with over 350,000 employees spread out over 127 countries, still uses joint ventures to attain world growth.

Roger Smith, chairman of General Motors admits that in order to prosper in the future, GM "had to reach out beyond our own resources for the best technology and best thinking available." The company, like the rest of the global automotive industry, reached out with joint ventures. The consequent linkages are often intricate. General Motors owns just under 42 percent of Isuzu, which in turn is involved in a joint venture with Subaru, which is partly owned by Nissan. Korean carmaker Daewoo is also half owned by GM, but manufactures cars for Nissan to sell in Japan. The latest twist is that Daewoo will be assembling cars designed by GM in Europe, carrying the Isuzu logo for sale to Japanese consumers. The Toyota joint venture operates in Fremont, California, and manufactures Chevrolets for sale in the United States. The Daewoo agreement reflects a more international thrust. Pontiac LeMans, financed in the United States, are

68

designed by Opel in West Germany, built in South Korea, and sold worldwide.

GM's latest linkup is with Sweden's SAAB. The joint venture, which cost GM $600 million, will provide staid GM with a product that appeals to young buyers, particularly in the United States. SAAB is able to take advantage of GM's size to reduce production and parts cost, as well as get an edge in research and development of new models to match SAAB's engineering savvy.

Charles Morris, a consultant with Devonshire Partners, a firm specializing in mergers and acquisitions, observes a lighter side of joint ventures as they relate to corporate image. For years Lee Iacocca has pitched buying a Chrysler as a patriotic act, a duty for loyal Americans everywhere. While jet planes streak overhead leaving red, white, and blue contrails, Iacocca blares, "Here's to you, America." What is not mentioned in the commercial is that Chrysler has the highest percentage of non-American parts in its cars than either Ford or General Motors. American Chrysler churns out nearly a quarter of a million cars a year with joint venture partner Mitsubishi. The cars are sold as both Chryslers and Mitsubishis. Even the jet planes used in the commercial are not made in America, they are French.

Elsewhere in Europe, Italian company Olivetti recently ended a seven-year joint venture with AT&T, whereby Olivetti provided the 6300 Personal Computer AT&T sold in the lucrative U.S. office computer market in direct competition to IBM and Apple machines. In addition to Olivetti, AT&T's European joint ventures include Dutch Philips, the United Kingdom's British Telecom, and Sweden's Nordic Cable and Wire. Perhaps the most successful joint venture in the 1980s was the European Airbus project established to manufacture wide-bodied jet aircraft. Launched as a challenge to the 90 percent market penetration of American-made Douglas, Lockheed, and Boeing aircraft in the international airline industry, the Airbus joint venture was headed by Roger Beteille, a French engineer and tough competitor who recognized the huge odds against success. World air travelers could easily identify 707s, 727s, DC-8s, and DC-9s, but could not tell a Viscount, Comet, or Caravell from a twin-engined Cessna. Nevertheless, after coordinating efforts across five nations, an almost impossible task in itself, Beteille saw his first plane off the ground, a scant four years into the project. An epitome of the joint venture philosophy, the craft sported wings from the United Kingdom, a cockpit from France, flaps from Belgium, a body from West Germany, and a tail from Spain. At first, the champions of the Airbus could only persuade relatively small airlines in Brazil, South Africa, and South Korea to buy the planes, but a breakthrough came when Airbus cracked the American market, selling four aircrafts to Eastern Airlines. By 1985, Airbus had captured 11 percent of the world's airline market and in 1988 edged out McDonald Douglas to occupy the number-two position in wide-bodied aircraft sales.

Joint ventures, or cooperative agreements between companies, provide a relatively inexpensive means for competitors to gain access to needed technology and to penetrate target markets. Most commonly, joint ventures establish a new company mutually owned by the venturing parties. In this way, each participant can maintain its own identity and management style, but still effectively compete through combined strength. Success of the concept, which lies so close to the heart of the new consortia, prompted Roger Smith to say that the "bottom line of the joint venture phenomenon is simply this: no manufacturer today can be an island."

Mergers. The number of mergers in Europe is at an all-time high and still climbing. The motivation behind the merger movement is clearly consortia development, suggests Peter Rona, CEO of the IBJ Schroder Bank and Trust Company. Rona sees the consolidation in Europe as "politically and economically driven rather than the financial phenomenon that happened in the U.S."

In Europe the question of merger is simple but painful. Does every country need to duplicate every industry, as traditional thinking about national interests suggests? The sheer emotion of the question is reflected in Italy's move to legislatively label its mineral water industries strategically essential to Italian national security. A more serious example is the 16 locomotive manufacturing companies that compete in Europe against only two in the United States. The fact that Americans are not as train-oriented as Europeans can be cited as a possible explanation for the difference. But Japan, which is as committed to train transportation as Europe, only has three locomotive manufacturers. Some of the European manufacturers turn out less locomotives in a year than their counterparts in Japan and the United States do in a week.

The country-by-country duplication occurs in almost every important product category. But this is changing as mergers increase. The white goods, or home appliances, business in Europe has shrunk from 22 companies in 1980 to just 5 today; coffee from 18 in 1979 to 4; metal and plastic packaging from 24 competitors in 1984 to just 5. But consortia mergers do not occur only among industrial companies. In 1989, Time Inc. and Warner Communications concluded a merger complicated by two years of negotiations and monumental legal battles with Paramount Communications (Gulf & Western) and even shareholders. Time Inc. CEO Richard Monro, dedicated to building a vertically integrated global entertainment machine, hopes to preside over an empire that, in his own words, "the media and entertainment businesses have never seen." The merger produces some globally significant results. Time Inc. can exploit Warner's marketing muscle in Europe and Japan, markets which account for over 40 percent of Warner's total sales. Warner, on the other hand, can use Time's lock on the cable television market to air programs from its television and movie studios. Such combinations will add a new competitive dimension to the rapidly expanding world broadcast market.

In contrast to the relatively loose joint ventures, mergers involve complete and formal integration of previously separate companies. In the Time-Warner merger, both CEOs will remain with the new organization, but with a stroke of the pen and some rather intense restructuring, the merger produced a more globally competitive organization overnight.

Acquisitions.   Outright purchases of other companies offer the quickest form of consortia growth. More comprehensive than a joint venture and more ruthless than a merger, the acquisition gives an impatient consortium a piece of market share immediately, but for a price.

The acquisition frenzy in the United States makes hungry sharks look like goldfish. Between 1981 and 1987, over 20,000 acquisitions took place in the United States, and many of these had a distinct international flavor. For example, in 1988, British companies alone recorded 385 acquisitions of American firms for a total of $32 billion, up not all that much from the 1977 figures— 262 U.S. companies for just under $31 billion. In 1988, American companies spent just over $9 billion buying roughly 100 European companies. The Japanese lag far behind both U.S. and EC buyers, with the exception of bank acquisitions in the United States.

The international nature of acquisitions eventually began raising some eyebrows. In 1978, Europe's Unilever shocked financial observers with its $484 million purchase of National Starch and Chemical of New Jersey. Though this large a transaction by a foreign buyer was very unusual at the time, a scant nine years later Unilever led a buying spree of foreign acquisition of U.S. companies with the $3.1 billion buyout of Chesebrough-Pond's Inc. The surge in Europe's purchase of American companies included $7.6 billion for Standard Oil (by British Petroleum), $5.7 billion for Pillsbury (by Grand Metropolitan), $5.2 billion for Farmers Insurance Group (by B.A.T.), and $2.6 billion for publisher Macmillan (by Maxwell).

The quest for buying businesses aims ultimately at increased market share and global dominance. Australian-based Rupert Murdoch publishes over 20 magazines in the United States and owns book publisher Harper & Row. The U.S. portion of Murdoch's consortium also includes Twentieth Century Fox Film Corporation and the Fox Broadcasting Network. Like the executives that shaped the Time-Warner merger, Murdoch wants to wield great power in global entertainment. Sweden's Electrolux wants to do the same in a different market. The 1986 takeover of White Consolidated Industries in Cleveland, Ohio, made Electrolux the world's largest white goods manufacturer, controlling lines such as Frigidaire and Westinghouse, both household words in America.

Direct Investment. This strategy represents the most patient form of consortia growth. Rather than joint venturing, merging, or acquiring, the direct investment approach either builds factories and service centers as a means of increasing market share or invests capital in existing companies without taking an active ownership or managerial role.

While the Japanese have been conspicuously absent from the merger and acquisition game and only play sparingly in a few select joint ventures, they have gotten into direct investment in a big way. Honda Motor of Japan built its own manufacturing plant in Marysville, Ohio, and quickly became the fourth largest U.S. auto producer. Since then, Mazda, Mitsubishi, Toyota, Subaru, and Nissan have all followed with American automobile plants. However, the Japanese are not the only global players who love direct investment.

In 1987, Scandinavian SAS Airlines tried to acquire control of British Caledonian Airlines, but an adverse political climate worked against its efforts to purchase 23 percent of British Caledonian stock. SAS has considerable experience with the direct investment method, having made investments in Continental Airlines and a 40 percent noncontrolling interest in Aerolineas Argentinas.

COUNTING ON CONSORTIA

Regardless of the methods they employ, consortia pave the path toward the global village predicted by the late Marshall Mc-Luhan. By hedging against the threat of restricted trade, they insure themselves pieces of market share regardless of unpredictable winds of national interest and political wrangling.

Business people who favor the balanced development of global enterprise can take heart that the United States and Europe have taken the clear lead in consortia growth, with Japan lagging desperately behind. However, that will not last long. Japanese joint venture and acquisition activity in Europe tripled in 1988 and 1989, although it still has far to go before it rivals United States activity in Europe or European activity in the U.S. Even as the Japanese attempt to play catch-up, the pace of consortia growth has accelerated, with Europe playing the pacesetter for a change.

CHAPTER THREE

Capitalism:
The Dominant
Methodology

*The Communists' idea of a good time
was going to a production meeting.*

PETER MATEFI
Romanian Worker

MANAGING COMMUNISM

In 1714, Germans Eberhard Gruber and Johann Rock formed the Community of True Inspiration and called its citizens Amanites. Community members lived simple lives bound by the word of God and economic necessity. In the mid-1800s, the group emigrated to America and eventually settled near Cedar Rapids, Iowa. Situated in seven villages, the Amanites peacefully farmed, manufactured home drugs, and produced woolen goods. From 1859 to 1932, the society practiced an almost pure form of communism. But when the century turned, the Amanites began to notice, with frustration and eventually longing, the material differences between their society and the surrounding neighbors. The initial prosperity of the colony, when there was nothing to do but improve, now paled against the seeming unlimited gains of the 1920s. Against the backdrop of the Great Depression, which warned of unbound capitalism, the community met on June 1, 1932, and 90 percent of the society voted to disband communism at the stroke of midnight. When they awoke on the morning of June 2, the Amanites were practicing capitalists. Their first major act was the founding of a refrigerator company in 1934. It carried the name of the original sect that practiced communism for over 80 years: Amana.

In East Germany and virtually every other Eastern European Soviet satellite, people are pursuing the Amanite transition from communism to capitalism. Like the Amanites, the change occurred seemingly at the stroke of midnight—the world woke up one morning to an additional 200 million capitalists. Unlike the Amanites, the transition is neither peaceful nor smooth, but even the Soviet Union sees it as inevitable.

"*Perestroika* is our last chance," said a grim Mikhail Gorbachev on January 8, 1988. "If we stop, it will be our death." This statement came 30 years after Nikita Khrushchev boasted, "Within a period of, say, five years following 1965, the level of U.S. production per capita should be equaled and overtaken.

77

Thus, by that time, perhaps even sooner, the USSR will have captured first place in the world, both in absolute volume of production and per capita income, which will insure the highest standard of living." But today, the USSR not only remains far behind the United States, but also finds itself embattled by upstart Japan and a rapidly uniting Europe. The clearly emerging victory of capitalism over communism has the Politburo worried and capitalist ideologists gloating.

Ever since Karl Marx issued the Communist Manifesto in 1848, both capitalist and communist ideologists, despite their opposing viewpoints, have promoted a single interpretation of world events. According to both camps, the so-called imperialistic bourgeoisie wages a daily battle against the forces of world revolution for the minds and hearts of nations. But the results of that battle seem undeniably conclusive according to Zbigniew Brzezinski, former Director of the National Security Council and a long-time communist watcher. His book, *The Grand Failure*, documents the fact that communism has not and cannot overtake capitalism. In obvious oversimplification, communist consumers, like the Amanites, glance at their capitalist neighbors with growing frustration. The standard of living gap which seemed to be narrowing when Krushchev debated then Vice-President Richard Nixon in Moscow, is clearly widening. To make matters worse, communist consortia have not and could not keep pace with capitalist consortia, ensuring that the gap between the capitalist haves and the communist have-nots would remain permanently in place. The gap was particularly hard to take when it glaringly existed just 20 paces across a wall between East and West Berlin.

While economic statistics and West German window shopping signal the apparent victory, the temptation to gloat must be avoided and the meaning of that victory must be carefully interpreted. Communism may have failed in its economic clash with capitalism, but that does not mean that the communist ideology will necessarily decline. The communist publication, *Marxism Today*, which pushes the concept of "market socialism," heralds a new-found flexibility that can keep communism alive. Like jumbo shrimp and military intelligence, "market socialism" is an oxymoron, but it does signal what may be the hottest issue of the 1990s: how can a generation of executives and leaders trained in communism make the transition to a capitalist world. To address this issue, it is first necessary to differentiate between ideology and methodology.

An ideology, the belief backing the -ism of communism and capitalism, uses ideas and words to capture the attention of people and nations seeking a way to attain progress and prosperity. In doing so, an ideology makes strong value judgments. In contrast, a methodology, the actual system that must put the words and ideas into action, operates more or less dispassionately. Ideology is an explosive fuel; methodology is a machine.

Evaluated in business terms, communism was a marketing success. It spread like Shacklee and Amway in countries plunged in political, social, and particularly economic chaos. Communism's ideas of equality and equal distribution of wealth played well to those who suffered severely under systems where the few gained extraordinary wealth at the expense of the many. The capitalist counter-idea that people should remain equally free to prosper or suffer has not played well with countries that have experienced only suffering, mostly at the hands of foreign rulers. The heady combination of nationalism and ideological equality effectively eradicated imperialism around the world in a relatively short 60 years. In doing so, it provided the natural yin to capitalism's yang.

Having achieved significant political success based on a gospel of equality, the converted communist countries then had to deliver material progress. Could they do so with methods consistent with their ideologies? At this point, the battle gradually ceased to depend on ideas and words and began to involve differentiated systems. Attention shifted from explosive fuel to efficient machinery.

A LEGACY OF FAILURE

The conflict between communism and capitalism reflects such opposing views of reality that they almost never draw the same conclusions from the same information. However, after decades of disagreement, the two factions now agree on one conclusion: communism has failed to deliver economic progress.

The failure is so complete, so encompassing, so well documented that the communists themselves can do little but sadly shake their heads. Communism as a management methodology has failed on three levels: developmental, competitive, and standard of living.

The Developmental Level. The Marxist ideology made notable headway in underdeveloped countries across three continents. Without exception, however, it failed to convert political power into economic progress since the Communist Revolution in Russia.

In the 1970s, a number of African countries opted for communism and began marching to the drumbeat of its tenets toward what they assumed would be sure social and economic improvement. Angola, Mozambique, Madagascar, Benin, Ethiopia, and the Congo aligned directly with the Soviet sphere. Algeria, Libya, Cape Verde, Guinea-Bissau, Guinea, Sao Tome, Zambia, Tanzania, and the Seychelles avoided direct Soviet alignment, choosing instead to stress nationally directed socialism.

Revealingly, those countries that aligned directly with the flagship of communism, the Soviet Union, languished the most economically. Angola has been torn apart by a civil war sustained by a 50,000-member Cuban military force financed and supplied by the Soviets. The Angolan internal strife has left the country economically devastated. In Ethiopia, the specter of starvation constantly lingers over a population with a per capita gross national product of only $110.

Those countries that favored national socialism over communism have fared slightly better, but far worse than their capitalist neighbors. On the east coast of Africa, socialist Tanzania posts a dismal record against prosperous Kenya, whose agricultural production has grown at a rate four times greater than that of its socialist neighbor. From 1980 to 1985, Kenya's gross national product has grown an average annual rate of 3.1 percent, while Tanzania has recorded a slow 0.8 percent each year. During the same period, industrial Kenyan production rose 2.0 percent annually, compared to a Tanzanian decline of 4.5 percent per annum. Consequently, Kenya moved ahead of Tanzania in most accepted social indicators of national well being, such as infant mortality, health care, and education. Other countries, such as Libya and Algeria, fare better, not due to socialist programs, but rather because of inherent wealth in oil reserves and close ties to France, their former colonial ruler.

Communism fared no better in Southeast Asia, where Viet Nam, Laos, and Cambodia continue the communist march of economic decline. Viet Nam cannot produce enough food to feed its own people, with rice production actually in decline. This fact has prompted Hanoi to request foreign assistance in feeding four million of its starving citizens. An inflation rate in excess of 700 percent per year requires more than $2 billion worth of Soviet aid just to keep the country afloat. The communist government of Viet Nam has defaulted on more than $3 billion worth of foreign debt, and foreign exchange reserves have dropped to less than $20 million. Neighboring Thailand, in contrast, enjoys an economic boom with a gross national product growth rate of about 5 percent. Sometime in the early 1990s, it will probably join the capitalist clique of nations referred to as the Four Tigers: South Korea, Taiwan, Singapore, and Hong Kong.

Finally, the economic record of communism in Latin America provides no surprises. Cuba still requires roughly $5 billion in aid each year from its Soviet partner. In 1986, Fidel Castro, Cuba's aging leader, announced payment cancellation on $3.5 billion worth of foreign debt, and he reported to the Central Committee that he had compiled a book of "economic irregularities" in which "every paragraph is a calamity."

The economy of the latest of communism's Latin American converts, Nicaragua, has run true to form. In 1987, it boasted an inflation rate of 1,800 percent, with real wages falling by 90 percent. Foreign debt has risen to $7 billion from $1.6 billion. Experts expect hyperinflation in excess of 10,000 percent to plague the country as it makes the transition to the 1990s. Already a can of pineapple costs 20 percent of an average monthly paycheck, and a pair of pants would require almost an entire month's earnings. The capital city of Managua lacks running water an average of two days a week, and it suffers electrical outages almost daily.

In country after country across three continents, the communist methodology has consistently failed to promote much-needed economic growth. As a result, many countries have launched a desperate search for alternative means by which they can increase the standard of living for their people.

The Competitive Level. Communism has also failed in established nations competing for a share of world trade. With over one-third of the world's population under communist rule, only 10 percent of the world's trade originates from those countries. The Soviet Union, while assuming the role of one of the world's top two superpowers, ranks only 15th in the exporting of manufactured goods, behind South Korea, Hong Kong, Switzerland, and even Taiwan. In 1985, Soviet exports totaled a mere $66 billion against $576 billion for the United States and $308 billion for Japan. Three-fourths of the Soviet trade volume consists of commodities, a fact that reflects the country's wealth of natural resources. Oil provides almost 50 percent of its total exports, followed by gold at 18 percent and timber at 4 percent. The disproportionate percentage in exports of commodities to manufactured goods and services underscores the weakness and lack of development of the Soviet industrial and business machine.

Communist China's total exports fare slightly better than the Soviet Union's. In 1987, China exported just under $80 billion worth of goods. The number is almost insignificant in light of the fact that Chinese industries produced 19.7 percent of the world's manufactured goods in the late 1800s. Comparatively, Great Britain, during the same period, slightly edged out China with a 19.9 percent share. Imagine, prior to the turn of the century, China actually ranked as the world's number-two producer of manufactured goods! While current Chinese efforts have pushed slightly ahead of the Soviet Union in terms of world trade, they have not even begun to match earlier Chinese economic achievements. The embarrassment will become especially acute for Communist China when it absorbs the capitalist ministate Hong Kong and adds an additional $60 billion to China's overall exports, an impressive 57 percent increase.

The competitive nature of Eastern Europe is less statistically damning of the communist methodology than it is subtle. At the end of World War II, Stalin formed Comecon, a trading alliance designed to rival the flow of capitalist goods in the free world. Most every communist country joined the organization, and for 40 years it controlled communist trade, with the Soviet Union as the largest partner.

All Comecon transactions are made in "transferable rubles." Soviet buyers used the invented currency to purchase merchandise made mostly in Eastern Europe, then accepted the currency in payment, mostly for energy resources sold to its European satellites. But Soviet shelves were (and are) chronically empty, and all of Eastern Europe's output was gobbled up as fast as production occurred. Meeting demand became the primary focus of Eastern European industry, and quality became the least important factor in the wave of five-year plans. As a result, the industries of Eastern Europe begin competition with the West never having sold against another product. Test marketing, comparative advertising, and incremental innovation are as foreign to East European managers as moral judgment was to Wall Street's inside traders. In a world where even the poorest mother surviving in the African bush has a choice between two competing brands of baby formula, Comecon has subtly robbed Eastern Europe of the tools of competition.

But the manufacturing and export failures of the communist system pale against the communist nations' inability to get abreast of changing technology. The knowledge explosion of the 1970s and 1980s rendered most forms of high technology obsolete every 18 months.

Technological change seems to thrust a giant monkey wrench into the communist methodology. In the mid-1960s through the early 1970s, the Soviet economy grew at a tremendous rate to reach a level more than half that of the United States, a significant achievement in the relatively brief period since 1917. But that growth primarily represented a transition from an agriculture-based economy to an industrial one. Alvin Toffler in *The Third Wave* labels the agricultural phase "the first wave," and the industrial phase "the second wave." The "third wave," or the information and knowledge explosion, has left the Soviet Union in particular, and the worldwide communist system in general, frantically treading water.

Standard of Living. The relative lack of exported goods and services indicates poor development of the communist manufacturing and service sector, which cannot even fulfill the needs of its own citizens. Forty years after World War II, the Soviet government still maintains a national meat ration and has done the same with sugar. In 1988, the Soviet weekly magazine, *Nedelya*, reported that residents of the city and region of Sverdlovsk needed to further *reduce* the ration of meat, butter, and noodles.

The increased flow of information in the era of *glasnost* reveals the saddest side of the Soviet system. The latest statistics indicate that roughly 40 percent of the entire population and 79 percent of the elderly live in conditions considered below the poverty level. Only one-third of the Soviet households enjoy hot running water, while one-third get no running water at all.

As information about life in the Soviet Union becomes available to the West, it grows obvious that the middle class in the Soviet Union subsists on the same level as people considered poor in the West. Under the communist methodology, what most of the people living in developed countries take for granted remains in short supply. Among the rank and file, cars, telephones, appliances, and other tools of modern living remain conspicuously scarce. The average family of four with the father working at an unskilled job must confine itself to living quarters measuring only 8 feet by 8 feet. The Harvard Center for Population Studies concludes that a male born today in the Soviet Union can expect to live fewer years than one born in Mexico.

The same conditions exist in Communist China, where they are aggravated by the fact that much of China still struggles to effect the transition from first-wave agriculture to second-wave industrialization. With the exception of coastal development, spurred on by foreign investment, most of China remains rural and even more devoid of modern conveniences than the Soviet Union. The one exception to China's general backwardness is television. The poorest of Chinese households manages to afford at least one TV. Not only does the government find the television medium an excellent means to bind a rather large country together, but color TVs also provide one of the country's major exports. Experts estimate that just over 2,000 satellite dishes lie scattered over mainland China, pulling in Western programs, albeit under tight government controls.

To better understand why the communist system has failed to rival capitalism in terms of economic development, the managerial methodologies of the two systems must be examined. Despite all the combative ideological rhetoric, both systems employ labor, expend resources, and distribute products and services; but they do so in starkly different ways.

DUELING METHODOLOGIES

Eugeniusz Piontek is a card-carrying member of the Polish Communist Party and a Rotarian. The Rotary Club, with its international headquarters in Evanston, Illinois, is understandably delighted that the Rotary is back in Eastern Europe after an absence of almost 50 years. Already there are clubs in Warsaw and Budapest, and even an outpost town in Siberia is looking into establishing a local chapter. At one of the first meetings of the Warsaw Rotary, Mr. Piontek was buttonholed by Ken Malli, a fellow Rotarian from Pittsburgh and not coincidentally an investor searching for Poles who want to start in business. The meeting of Piontek and Malli is both a historic event and a warning. The return of service-oriented Rotary to Poland and Rotarians who are card-carrying communists is not exactly a duplication of Rotary activity in Duluth, Iowa. The small meeting held at 7:00 on Wednesday morning is certainly Rotary history. But the warning is also clear. If you own something, run something, or have letters after your name, you qualify for Rotary. It is a club, dedicated to unparalleled community service, and a never-ending business network that circles the globe. In a sense, Rotary and Rotarian Ken Malli are the advanced guard of capitalism; while they do not quote Marx, they did make the book *Swim with the Sharks Without Being Eaten Alive*, a runaway best seller.

The imperialist West are no longer enemies, just competitors. But they pursue the rewards of capitalism with the same, if not greater, fervor that once spread communist revolution throughout the world. To survive or maybe even dominate, Eastern Europe must use its new-found freedom to radically alter their executive thinking.

It is customary, particularly in the press, to categorize communism and capitalism in terms of a controlled versus a free market system. While this comparison may contain some ideological truth, it falls short of describing just how the two systems differ in a nuts-and-bolts, day-to-day way. To get at those rudimentary differences, the key business tools both systems use, noting how individuals in each actually apply them, must be examined. Analysis of four common business denominators can demonstrate important differences: planning, management, information, and ownership.

Planning. Communism relies on central planning, while capitalism relies on decentralized planning. In the communist system, a bureaucracy rigidly controls all elements of the industrial, manufacturing, distribution, and service sectors, most notably under the now infamous "five-year plans." To exercise its control, the Soviet central planning authority must develop plans for over 24 million products each year. Driven by a free market economy, the capitalist methodology permits individuals, institutions, and companies to take their own best shots at the future. The amount of freedom varies, however, from country to country. Japan, for example, encourages more government intervention than does the United States, although the U.S. government has come under increased pressure to take a more direct role in national industrial planning.

On the practical day-to-day level, the communist executive will look to the central planning authority for social indoctrination, role assignment, and division of labor.

The heavy emphasis on equality in communist societies demands that somebody take responsibility for distribution of that equality. Self distribution or insuring one's own share runs against equal distribution, at least in theory. Thus, managers feel tremendously pressured to trust the central planning authority, regardless of personal convictions and opinions. Further, each citizen performs an assigned role, even those in the central planning authority. If anyone challenges the planner's role, they would be guilty of creating duplication of effort and subsequent waste. Further, to challenge the planning authority would require a commitment of time and energy so far beyond an executive's normal role, an effective challenge could hardly arise. As a result, managers resign themselves to a forced and largely cynical reliance on the planning authority to deliver the future promise of the communist system.

Since the planning authority receives virtually no constructive feedback and relies on final tallies of winners and losers, each five-year plan is little more than a capricious roll of the dice. Understandably, then, planning executives spend as much time creating loopholes and protective excuses for planning failures as they do creating effective plans. No one tries to bridge the gap between planning and implementation, because doing so would make it easier to pinpoint blame for planning failure on the shoulders of individuals. In the recent past, such blame could result in the *gulag* or death.

In contrast, capitalist executives assume that any plan originating from a central source will be tragically flawed, and they tend to discount any government projections about the future. Since capitalist executives advance or fall back based on the success or failure of a plan, they shy away from trusting that function to others. Should a plan fail, the whole business may well go down with it, leaving little room for midstream correction. Further, without central direction, every business person must constantly anticipate the future, a fact of life that invites inherent risk. Since not acting carries the same risks as acting poorly, each executive feels a constant incentive to plan. This makes the individual and organization more self-reliant in terms of survival. Although central government may intervene in times of crisis, even then the typical executive expects little or nothing of value to come from that assistance.

The lack of trust in central authority assures that individuals and companies constantly design and implement plans regardless of the state of the organization. This continual planning activity ensures an ongoing rejuvenation that can outlast temporary lapses by a government or even a megacorporation behaving like a government.

Management.   The central planning approach requires a tremendous number of managers to operate and oversee the system. Communist management breaks down into two functions, a bureaucracy to operate the actual planning process and a working management to insure that directives get carried out. *Izvestia*, a Soviet publication, estimates that over 15 percent of the Soviet work force is managerial, roughly 18 million managers, or one manager for every six workers. Given the communist emphasis on control, a manager at the working level does nothing but implement directives. Any changes must come, of course, from the central planning authority. The lack of central planning in capitalist countries eliminates the need for a vast planning bureaucracy. Rather, executives responsible for planning often function at the working level. With the exception of the late 1970s, capitalist managers combined the planning and implementation roles, maintaining a ratio of managers to workers much lower than the one required by the communist system. Further, capitalist management can tinker with plans as they unfold and often serve as a resource for workers, rather than as enforcers of a central plan.

In the communist system, management serves as a tool for enforcing the dictates of the central planning and distribution authority. Not surprisingly, the system discourages managerial differentiation in its quest for the most uniform method of keeping workers and organizations within prescribed boundaries. Since performance in the party can parallel managerial promotion, keeping within boundaries becomes crucial to managers' careers. Communist managers concentrate heavily on rules and roles, feeling little incentive for self improvement and skills enhancement in a system where promotion mostly depends on avoiding error and fostering party relationships. The connection of party to performance also links the talent pool of communist countries. The best and brightest within government play similar roles in industry, quite effectively eliminating constructive interplay among opposing ideas and solutions.

The capitalist methodology makes management a commodity, not just a tool, and managers feel constant pressure to grow and enhance their skills. The incentive for constant personal improvement results in a continuous stream of aggressive and assertive individuals. Further, these managers enjoy great mobility, with the best and brightest managers often gravitating toward the hottest sectors of the economy. In the capitalist system, the executive talent pool does not correspond with the talent pool in government or a given political party. Even with an inept government, a country could still maintain a highly productive managerial core. In fact, most capitalist executives assume a level of superiority to their government counterparts and rarely accept official government opinion as valid or binding in the long run. This attitude promotes even greater risk-taking by executives, not necessarily out of a desire for further risk, but rather out of an assessment that a vacuum of executive risk will likely invite the intrusion of inept government interference.

Information.   Both systems recognize information as a valuable commodity. Under the communist methodology, information, like planning, is centralized. Subsequently, the distribution of information also comes under rigid control. Information, regardless of origin, is a key party resource and thus belongs solely to the state. In a capitalist environment, information also comes under rigid control, not by the state, but by its owner or that person or company who holds the legal right to use the information. In this sense, information falls into two categories, public domain and private property. Theoretically, information in the public domain remains freely available to all, while private property information can be made selectively available at a price the market will bear.

Communist executives assume that the central planning authority has properly allocated the information necessary to meet the established goals, and they expect nothing more. Since executive decisions should derive only from the information allocated directly to a given task, even communist executives who possess information beyond that provided by the central planning authority will not likely incorporate it into the decision-making process. To do so would invite questions as to how the executives obtained information outside of their assigned role and irritate those with planning authority who may not possess the same information. The communist attitude compartmentalizes information, expecting that information, like roles, must be assigned and never altered or challenged.

On the other hand, capitalist managers constantly seek more and better information. A good decision depends on complete and accurate information. Contrary to their communist counterparts, capitalist executives refuse to work within the confines of the information provided and strive not only to expand available information but also to integrate any and all of it. The drive for self improvement, coupled with a large dose of career mobility, produce a relatively large personal information bank for managers, who combine and analyze it all for each decision they make. The resulting noncompartmentalized information often integrates diverse experiences and interpretations to arrive at surprising and innovative solutions.

Ownership. For the purposes of equal distribution, the communist approach traditionally eliminates individual in favor of state ownership. Capitalism, on the other hand, leaves ownership in the hands of the general population and accepts, as a matter of course, that the distribution of wealth will never be equal. Of all these issues, the one of ownership provides the starkest contrast between communism and capitalism. It also reveals the broadest rift in executive attitudes. At the same time, discussion of ownership becomes quite difficult because it seems to run so deeply into the core of human nature. Whereas planning, management, and information represent relatively dispassionate mechanisms for getting things done, ownership seems to provide the deepest and most passionate reasons for doing things at all.

Each country, communist and capitalist alike, defines ownership in a slightly different way, but ultimately, the issue boils down to who controls surplus. Communist executives, lacking access to the rewards of surplus, have little incentive to run the risks leading to increased production. Rather, they focus attention on the negative consequences for failing to attain established goals, a focus that results in a disposition toward simply making quota or finding acceptable loopholes or official excuses for not doing so.

The availability of surplus in the capitalist system motivates executives to take high risks to obtain it. Capitalist managers constantly balance the potential for gaining surplus against the possibility of courting failure. Within the equation exists a legitimate choice that does not even occur to the communists, at least in theory. So entwined in human nature is the concept of ownership that the communist system has created a hidden system of surplus in preferred access to goods and services for ranking members of the ruling elite. While the system officially prohibits direct access to surplus, certain individuals do receive privileges beyond the reach of the rank and file. As George Orwell observed in *Animal Farm*: "All pigs are equal, but some pigs are more equal than others."

LESSONS IN IRONY

In light of this brief and admittedly superficial examination of the reasons for the triumph of capitalism as a methodology, it seems clear that the capitalist methodology will continue to dominate international business affairs as the world enters the 1990s. More and more, the members of the global economic community, and especially the constituents of the European Community, will divorce methodology from ideology. It will not come about easily, as a ten-year snapshot of two countries, Communist China and the United States, amply illustrate. The picture of China from 1977 to 1987 shows the progress that can occur when a communist ideology embraces the capitalist methodology. And the United States in the span of the 1970s exemplifies the decline that can occur when the communist methodology infiltrates the capitalist ideology.

China.   In the late 1950s and early 1960s, Mao ZeDong's Great Leap Forward landed flat on its face. In the period between 1958 and 1962, agricultural output declined by 28 percent, light industry by 21 percent, and heavy industry by 23 percent. As a result, China, from 1966 to the mid-1970s, was racked with economic disasters and subsequent leadership and management purges. After Mao ZeDong died in 1976, subsequent economic reforms ignited a ten-year run of economic growth fueled by a partial adoption of the capitalist methodology.

The 107 state planning departments were scaled down and purged to make them more responsive to regional needs. Industry management gained a freer hand in local operations, and information, particularly from Western sources, became more readily available. The government established economic zones along the coastal regions and permitted farmers to control a portion of their excess and sell it in a relatively free market. By the Thirteenth Party Congress in 1987, the reforms had netted staggering results.

The U.S. Central Intelligence Agency reported in 1988 that 300,000 small businesses had sprung up in China, not counting over 20 million single person or family business enterprises, *in a single year.* Gross agricultural output grew by 9 percent in 1978, 11 percent in 1982 and 14.5 percent in 1984. In the period from 1981 through 1986, agricultural output increased a remarkable 400 percent, 37 percent in 1987 alone. The designated special economic zones along coastal China exploded with foreign participation, resulting in $80 billion of trade, four times the level at the time of Mao's death and surpassing the Soviet Union. Since 1978, the gross national product of China has doubled.

United States. Ironically, during a ten-year period spanning the 1970s, the intensely capitalistic U.S. industrial sector adopted a series of academically inspired organizational changes that represented a partial adoption of the communist methodology. Entire central planning departments sprang up in corporations across the nation, and legions of bright but inexperienced MBAs pirated the planning function away from line management and into corporate headquarters. There grew an immediate and widening gulf between the real world of the factory and distribution centers and the carpeted white noise of corporate headquarters, sometimes isolated thousands of miles away. Management energy shifted from productivity to playing the corporate political game with the ruling party, with everyone scrambling for loopholes and looking for scapegoats to blame for declining performance.

During this period, management ranks swelled in a bureaucratic bloat that added layers of middle management that accomplished little more than frustrating the work force charged with the mission of increased productivity. Information became restricted, not necessarily by intention, but by the months it took the data to traverse the bureaucratic network. Finally, in the ultimate irony, ownership interests, in the form of stockholders, received scant attention as professional managers established self-serving access to the "surplus" that included corporate jets, condominiums at ski resorts and tropical hideaways, fleets of chauffeur-driven cars, country club memberships, and expansive office buildings with millions of dollars worth of amenities.

During this period, US industrial profitability stagnated, assets were under-used and subsequently undervalued, and great amounts of market share fell to foreign competition. Fortunately, the early 1980s brought a wholesale purge in the form of leveraged buy outs and hostile takeovers. Entire planning departments disappeared as quickly as they had accumulated, and layers of bureaucracy vanished. Corporate privileges and perks came more in line with reality, and stagnating assets were sold or re-evaluated for better utilization. More important, the ownership, in the form

94

of stockholders, voted with their shares, tendering millions of them to raiders in contempt of management and hand-picked boards of directors.

The unintentional transition toward a communist methodology by America's devout capitalist industrial CEOs did such damage in a short ten-year period that the prospering mergers and acquisition sector has become a booming industry. The purge continues to move through corporate America.

CAPITALISM, THE ONLY CHOICE

At the EC summit in Strasbourg in December, 1989, consideration was given to the establishment of a development bank, capitalized with $10 billion, to assist in Eastern European economic growth. To the surprise of all, the sponsor of the initiative was France. In the mid-1970s and early 1980s, semi-socialist France was the epitome of anticapitalism and a major carrier of Eurosclerosis. But in 1990, French industries are vibrant, French banks are merging, and the number of new businesses started in 1989 was up 20 percent from the previous year. France had gone capitalist.

Language barriers and an international reputation for a lack of hospitality make following internal French evolution difficult. The same conditions do not exist in the United Kingdom, and Britain's transition from tinkering with socialism to converting to capitalism has been closely watched. Prime Minister Margaret Thatcher has privatized previously nationalized industries, which has pumped new vigor into the United Kingdom as a global competitor. Apparently, the world has taken the British transition seriously, making London, not Bonn, the European international money center, and the British have become the largest foreign buyer of operating companies in America. The transition comes just in time.

The experiences of China, the United States, France, and Britain highlight the possibility of unlinking ideology and methodology in contemporary society. Indeed, increased global competition demands that each country, regardless of ideology, shift its attention to methodology in the effort to increase overall productivity. This challenge now faces Eastern Europe. In addition to establishing new governments, the Warsaw Pact nations must also make the transition to the capitalist methodology if they are to survive ultimate competition with the West. If the EC were not proficient and poised to serve as tutor, Eastern Europe would be forced to turn to the United States as its sole source. But the EC has not passed up the challenge. While President Bush earmarked $800 million for the building of the Polish economy, West Germany alone has pledged over one billion dollars. EC assistance is certain to geometrically increase as other EC members pitch in. But do not count the Americans out. General Electric is headed for Hungary with the acquisition of Tungsten, the largest manufacturer of lighting equipment in the country. Even the entrepreneurial segment of U.S. business is already booking flights to Budapest. New York barterer Morton Binn has opened offices in Hungary, Poland, East Germany, and Czechoslovakia; and Silicon Technology Corporation of Oakland, New Jersey, is negotiating to sell its semiconductor manufacturing gear in East Germany and Czechoslovakia.

To be sure, the ideological battle between communism and capitalism will rage into the future on its old momentum. But recent history has clearly demonstrated which machinery works. Despite the setbacks, such as the 1989 communist crackdown on students in China, the capitalist methodology will drive communist nations worldwide, each on its own schedule and each with its ideological cover-ups explaining past failures.

For capitalist countries, the challenge will come in keeping the methodology free from issues and infringements that would alter the productive attitudes that make the methodology work. Central planning, restricted management, limited information, and lack of ownership initiate decline, regardless of ideology.

The shift of all countries to the capitalist methodology calls attention to another shift, from a disjointed Europe to the reality of EC92, the making of a world superpower. If consumers, consortia, and capitalism are the key forces in an evolving global trade war, then the newly united Europe is on a line drive to the centerfield of world power.

CHAPTER FOUR

Europe 1992
and World Change

*These opportunities only happen once—
we have the best chance since Japan
of changing the World.*

SIR JOHN HARVEY JONES
Former Chairman of ICI

HISTORY 11 UNIFICATION 0

In the Leviticus Chapters of the Christian Bible appears the prediction of a time when "ten women shall bake their bread in the same oven." According to the ancient scribes, this symbolic event would signal the impending end of the world. Amazingly, a core of ardent Christians point to the unification of Europe into one common market as the prophesied event. Whether the unification of Europe embodies a spiritual warning or not, the fact remains that Europe 1992 signals the end of one, and the beginning of another, international world of business.

The unification of Europe (or EC92) will surpass the Japanese rise to economic dominance when future historians analyze post-World War II change. Ironically, while the United States' gaze remains fixed on the skyline and ticker tapes of Tokyo, Europe has been steadily growing into an economic power that will challenge and ultimately stifle the current samurai siege on world economics. A few keen eyes have seen the light. Jack Welch, CEO of General Electric, warns that the new Europe will make experience with Japan seem "like a cakewalk."

Ever since the passing of the Roman Caesars, the dream of a united and powerful Europe has met with failure, victim of the fierce independence permeating the various countries who share geographical borders, but little else. The late President of France, Charles de Gaulle, warned that one cannot expect to effectively govern a country that has "over 385 different types of cheese." And that's just France. Armies and navies, popes, priests, and possessed politicians have all striven for and failed to grasp the holy grail of unification. No wonder that so many present-day pundits predict failure for EC92. History clearly argues against success.

However, three contemporary phenomena separate the latest thrust for unification from purely historical precedent, and they link EC92 more to a bright future than to a dim past. First, the current drive for unification does not spring from the heart or mind of a single person, party, or philosophy. Instead, its roots run deep in populist sentiment. Second, the target date of December 31, 1992 marks less of an end result than a fresh start. As a populist movement, EC92 provides the European soul, expanding in all directions and adjusting to every shift in the winds of global change. Finally, the quest does not aim for world dominance, but for global equity. Desiring to escape its current role as an offshore playing field for two flailing economic powers, Europe wants to play on fair and equal terms with Japan and the United States. Each of these three phenomena should be examined closely.

The Populist Revolution.   Admittedly, the notion of unification as a populist, not a political, revolution seems to run counter to all the political circus reported almost daily by the press. British Prime Minister Margaret Thatcher performs in the center ring, seeming to pull off the impossible feat of championing unification while stauchly attacking it at the same time. All this political juggling and sleight-of-hand should not, however, fool anyone.

EC92 grows more out of a sense of pan-European political failure than out of any sort of grand political vision. Despite the seeming strength of the United Kingdom and West Germany, Europe in the late 1970s and early 1980s stagnated, while the United States and Japan surged ahead in economic growth. While unemployment rates of nearly 12 percent ravaged the continent, business, divided by national loyalties and geographical restrictions, fell victim to American and Japanese expansion. During this period, only a surface prosperity masked the reality of internal stagnation. During the mid-1980s in West Germany, for example, the autobahns, skyscrapers, and trade surpluses drew attention away from an unemployment rate that hovered near 8 percent. During the same period, while Japan boomed ahead at an incredible 11 percent growth rate, West Germany limped along at 2 percent. The truth of stagnation becomes most apparent when the drop of West German domestic investment is considered. It went from 9 percent of output in the mid-1970s to 5½ percent in 1985.

By 1980, Eurosclerosis political rhetoric ran high, with no rescuing doctor or miracle cure on the horizon. That is precisely the climate in which a populist movement can come alive. In Europe, the fledgling movement was not violent, vocal, or even visible. Rather, the people of Europe, wearied by the masses of stagnation and decline, revolted calmly and silently, redefining the very nature of nationalism.

Despite all their differences, all the European countries share the characteristic of fierce nationalism. The West Germans puff up with pride over their homeland, as do the English, the Italians, and the Dutch; and every country cherishes its dissimilarities from the French. So intensely does Europe's nationalistic fervor burn, that citizens revere country even over God, particularly a God inhabiting the Vatican and represented by the pope.

In 1956, two French visionaries prophesied a united Europe: Robert Schuman and Jean Monnet. At the time, Schuman was France's Foreign Minister and Monnet was the Chairman of the Action Committee for a United States of Europe. Together, they pushed for the Treaty of Rome, which created the European Common Market in 1956. However, the dream soon drifted, with individual countries unable to set aside national history, sovereignty, and competitive options in favor of united power. Uniting Europe seemed once again doomed to failure. Halfway around the world, however, another man saw a vision, one that would unite Europe more than any European politician could ever dream.

In 1957, Soichiro Honda oversaw a company consumed by corporate debt, but nevertheless felt a burning passion to become the Henry Ford of Japan. At the time, Honda's company was fighting for market share in a motorcycle industry dominated by much bigger Tohatsu. Tohatsu's after-tax profit stood at 8 percent of sales, while Honda's lagged at 3.4 percent. When the market for motorcycles started growing at 40 percent a year, Honda seized the moment by initiating what at the time appeared to be a recklessly aggressive marketing program. Market leader Tohatsu sat back complacently. Seven years later, Honda had captured 11 times Tohatsu's market share, a statistic that contributed to Tohatsu declaring bankruptcy in 1964.

By the early 1980s, Soichiro Honda aimed his competitive drive and market ruthlessness at Europe. Now, however, the dream was no longer one man's but an entire nation's. This time, that nation had money to burn, or, more accurately, invest. The quest remained constant—market penetration—followed by complete market dominance.

The shock to Europeans of a future world dominated by two foreign economic superpowers sowed the seed of a new loyalty. A pan-European economic loyalty that would ultimately accomplish what 2,000 years of history had failed to do.

To put pan-European economic nationalism into perspective, one should consider the residents of New York and California. The United States may operate with one currency, one system of national law, no interstate border restrictions and one flag, but that does not make Californians and New Yorkers identical twins. An executive from California's Silicon Valley, hailing a taxi in New York City may feel as if he or she has landed on a remote planet where no one speaks English, while a Wall Street financier will feel just as disoriented in a San Francisco conference where no one else is wearing a suit. Still, the two coasts conduct business quite comfortably with one another. In much the same way, the populist mind in Europe reasoned that a united Europe need not make the British less British or the Germans less German, though it can make the Japanese and Americans less overpowering.

Some numbers should be considered. The combined population of the proposed EC will surpass that of Japan almost two-and-a-half times and the United States by 70 million. While the individual EC countries merely cause a ripple on the wave of world trade, the combined power of Europe would create the world's fastest rising tide, passing up the combined trade output of the United States and Japan.

Sprouting firm the seed of economic self-defense, populist reasoning grew to challenge and redefine the very notion of national sovereignty. In the absence of war, national identity derived not from combating an enemy or from the army or government, but rather from images on the movie screens, products on grocery store shelves, the wares of sidewalk vendors, and the revolving contents of washing machines. Unification may involve Eurocurrency, Eurobanks, and Eurolaws, but as happens in California and New York, McEuro will be selling distinctly British, French, Greek, and Dutch sandwiches. The reality of uniting Europe will not prompt conservative Park Street executives in London to wear their wristwatches over their shirt cuffs, as do the executive elite in Italy, including Giovanni Agneli, head of Fiat; but both will be wearing the same watch assembled on the same bench in Lucerne. The concept of an economic Euronation stops short of socially defining a Euroman or Eurowoman. In fact, any definition may lie beyond human language, as the simple example of washing machines illustrates.

Reporter Barbara Toman, writing for *The Wall Street Journal* observes that the British definitely favor front-loading washers, while the French demand top loaders. The Germans want washing machines with characteristics much like their cars, plenty of electronic settings and very high-speed spins. The Italians, on the other hand, favor slower-speed spin cycles, a preference that parallels their affection for leisurely lunch hours. Even soap, or rather soap advertising, falls prey to national preferences. While Italian television advertisers employ glamorous models to hawk cleaning agents, their French counterparts prefer a business-like image. The English see a cross between Mary Poppins and June Cleaver, a conventional housewife even down to the crisp starched dress. Despite this sort of day-to-day national diversity, however, economic nationalism will put the same brand names in the laundry rooms of households from Lisbon to Bonn.

Economic nationalism draws on different symbols and mores rather than military or political nationalism. The 1990 European residents care less about defending the old icons of political nationalism than obtaining the higher quality of life represented by the new icons of economic nationalism. Even so, certain cynics reason that the Eurocrat will look and act much like their British or French national counterparts. Eurotaxes will hurt just as much as Spanish taxes, vague Eurorhetoric will flow just as freely as Italian rhetoric, and Euroscandals will create headlines just as big as any the British have managed to concoct in recent decades. In an economically united Europe, the more some things change, the more they will stay the same; economic nationalism does little to alter cultural nationalism. At the same time, however, economic unity will challenge power and political domination that have ruled Europe's countries for centuries, more often than not at the expense of the people.

The Organic Revolution. Unlike revolutions spawned by the dreams and vision of one person or one party, European unification represents the confederation of the hopes and expectations of a diverse collection of peoples. To those in the United Kingdom and West Germany, 1992 offers the chance of increased trade competition and greater international banking dominance. To Portugal, Spain, and Greece, it spells more jobs as industries shift south in search of lower labor costs. Of course, the diversity of expectations creates a political cauldron for those at the controls of the mechanical processes that will make it all happen. Every attempt to draft EC legislation gets ensnared by crafty national interests committed not only to unification, but also to as much self-gratification as other members will tolerate. So complex can this blending of national wills become that it prompted *Wall Street Journal* reporter E.S. Browning to describe it as a very "sticky solution," especially when the best and brightest minds of Europe came upon the issue of strawberry jam.

Because the Dutch spread jam on bread for breakfast, they like it smooth and loaded with sugar. The French, however, would rather treat visiting American tourists with respect than spread jam on anything. Jam, they insist, should go directly via spoon from jar to mouth. Consequently, French jam is chunky and chocked full of fruit. Across the English Channel, the British disdain jam in favor of marmalade, a concoction dismissed by the rest of Europe as poor quality jam, much to the chagrin of the British. This disparity of perceptions and taste led to a whopping 25 years of negotiation to develop a European labeling standard that finally emerged in 1979. The French, ever so conscience of the historical fact that French jam dated back to the 13th century, held fast against the standard for another four years until finally agreeing in 1984 to a pan-European jam consensus. Europe sighed as history recorded some progress in a very sticky area, then it held its breath once again as the next major obstacle to unification erupted: mayonnaise.

The Eurojam debate demonstrates the difficulty surrounding the mechanics of unification, but it also points out a major strength. European minds join forces in a combined consensus that unification represents a positive move toward the future well being of all concerned. To be sure, a multitude of "sticky issues" will crop up along the way, but no single one of these can shatter the unification dream itself. EC92 will continue to evolve as a living system of change, propelled by its own momentum, toward the objective of a united economic zone. The fact that no single dogma or doctrine guides unification allows the process to incorporate issues unforeseen at the beginning of the journey.

For example, on the more serious side, the events surrounding the changes in the Warsaw Block can bring monumental forces to bear on the unification process. West Germany, which stands to gain significantly from future Eastern European economic ties, reacts sympathetically to overtures from previously isolated Communist countries that East and West strengthen their economic ties. In fact, rumors have been circulating that Hungary's entry into the EC may come within the next five years, tossing the old Cold War alliances into a cocked hat. One EC company has already begun turning the rumors into reality. In Italy, financier

Carlo De Benedetti has set up a holding company to buy controlling stakes in Hungarian firms. "The guy who arrives first has more room to maneuver than the others," said an unidentified Hungarian official, commenting on Benedetti's interests to *The Wall Street Journal*.

Another strength of the unification movement's organic nature protects the EC from instant death at the hands of an issue that has so far reached a political impasse. The Madrid Summit of 1989 ran hard up against it when it faced down Margaret Thatcher's strident resistance to a common currency and a central bank. Although a considerable gap exists between these goals and any semblance of reality, the EC members warned Thatcher that it would move ahead on both fronts, with or without the United Kingdom's support. Up to that point in EC development, a united Europe without Great Britain might look to be politically impressive, but it would undoubtedly be weak. The 1989 summit in Spain so reversed the perception that British citizens have begun warning Prime Minister Thatcher that a Britain isolated from the EC cannot prosper. John Young, economic advisor to Lloyd's Bank argued that "the longer Britain stays out of the EMS (European Monetary System), the greater the likelihood that a Federal Reserve bank located in Frankfurt might ultimately become the operational centre of foreign exchange and money market intervention in the Community, posing a further threat to the pre-eminence of London among Europe's financial centres." Once again, the populist amoeba of unification surrounded and gobbled up an invading issue that might have otherwise spelled sure death for embryonic unification.

To Europeans, as well as to the outside world, it seems clear that more obstacles lie in ambush than the unification process has ingested to date. However, it also seems increasingly obvious that the movement can ingest even the most distasteful of those obstacles as it marches headlong to the tune of a united Europe.

The Quest for Equality. Since the Roman garrisons marched on dusty roads to Gaul, all attempts at European unification have aimed at world dominance. The Caesars, Napoleons, and Hitlers all gazed beyond national, European, and even global borders in their efforts to consolidate power and wealth. Even when people perceived that the world ended abruptly just off the shores of Anglo-Saxon Britain, the global drive for domination burned in the hearts of ambitious conquerors. From the viewpoint of the conquered, the struggle seemed to involve little more than seeing who would be the last one eaten by the alligator.

EC92 is different. As seen earlier, no one person or party paves the way with the glint of global fanaticism in the eye. Instead, the movement is carried forward on the shoulders of unemployed southern Europeans seeking jobs, northern and central European managing directors and CEOs looking for broader markets, and pan-European consumers wanting the highest-quality goods for the lowest prices. Consequently, the obstacles to unification come from within rather than from without. In fact, the strongest argument that the rest of the world has been able to conjure up against EC92 is the unfounded fear of a so-called Fortress Europe.

Antagonists, or perhaps paranoids, have dredged up the code word Fortress Europe to sound the warning that a united Europe will restrict influx of trade with tall ramparts. The argument not only deserves little thought, but it makes no sense coming from the United States and sounds absolutely absurd coming from Japan.

Two factors undermine the argument. First, the world has not witnessed anything resembling free trade for the last 20 years. Each nation, even the United States, has vigorously protected one industrial segment or another. The perception that a united Europe will automatically restrict a previously open flow of goods and services may make good political fodder, but when the attractive rhetoric is pulled away, nothing is left but soggy newsprint.

The second factor dictating against Fortress Europe stems from Europe's current dependence on foreign trade. If Europe were to brazenly escalate the existing level of trade restrictions, particularly with respect to the United States and Japan, countermeasures would come swiftly and devastatingly. Trade limitations would add up to little more than global suicide for the newly unified economic zone.

The irony of the United States' concern for a trade-restricted Europe resides in the record of former President Ronald Reagan, whose "free market" rhetoric drowned out the steady throb of trade restrictions executed under his administration. In fact, economists identify Ronald Reagan as "the most protectionist president since World War II."

During Reagan's presidency, the United States initiated or increased protection against a host of imports, including steel, automobiles, sugar, semiconductors, lumber, machine tools, and processed meat. Government subsidies for agriculture, which create unfair competitive advantages for domestic over imported food, scaled to new heights between 1980 and 1988. In a 1987 speech, then Treasury Secretary James Baker acknowledged that Reagan "has granted more import relief to U.S. industry than any of his predecessors in more than half a century."

The discrepancy between the former president's rhetoric and reality may make any U.S. cries of "Wolf!" over Fortress Europe seem silly or even hypocritical. They, however, do not sound nearly as absurd as the cries emanating from Tokyo.

Japan's argument is like the one Colombian cocaine distributors made when they agreed to freeze drug activities at current levels if the government would only cease its war on drugs. In a like vein, Tokyo has been pressuring Europe to cement in place existing trade agreements, imbalances included, and then proceed negotiating one discrete issue at a time. On the surface, the suggestion seems logical, until it is realized that Japan's trade with Europe, like its trade with the rest of the world, dramatically favors Japan. The Japanese approach would freeze the current imbalances and allow equality to arise on a hard-fought, case-by-case basis.

Meanwhile back in Colombia, a noted cocaine cartel member sent a letter in September, 1989, to the President of Colombia, offering to invest all his drug profits, some $3 billion, directly in the Colombian industrial economy, provided the government ease its attack on cocaine production. At the center of the drug runner's proposal lay the notion that the march to future prosperity should erase all previous ills. The Tokyo message to Europe in essence says, "Forget how we bashed you in our quest for the top, let us learn to live as friends, with you staying where you belong—on a lower rung of the ladder."

In light of the reality that much of the motivation for uniting originates with the European fear of Japanese domination, it seems quite unlikely that Tokyo's bemoaning Fortress Europe will gain much sympathy in Europe or in the rest of the world, which silently applauds the European stand against the once-unstoppable Japanese trade machine.

GLOBAL CHESS AND EUROCHECK

Although the EC has been racing toward unification since 1985, the significance of a united Europe has largely escaped world attention. The first official mention of EC92 by the United States did not come until August of 1988, and even then only by former Deputy Secretary of the Treasury Department, Peter Mc-Phearson. Before condemning the United States for its near-sightedness, however, it should be revealed that a 1988 British survey of 200 major European companies reports only 7 percent of the managing directors surveyed had appointed an executive or team to prepare for 1992. Europeans, it turns out, have paid little more attention to the impact a united Europe will have on world events than have the Americans.

Most of the impact studies published thus far on unification have limited their analyses to the internal changes that will flow from a united Europe, many of which will be reviewed in the next chapter. However, it is the external changes wrought by EC92, the ones that will create a new pattern of global power, that really matter. Like an unforseen power move in a high status chess match, European agenda will put the United States and Japan on the defensive as it creates a new game of multidimensional competition with more players and new moves. Certainly, EC92 cannot claim sole responsibility for these pending world shifts, but it does play a crucial role as the world migrates toward the reality of a global village. Four other large shifts will combine forces with changes in Europe.

Shift #1 The Decline of Japan.   Ford engineer and one-time Iacocca protege, Hal Sperlich, compared the conditions surrounding the Japanese entry into world trade to a pleasant suburban country club, where gentlemanly amateur players abided by gentlemanly rules. "And then one day," he said of the Japanese, "Bjorn Borg and John McEnroe walked on the court." The game suddenly became world-class and, at times, ugly. By 1989, of course, Borg had retired, and McEnroe was trudging dejectedly toward the exit, both players having fallen victims to much younger and more agile competitors. Tokyo will pay the same piper.

This would seem an odd prediction in light of Japan's present trade dominance and its ever-expanding capital capabilities. In 1989, eight of the ten largest banks in the world were Japanese. But countries, like tennis players, reach a peak and decline, a fact of life from which Japan is not immune. For 40 years, the Japanese have concentrated their energy on carving out hefty chunks of the world market, but that energy took a lot of sacrifice. Now, in the verge of a "midlife" crisis, Japan has begun to reevaluate itself and readjust its priorities.

Executives like Takashi Sakai, after working for years away from corporate headquarters, refuses his transfer back to Tokyo, preferring instead to become a U.S. merchant banker. He no longer wants to subjugate his personal welfare and fortune to the harmony and growth of the Japanese machine. All over Japan, work crews are repairing and installing sewage systems as its citizens grow less tolerant of a policy that sacrifices domestic well being for international growth. Finally, the rising generation of Japanese worker questions the seeming sacred ritual of investing untold hours and unquestioning loyalty in the quest for world dominance and would rather live life as consumers than as corporate cogs. While the Japanese could adequately address each of these issues independently, it can be swamped by their combined pressure. In the near future, Japan faces the type of across-the-board change that swept through the United States in the 1960s.

Japan bashers should not make the mistake of relishing this turn of events. Decline in global clout, like decline in baseline power, is relative. A McEnroe in decline can still whip the shorts off the duffers at the country club. When the post-1992 dust settles, sometime in the next 30 years, Japan will have slid from dominance to equality, not really a bad place to be. Equal partners court fewer enemies.

Shift #2 American Resurgence.   The United States has experienced more than its share of change. Those who grew up in the 1960s with its controversial war, undermanaged industrial sector, and misdirected political ambitions, have become the business, political, and educational leaders of today. For the nation to prosper and remain competitive in a tougher world, this crop of American leaders must pull two smoldering issues from the back burner to the forefront of American priorities: the need for dramatic educational reform and emphasis on the national debt.

Basking in cool alpine air and surrounded by breathtaking mountains, Salt Lake City, Utah, provides as accurate an image of mainstream America as any other city in the United States. In September of 1989, Salt Lake City made national headlines as some 20,000 teachers walked off the job, stranding almost 400,000 children in schools without adult supervision. The besieged school administration was forced to turn those kids loose on the streets. The demands that forced the strike did not surprise the American public: more money per teacher and fewer students per class. The demands seemed justified, except for one small detail. American high school graduates, the final product of the national educational system and its teachers, scored dead last in competition with their peers in other developed countries. The teachers' strike in Salt Lake City or any other American city comes off sadly like automobile workers in Detroit demanding more wages to continue building Edsels.

For years, the educational debate in America has raged over the issue of value. What do Americans get for their educational dollar? How much is a good teacher worth? While Wall Street bankers and lawyers pull in millions per year, school teachers in Boise take home an annual wage that totals less than the annual tax payment of senior corporate executives. While the rich get richer, the dumb get dumber. The debate would most likely never end save for the issue of competitive advantage. Though the futurists like to predict that the United States will lead the world in the new industrial sector knowledge, the major raw material of such an industry comes from strong minds, the sort not being matriculated from American schools. Consequently, the country has two alternatives: completely restructure its current means of education or import knowledgeable workers from other countries. For a country trying to come to emotional grips with the fact that it has become an import junkie, it seems unlikely that importing the by-products of foreign educational systems will appeal to the American psyche.

When President Ronald Reagan ended his second term, one out of every two Americans received some form of government "transfer payment." This payment is money gathered by taxation and then transferred to individuals on the basis of need. Thirty-eight million Americans receive Social Security payments, over 30 million get Medicare, and 23 million are covered by Medicaid. Over 20 million buy groceries with food stamps and children from 6 million families enjoy government-subsidized school lunches. Another 4 million receive Supplemental Security Income and 11 million recipients are covered by Aid to Families with Dependent Children. While American charity is commendable, it also costs. Since 1965, transfer payments increased from 24 percent of federal spending to over 41 percent of every government dollar circulating in the economy. The cost of American social sensitivity exceeds $500 billion per year, with less than 20 percent actually reaching the truly needy. The balance is nonpoverty transfers for Social Security, Medicare, and federal employees' retirement.

The American social conscience has forced the government to consistently spend more than it collects in taxes; the difference is borrowed. In 1985, the United States joined Mexico, Argentina, and Brazil as a debtor nation. Basically, the United States borrowed, mostly from foreign sources, more money than it invested abroad. This condition has doomsayers delighting in projections of economic decline or outright disaster. The government debt exceeds $2 trillion. The amount seems disturbingly large, but compared to what? The very question results in a war of words for American economists attempting to link deficit-spending and the debt to the future. Whatever the conclusion, the entire issue is one that must be addressed by the nation as it assesses its position in the new game of international power.

Shift #3 Spiralling Innovation.   In 1967, the *Wall Street Journal* predicted that Americans would be tapping away at the keyboards of 220,000 computers by the year 2000. Today, a decade short of the new millennium, the United States boasts 45 million machines. In the same issue, the *Journal* suggested that humans would stroll on the surface of Mars before the end of the 20th century. No one has even gone back to the moon. To see the basic change, the application of the concept inherent in any attempt at "elasticity" to such prognostication must be contemplated.

Elasticity treats technology like a rubber band with one end nailed down at the current point of development. To pinpoint the future, the rubber band is stretched to its perceived limits. Then one postulates how far the stretched end of the rubber band has reached. If in 1967, the secured end of the rubber band was tacked at 1,000 very expensive computers in the hands of government and large business users, then the stretched end, in 1989, would logically reach over 200,000 computers in the hands of more government and business users. Of course, the phenomenal explosion of faster, cheaper, smaller machines in the hands of writers and housewives and schoolchildren is excluded. Likewise, the band could certainly be stretched from a man on the moon in 1969 to a man on Mars in 1989. But that prediction would overlook a dramatic shift in American priorities during the intervening years.

Technological change, it turns out, progresses in a far less linear fashion than even supposed in the 1960s. While behemoth computers and Mars may have lain on a straight line drawn from 1967 to 2000, the folks with the crystal balls did not account for microchips and the fact the nation might want better televisions, a different concept in ovens, and a novel way of sending letters over the telephone even more than it wanted to visit Mars. As the year 2000 approaches, technochange follows more of a spiral than a straight line. Always moving vertically, change simultaneously moves in large horizontal ripples that lengthen the time it takes to get from point A to point Z. Once point Z is reached, a lot of surprising tidal waves have grown out of all the ripples.

When looking at the technological spiral over the last 20 years, the quest for new frontiers drives the spiral up, while the demand for consumer applications pushes the spiral sideways in wide circles. Walking on the moon sparked imagination and knocked civilization one notch higher, but the widening circle of digital watches, microwave ovens, fast food, and microcomputers changed the tone of everyday life from Iowa to Istanbul.

The unification of Europe in 1992 and a revitalized United States will help explode innovation sideways in tidal waves of unprecedented scope. Consumer demands, fueled by capitalist investment and development efforts of consortia, will transform each upward click of technological change into ten widening waves of lifestyle change. Why the link to EC92? Percy Barnevik, CEO of Europe's ABB, suggests that the answer lies with market generation. Barnevik believes that businesses across the globe will consolidate into consortia for the sake of grabbing world market share. When the consortia have divvied up the market share, they will look for the quantum leaps of applied consumer technology that will create new markets.

A striking example of technological market generation can be found in the world of television. As the international market for television approaches almost saturation levels, the introduction of higher resolution TVs (HDTV) creates a totally new market for television manufacturers. Owners of existing television sets, which cannot receive HDTV transmissions, must buy new sets. Compact discs performed the same feat in the audio realm. In theory, the entire world television market doubles as the HDTV receivers replace existing sets. Fortunately, the old market does not shrink and disappear overnight. Consequently, the industry enjoys a new boom while not giving up its current business. This technomarket rollover will occur in all products from transportation to telephones and from computers to college textbooks. As a result, not only will consortia tap more markets and reap greater profits, but consumers will enjoy an astonishing array of new products and services.

Shift #4 Realigned Spheres of Economic Influence. The last 40 years has seen the world carved up into political, ideological, and military sections, and all the geopower slicing and dicing has resulted in a world map that makes little sense in the absence of war. For example, Cuba, the floating military base near the U.S. border, makes only one trade contribution to the Soviet Union, sugar. At the tune of a $4 billion per year subsidy to keep the island economy afloat, Cuba may be a sweet tooth Gorbachev can ill afford. However, Cuba also reminds the world of the bipolar military tension between the United States and the Soviet Union, a tension that has drawn a good many of the lines on the map of political geography.

But there is another force, geo-economics, which will sketch in some new lines. Observers from Kenichi Ohmae to Peter Drucker have already described this new force in world map-making that will enable EC92 to accelerate certain global adjustments. Basically, while the old military maps remain on crumbling walls, three new spheres of economic influence have begun their quiet restructuring of the globe: Asia, the Americas, and Europe.

Prior to its last-ditch attempt to maintain the old order, Communist China was riding a rocket toward economic prosperity and development. Highlighting China's acceleration into the 21st century, fresh food and hoards of Japanese businesspeople crowded the Chinese marketplace. The spring 1989 student revolt, and the vicious response by China's aging leadership, may have slowed the schedule, but only for a time. In this era of consumer longings and concurrent yearnings for democracy, the forces of change can be crushed but not killed.

Financing the development of Communist China and the rest of Asia, cash-rich and market-minded Japan foresees a booming manufacturing-consumption mecca right in its own backyard. The loose economic affiliation of Communist China, the Four Tigers (Hong Kong, Taiwan, South Korea, and Singapore) and the emerging kitten Thailand promises to exploit the dynamics of technological enhancement and quick turnaround production.

Finally, in a world where flash, particularly potential nuclear flash, attracts immediate attention, the years of favorable relationships between Canada and the United States have gone largely unnoticed. In legislation scarcely visible in the stream of world events, the already open trade borders between the two countries have all but vanished. While the two burly North American neighbors surely function as one big happy market, the explosive growth lies to the south.

According to traditional political logic, the Soviet Union has been smart to foster alliances smack in the southern backyard of the United States. However, the shift to a geo-economic perspective and the advancement of nuclear delivery systems, particularly submarines, has eroded the strategic value of South America. During Gorbachev's summer of 1989 visit with Fidel Castro, the forward-thinking Soviet leader advised the throwback Cuban leader that the export of revolution to South America no longer met cost-benefit criteria. The decline of South American strategic value is offset by the rise of its economic value. If properly cultivated, South America becomes the most proximate, highest growth potential market for United States and Canada. It also becomes a wonderful platform for the manufacture of products for competition with the Asian and European economic spheres.

The rise of three economic spheres in no way excludes potential business development that spans the spheres themselves. In fact, consortia make that not only viable, but inevitable. Unlike the old political or military alignments, which united for common aggression or defense, the new spheres pragmatically exploit the reality of proximity. A nation's future economic well being, assuming world peace, will rest on its ability to produce and consume. In the quest for lower cost production and increasing markets, the world trade leaders—the United States, Japan, and Europe—are sitting on vast untapped pools of underdeveloped markets, labor, and real estate right in their own backyards. Clearly, it would be more logical for Japan to drive the development of Communist China while taking the backseat role in South American growth. The United States, on the other hand, could attempt to compete with Japan for China or with Europe for Soviet developmental rights, but it could accomplish so much more with far fewer resources in more proximate South America. Regardless of the new alignments, of course, considerable overlapping will occur as the scramble to develop new markets takes shape.

THE WORLD AFTER EC92

The unification of Europe does not cause these global shifts, but rather like the shifts themselves, it occurs as a natural consequence of world events spurred on by the forces of consumers, capitalism, and consortia. Even so, European unification greatly accelerates the other shifts. For example, Japan would obviously prefer a lengthy time period to even out the imbalance of trade at its own pace, but the new Europe will not likely tolerate Japanese foot-dragging the way the United States has.

Throughout each global shift, Europe assumes responsibility for forcing each issue to a quicker resolution than would otherwise occur. This acceleration makes new global linkages a fore-gone conclusion, the waves of trade make the physical isolation of nations a dream of the past, and the flow of information makes political and social isolation impossible. In the "linked and shrinked" future, a country cannot seal its borders and survive. Whether they like it or not, Tokyo politicians must not only further the interests of Japanese voters, but also of Japan's American constituency. The lack of support from either group would bring Japan to its knees even more quickly than it gained world dominance. Likewise, American education must compete head-on with every developed country. Winning this competition for knowledge will not come through the control of local school boards or state educational budgets, but as a result of global interaction that demands a stronger emphasis in international strategy. A shrinking world is a very dangerous place for small minds.

CHAPTER FIVE

The Three Faces
of Europe

There is no way back.
The critical mass to unify Europe
has already been achieved,
there will be implementation.

DR. PETER WALLENBERG
Swedish Financier

MULTIPLE OUTCOMES

As 1992 approaches, Rome must recover from an uppercut delivered by unification legislation. A ruling issued by the European Community's Court of Justice struck directly at the very symbol of Italian nationalism, pasta. Italians prefer their lasagna and fettucini *al dente*, or firm to the tooth. Since a cook can only achieve the ideal texture by using durum wheat flour, ever since 1967 Italian law has dictated that only durum wheat be used to make pasta. In 1988, however, the EC ruled that Germany and the Netherlands could begin exporting what the Italian newspaper *La Republica* called "gluey and insipid pasta" to Italy. The Italian government fears that its constituents will munch the cheaper counterfeit pasta, without durum wheat, and thus lower Italian culinary standards, not to mention the profits of local pasta manufacturers. In sympathy, Brussels, the EC capital, suggests that "sacrifices will have to be made by every country" in order to achieve unification by 1992.

This may seem like a tempest in a teacup, until it is considered that just under 300 directives, all designed to facilitate unification, will force similar or even greater sacrifices by citizens in all 12 EC countries. The directives range from setting standards for European television to controlling the value of the ECU (European Currency Unit), the new common currency of the EC. While each country views and values each directive differently, the collection of directives mandate a massive give-and-take proposition, with each nation giving up something with the left hand in order to gain something with the right.

The actual passing of the 300 directives will take a lot of tedious, time-consuming discussion, and the whole process would bore even the most eager observer, even the Europeans. However, the eventual outcomes, set in motion by the approved directives, formalize Europe's role in what communications guru Marshall McCluhan dubbed the "global village." Rather than dig into the nuances and details of the directives, this chapter focuses on the outcomes, of EC which range from the EC becoming merely a joint economic zone with relaxed borders, all the way to the EC emerging as a full-fledged international power complete with a central bank and a united military force.

As outlined in Chapter 4, unification entails a living, growing movement, not confined to an arbitrary deadline of December 31, 1992. Nor is it limited to the 12 countries currently comprising the EC. While no one will know precisely to what extent unification will ultimately redefine Europe until the middle of the next century, three basic outcomes will most likely occur.

EC The Economic Zone. This outcome attracts the most attention and is the greatest concern to business people in the United States and Japan. James Olson, the late Chairman of AT&T, noted that "70 percent of all American-made products have intense foreign competition in the U.S." Most of the attention regarding increased foreign competition has been focused on Japan, but as the discussion of consortia in Chapter 2 pointed out, a fair share of the competitive challenge is coming from Europe. The EC economic unit will almost certainly sharpen the edge of European competitiveness. In a Booz Allen survey, over half of the American executives questioned predicted "that European-based firms will gain such strength from Europe 1992 efforts that they will be more effective competitors in the U.S." If the Americans are concerned, the Japanese are panicked.

Tadahiro Sekimoto, President of Japan's NEC Corporation, when discussing the challenges of management, suggests that "the problem most frequently encountered is trade friction." The solution, Sekimoto adds, is "an all out effort to solve the problems involved in internationalization and globalization." Of late, most Japanese attention was aimed at preventing an American backlash to Tokyo's trade superiority. Now, Japan faces the potential of an economically united Europe whose market size and clout exceed that of the United States and whose anger toward Japan may also. Kichiro Ejiri, President of Mitsui & Company Limited, suggests that Japan's closed domestic market and predative pricing is "an underlying cause of the problems in Japan-EC economic relations."

The creation of a single European economic zone assumes that the roadblocks that keep each country economically distinct will be reduced or eliminated, and that the combined countries will function as a unified economic power. The pursuit of this outcome concentrates effort on physical, technical, and fiscal barriers that separate the EC members.

EC The Global Trader.   Ironically, most discussion of EC92 is coupled with fears of Fortress Europe—a closed consumer market, off limits to non-European participants. "Fortress Europe is very real," argues J.N. Garrow, Managing Director of Salomon Brothers in London. Garrow predicts a surge of American activity just prior to 1992, as the fortress walls go up. But concerns over Fortress Europe cover up what is a far more likely outcome—rather than retreat behind trade walls, Europe opens up with a vengeance and goes after American and Japanese markets. Jan Carlzon, CEO of SAS, the Scandinavian Airline consortia, is far more cryptic: "Fortress Europe? I don't think so." Carlzon cites SAS's Amadeus Project as proof that at least European aviation is advancing on the world, not retreating within Europe. Amadeus is a reservations booking system to rival the massive systems being used by American and Delta Airlines. The project is a joint venture between three competing airlines, Iberia (Spain), Lufthansa (West Germany), and SAS (Sweden, Norway, and Denmark). Development headquarters is in Madrid, but the practical development of the system is occurring in southern France, because of local software expertise. The system will be installed in Munich, where telecommunications are advanced. The management of the entire project is from Scandinavia. Carlzon claims that motivation for development of Amadeus is not consolidation of European airlines into a domestic power, but rather "staging for international competition." Underscoring Carlzon's comments are investments by SAS in Continental Airlines (U.S.A.) and Areolinus Argentina. Both investments are on the wrong side of Fortress Europe, if indeed Fortress Europe becomes a reality.

Refuting accusations about Fortress Europe, Giovanni Agnelli, Chairman of Italian carmaker Fiat, advised critics not to "forget that 45 percent of American capital currently invested overseas is in equity ownership within Europe." Agnelli then comments that "it is a very strange fortress indeed that welcomes its enemies to buy parts of its fortifications." In 1989, Fiat took the step of listing its stock on the New York Stock Exchange— again an odd move for a company if it were preparing to hide behind castle walls.

An internal economic zone does not automatically guarantee that Europe will be able to compete against the United States and Japan, particularly in the area of technology. To achieve its desired global status, Europe must go beyond physical, technical, and fiscal barriers and emphasize coordinated industrial development backed by a strong central bank.

EC The World Power.   For the most part, talk of unification involves economics more than politics. But the Japanese emergence and the subsequent pressure on Japan to assume the responsibilities of a world power suggest that Europe must accept similar responsibilities in exchange for the privileges of global influence. This outcome revolves around the two most sensitive post-1992 unification issues: foreign policy and a combined European military.

The potential outcomes of the EC as an economic zone or as a global trader ignite fierce debate between their committed followers and caustic critics, although all parties lower their voices when entertaining the third, particularly West Germany. Since the shadow of World War II has not completely faded from European consciousness, the rise of a united European nation with strong and influential West Germany at its geographical core causes some concern to all EC members. Still, the third option that Europe emerges as a world power, with a single foreign policy and a pan-European military to back it up, seems logically inevitable and perhaps even visionary. Stanley Hoffman, Chairman of the Center for European Studies at Harvard University, believes that Jacques Delors, who will head the EC through its birth in 1992, is ultimately committed to the "construction of a federal state." While soft-spoken Delors' vision significantly impacts current issues, Hoffman adds that the members of the EC are reluctant to act on Austria's application for membership "because Austria's neutrality is seen as a handicap for the common diplomatic and defense policy of the future."

The quest for unification may originate with an impulse for economic survival, not the wish for world dominion. EC members may not be able to separate the goal of economic well being from the tools of foreign policy and military strength. In addition, the momentum generated to achieve the first two outcomes will likely spill over into this sensitive area. As EC members ease themselves into a cohesive economic zone, they may find it an easy progression to the next step of a United States of Europe. Finally, regardless of the motives and actions of world events, such as the economic and political breakdown of the Warsaw Pact nations, the EC may be forced into the role of world power broker whether it wants that responsibility or not. Each of these three major outcomes should be closely examined.

EC THE ECONOMIC ZONE

A truck transporting goods from Rotterdam, Netherlands to Genoa, Italy now averages slightly less than 20 kilometers (12.3 miles) per hour over the entire distance because of border delays of up to eight hours (often the rule rather than the exception). Some trans-European trucking actually moves more slowly than world-class marathon athletes can run.

Developing the EC into a competitive economic zone involves eliminating the barriers that impede shipments of goods. These barriers fall into three main categories: physical, technical, and fiscal.

Physical Barriers. While these tangible and relatively easy-to-move obstacles pose the least of the EC's problems, their importance to each country cannot be underestimated. In essence, what a country allows to cross its borders reflects its nationalism, its hopes, and its fears. In Italy, for example, "inferior pasta" ran into a stone wall at the border, which often caused trucking delays of eight hours or more. France gets equally touchy about cheese, West Germany about beer. In each case, the border provides the first line of defense.

Borders, however, also affect issues with even more political calories. The EC lines up along a North-South divide that Europeans call the "two-speed" economy. The North, represented by the United Kingdom, France, West Germany, the Benelux nations, and Denmark, enjoys an economically more advanced status than the southern group of EC members—Greece, Spain, Portugal, and parts of Italy. Currently, the borders keep the economic prosperity in the North from luring relatively cheap labor and its accompanying urban stresses from the South. Border red tape also discourages northern industries from relocating production in the South where they could benefit from generally lower costs. The economic nature of these concerns can be measured. For example, the average hourly wage in Spain is not a national secret and is easily compared with wages in West Germany. The comparison can then be used as the means of negotiating some sort of solution. Not all border issues, however, are economic and solvable by rational debate. In 1975, at least one sector of noneconomic problems of a borderless Europe was addressed by EC ministers meeting in Trevi, Italy. Their conclusions, implemented as the Trevi Process, addressed such unpopular issues as drugs, crime, and terrorism and called for pan-

European cooperation of police and intelligence agencies. The Trevi recommendations sat largely idle until a group called The Solidarity Committee for Arab Prisoners initiated a series of bomb attacks in Paris, demanding the release of three Arab terrorists. The attacks, which occurred in the spring of 1986, rekindled focus on the Trevi Process, by that time ten years old and largely forgotten.

The Trevi Group consequently reconvened in an emergency meeting in September, 1986, at the end of which it authorized an agreement to further the level of intelligence and police co-operation. In October, 1986, when the EC Interior and Justice Ministers met to discuss the security implications of the proposals to abolish internal frontiers by 1992, they agreed to "launch a concerted assault against terrorists, drug traffickers, criminals, and, for the first time, illegal immigrants, while simultaneously pledging themselves to the goal of free movement around the Community for all law-abiding citizens." They set an immense task for themselves. In 1988, the annual meeting of the International Union of Police Federations, which represents 500,000 officers, passed a resolution *opposing* the abolishing of frontier controls. The resolution gained a majority by a single vote.

Relaxed or abolished borders will carry an impact beyond the human element. According to data gathered by the International Organization of Epizootic, 19,000 cases of rabies were recorded on the European continent in 1985. Of this total, 14,000 involved foxes, 3,000 other wild animals, and 2,000 involved domestic animals. Only one known case of rabies occurred among the human population in Finland. The EC soon recommended a Community-wide eradication and vaccination program to be implemented in 1990. The motivation? Britain, a 100 percent rabies-free country, hesitates opening its borders until rabies no longer exists in the entire Community.

What are the odds that the borders will vanish? Travelers landing at Britain's Gatwick Airport form two lines through customs, EC passport holders and foreigners. European industry is consolidating as if the borders are already gone. When Zurich-based Asea Brown Boveri closed down a plant in West Germany, German union leaders accused the consortia of favoring labor in its home country. The only problem was that the leaders could not determine the home country. SAS's Jan Carlzon again cryptically addresses the future with an obvious statement about the present: "it is impossible to run a national policy *anymore*."

Technical Barriers.   In most developed nations, most people count themselves happy if they can avoid all contact with lawyers. Before they could avoid lawyers in Europe, however, they would have to be able to identify them. Just what constitutes legal training in Europe? As *The Economist* points out: "In Italy, a young person hoping to be a lawyer completes six years of university, professional training and apprenticeship before qualifying, aged about 25 . . . In Spain, the usual starting age is 17, with new lawyers qualifying at 22. In France, the age of 18 marks the onset of four years of university education for prospective lawyers, followed by a year of professional training, and then two subsequent years of apprenticeship, culminating in entry to practice at age 25. In West Germany the studies and training go on until 26."

This definition or standards problem spans the spectrum of matters, from serious health issues such as prescription drugs to such mundane issues as the labeling of jam, jellies, beer, and biscuits.

In 1957, The Treaty of Rome provided a mechanism to harmonize technical differences, one issue, one item, and one product at a time. This approach, which was illustrated in the jam example in Chapter 4, required years of "tortuous negotiations to arrive at a common position for a single product standard, was inherently bureaucratic, extremely unpopular and very time consuming." In 1985, the EC decided to limit standardization to those areas "where it is considered vital to create a uniform Continental market." For those products not considered vital, individual countries can set their own standards, but cannot restrict product flow based on those standards. This basically means that France cannot impede a product such as a hair dryer, simply because the French deem the appliance "not up to our standards."

Standardization makes enormously good sense in light of the fact that, currently, some 100,000 technical specifications differ across Europe, costing industry billions of dollars in adaptation. A study of the European telecommunications sector suggests that the divergent technical standards imposed on telephones, facsimile, telex, and transmission equipment adds an additional $8 billion to overall costs. Electrolux, the world's leading appliance producer, must alter the same item six times to meet the different electrical specifications throughout Europe.

In the area of pharmaceuticals, manufacturers must submit new drugs to 12 different registration authorities, each with different requirements. On average, the approval process takes two years per nation. European pharmaceutical companies maintain that it takes ten years and roughly $85 million to develop a new drug from pan-European use and that standardization would save the industry $350 million per year.

The construction industry also suffers from lack of coherent standards. In 1985, the EC determined that the construction products market turned over roughly $110 billion a year. However, tremendous variations in customer specifications for materials such as glass, bricks, concrete, aggregates, timber, and steel severely restrict industry growth. The EC estimates that standardizing the industry would encourage an additional $2 billion of yearly growth in construction.

Perhaps the greatest gain for standardization will occur in the financial industry. The cross-border standardization of financial services such as insurance policies, mortgages, consumer credit, and trusts will pop the cork on the banking and insurance industries. Standardization will allow Britain, West Germany, and France to spread over Europe, in many cases overpowering domestic competition for basic services. The so-called "southern" members of the EC, generally lacking strong banking systems, could suffer a real blow in the wake of financial standardization. Standardization, however, cuts both ways, allowing professionals and goods to migrate north and compete costwise with relatively overpriced products and services.

Fiscal Barriers. Tariffs and taxes stand as the major fiscal road-blocks to European unification. Any changes to existing ones will bring such direct financial consequences that Europe tackles them with extreme caution.

Tariffs are the costs countries tack onto imported goods in order to make them more expensive and less competitive with domestic rivals. Almost all countries impose tariffs to some de-gree, but they touch a real nerve in Europe because of the prox-imity of national neighbors. The average tariff level across Europe amounts to slightly under 10 percent, with specific tariffs by product varying from country to country. To see the impact of tariffs and the way they favor selected domestic industries, prices across Europe for the same commodities need only be compared. In Table 1, Belgium produces the price standard to which four neighboring countries are contrasted.

Without tariffs, European consumers would engage in "cross-border" comparison shopping, buying goods and services from the least expensive suppliers. A Londoner might buy a German car in Belgium, antihistamines in France, and life insurance and domestic appliances at home. The tariffs and the borders have traditionally erected a sturdy defense against such a practice. In 1968, the EC adopted a common customs tariff that will stan-dardize the border tack-ons by 1992, thus making imported prod-ucts more competitive. This will greatly benefit consumers as prices generally drop, but it also rings the death-knell for pre-viously protected industries that cannot compete with higher-quality and lower-priced imported alternatives.

Taxes provide an even more explosive issue. Most nations view the right to levy and collect taxes as an extremely important prerogative and even proof of national sovereignty. For countries with a fanatical commitment to independence, such as those in Europe, EC measures to set tax limits strike at the core of their being. The main blow comes from something called the Value Added Tax, or VAT, which adds a notch of taxation in each stage of product development. The added cost of the tax gets tacked onto the price of a product until it ultimately reaches and is paid for by consumers. Along the tax chain each product "handler" remits the appropriate tax to the government.

In the United States, state and local governments raise funds via three main taxing mechanisms: personal/corporate income tax, property tax, and sales tax. The EC members also use the first two taxing methods but prefer VAT over sales tax. Each country mandates a different rate. If VAT rates do not become harmonized among EC members, internal trade will suffer two restrictions. First, taxation for products manufactured, distributed, and sold across national borders cannot be easily enforced. This problem does not occur when production stays in one country and all VATs along the production chain flow to the same

TABLE 1: Comparitive Prices in European Markets

	German Cars	Pharma- ceuticals	Life Insurance	Domestic Appliances
Belgium	100	100	100	100
France	115	78	75	130
West Germany	127	174	59	117
Italy	129	80	102	110
Netherlands	N.A.	164	51	105
U.K.	142	114	39	93

SOURCE: *European Economy*, March 1988; Nicolaides & Baden Fuller, 1987.

government. But in the manufacturing process, if a product crosses a national border, say between Spain and France, the French manufacturer in the subsequent step cannot get excited about remitting a value-added tax to the Spanish government. Second, variations in the VAT rate make production more attractive in some EC members than in others. If the physical border restrictions and the tariffs fall away, then those countries with lower VATs will automatically become more competitive, drawing manufacturing and consumption away from high VAT nations, which usually depend heavily on VATs for national revenue.

While EC members see the value in harmonizing VAT rates, they know they must set rates cautiously so as not to help or harm a particular nation arbitrarily. Table 2 indicates that Denmark, Ireland, and France derive a greater percentage of gross national product from VATs than other EC members.

If a country must lower its VAT rates, it will incur a shortfall of revenue. On the other hand, if a country must raise its VAT rates to a level acceptable to other countries, it will enjoy increased revenues, but at the cost of higher consumer prices. This destroys one of the supposed major benefits of unification: lower-cost products. The latest efforts to resolve this sticky problem have resulted in a compromise solution. It sets two VAT categories, with product groups such as food, drugs, and cars assigned to one or the other. While the EC members can set VAT rates within an established range, they cannot switch a product group from one category to another. Thus, if an EC member wanted to become more competitive with its food products, it would adopt the lowest VAT range possible. The member might also charge the highest tax possible for automobiles, where it does not care to become more competitive.

Eliminating, standardizing, and harmonizing the barriers to unification will clearly provide an economic shot in the arm for EC members. At this stage of unification, the analysts' projections vary considerably, but the report drawing the most attention is

"The European Challenge 1992: The Benefits of a Single Market." This report was compiled under the chairmanship of Paolo Cecchini, a special adviser to the EC. The results are based on a survey of 11,000 business executives, conducted by 15 separate groups of consultants, academics, economists, and EC administrative personnel. According to the report, lifting the physical,

TABLE 2: VAT Contribution to Gross Domestic Product

Country	*VAT as Percentage of Gross Domestic Product*
Belgium	7.67
Denmark	9.84
West Germany	6.34
Greece	—
France	9.19
Ireland	8.22
Italy	5.48
Luxembourg	6.04
Netherlands	6.83
Portugal	—
Spain	—
U.K.	5.22

SOURCE: Completing the Internal Market, European Commission White Paper, 1985.

technical, and fiscal barriers will generate over 200 billion ECUs or $220 billion in cost savings, roughly 5 percent of the gross domestic product of the combined EC membership. Consequently, consumer prices should drop by 5 to 7 percent, and 12 million new jobs should be generated. Of course, no projection of a newly revitalized European economic zone can insure that the EC will experience a similar lift in world trade. In fact, the Centre for Business Strategy at the London Business School warns Europeans to look "beyond the—often absurd—hype" which often promises economic windfall to the EC after 1992. *The London Times Guide to 1992* takes a softer approach, admitting that "the report's estimates have been the subject of a heated dispute" but concluding that "few have denied that they [the estimates] are pointing in the right direction." The debate over Cecchini's optimism will certainly heat up as 1992 approaches, but one issue is clear. In order to accomplish a significant economic windfall, the EC must look beyond immediate barriers toward the possibility of forging a truly unified nation.

EC THE GLOBAL TRADER

The easing of limitations to intra-European commerce may set the stage for a more internationally competitive continent, but reaching that stage will take far more than disapproving internal borders. The EC will have to embark on a program of full competitive coordination. Otherwise, Europe can never expect to hold its own against Japan and the United States. The only other alternative, blatant protectionism in the form of Fortress Europe isolating the EC from global trading partners, would never survive. Three categories of coordination must come about before the EC can emerge as an equal trading sphere vis-à-vis Japan and the United States: industrial, financial, and trade coordination.

Industrial Coordination. Although unified under the EC banner, Europe's industries engage in a hodgepodge of duplication as each country defends its home-grown favorites. In the past, this worked just fine. Why, for instance, should France and Italy abandon their auto industries just because West Germany had forged a better track record of export success, especially to Japan? Why should the French consumer give a hoot about West German car sales volume? In the case of banking, Greeks automatically assumed they needed Greek banks, while Spain certainly required a Spanish telephone company. In light of the old logic, each EC member must duplicate every key industry or service. But if Europe unites into a single block of consumers, competing as one entity against the United States and Japan, then duplication becomes an unwise allocation of resources and effort. Table 3 demonstrates the redundancy in four relatively mundane categories. In each case, there are too many suppliers competing for too limited a demand.

Does the EC need ten turbine generator manufacturers when it takes only two to service the entire U.S. market? The same question can be posed about a thousand other products and services. If the new logic prevails, Europe will embark on a massive consolidation of goods, producers, and service providers that will,

TABLE 3: EC Duplication of Industries

	Number of EC Producers	Number of U.S. Producers
Boilermaking	12	6
Turbine Generators	10	2
Locomotives	16	2
Telephone Exchanges	11	4

SOURCE: Adapted from J.A. Kay, *1992 Myths and Realities*, London Business School, 1989.

with luck, avoid the inefficiencies of a monopoly, but at the same time reduce the waste of redundancy. Oscar Fanjul, Chairman and CEO of Repsol, Spain's largest petroleum company, sees eventual consolidation as "the only means by which competitive companies can afford the inevitable rise of research and development costs in the future." Harvard-trained and impressively aggressive, Fanjul symbolizes a new breed of Spanish executive who thinks beyond Spain to the EC and global vista. Under his direction, Repsol, whose stock trades on the New York Stock Exchange, will try to engineer a string of acquisitions in a quest for global competitiveness.

Fanjul's argument for consolidation does not account for the emotion that is certain to erupt. Unemployed assemblers in France cannot feed their families logic when the production facility moves to Spain, which sports a lower labor cost. When 500 scared and out-of-work French citizens march in protest to the home of their elected representative, logic will be the last human trait on anyone's agenda. But French jobs are already in jeopardy, as are employees of all EC members. Barring blatant protectionism, French workers do not just compete with Spanish labor, but also with the sweat shops of South Korea and the hand labor of Hong Kong. Steel workers in Pittsburgh made the error of assuming that their competition was around the block rather than across the ocean. When factories closed in Pennsylvania, they did not reopen in California. The EC accepts the risk of an emotional response to free market forces that motivate a change of venue from one country to another. At least the new location remains in Europe, which, according to the new logic, is basically one entity.

The concept of industrial coordination will continue to spark intense debate among politicians, but among European CEOs and directors it looks like a sure bet. The most imaginative are already scrambling to form the one or two dominant competitors in each sector. Any hesitation could cost them the opportunity, not only to another EC company, but perhaps to a global adversary. Ford, already well established in the EC, considered acquiring Porsche and SAAB before finally settling for Jaguar, at a sticker price exceeding $2 billion. Then General Motors snatched up SAAB. The European CEO's sensitivity to this issue fuels the dramatic rise of mergers in Europe since 1984. See Table 4.

If the EC restricts or delays the movement toward consolidation across national borders, Europe will fail to realize its full global competitive potential. Would California succeed in taking on Japan all by itself? To be sure, Europe would still be productive and would offer a market too large to ignore, but it would lack collective muscle. In order to compete effectively, the EC must make its mark with an elite and powerful industrial front, represented by a smaller number of more aggressive competitors in each category. It must butt heads against the Toyotas, Nissans,

TABLE 4: European Merger & Acquisition Activity

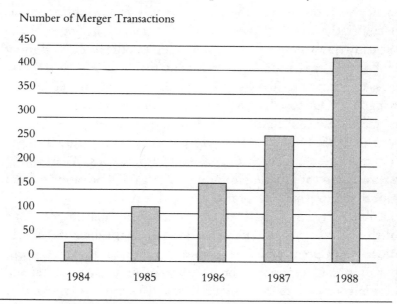

SOURCE: Klinewort Benson

and Hondas with Fiats, Benzs, and BMWs, rather than the second-rate offerings of 12 smaller squabbling car companies, each championed by national interests, but each technologically deficient and undercapitalized.

Financial Coordination. Capital represents the newest commodity in the flow of global trade. Donald Marron has a special interest in EC efforts to engage in world competition over capital. As CEO and Chairman of Paine Webber, he manages a financial institution in a world where hundreds of billions of dollars are moved through international financial markets every 24 hours. Marron labels the future financial market as "an explosion of choices" as 1992 draws nearer, and warns that three trends merit special attention: globalization, computerization, and deregulation.

Globalization is the increasing tendency of capital to cross, recross, and almost totally ignore national boundaries in the unceasing quest for maximum return. The challenge is to have money working around the clock, literally following the sun as it circles the globe. This demands that money managers make the daily transition from one major market to the next. Beginning in London, traders make transactions that flow to New York, cross the Pacific to Tokyo, and start all over again in the United Kingdom. On most days, $200 billion worth of foreign exchange is traded between these three markets, more than twice the volume in 1985. Only a tenth of the currency traded is used to pay for transactions between the world's corporations. The balance is directed toward trading for profit. While the motivation behind global trading may be profit, the entire phenomenon is made possible by technology. Deregulation, the dismantling of many of the rules and restrictions that long kept the financial world orderly and predictable, has created many new investment opportunities. Computerization harnesses technology to gather and disseminate information about financial events, links together widely separate exchanges, and supports trading in stocks, bonds, and other financial instruments in ways that do not depend on the physical presence of traders or even an exchange floor.

In 1971, technology took on Wall Street with the debut of the National Association of Securities Dealers' automated quotation system (NASDAQ). The system was a patchwork electronic quilt of 20,000 miles of leased telephone lines, some video terminals, and one central computer. Today, the world markets are on-line—computer linked to give instant information and access to money managers around the clock. The extent of technology's role in international finance is evidenced in the computer linkage between the Chicago Mercantile Exchange and the Singapore International Monetary Exchange that has been in place since 1984. The system operates 24 hours a day, making transactions between these two off-Wall Street and off-Tokyo exchanges almost instantaneous.

The transition of trading from paper to optic fibers made moving money around the world a matter of keystrokes, not postage stamps. Consequently, money, like liquid, was following the path of least resistance, to those countries that enforced the fewest rules. Between 1966 and 1980, the Eurobond market grew almost 30 percent a year from $17 billion to $575 billion. American money managers were tired of U.S. rules, regulations, and returns. While European financial centers gloated, the U.S. government got the message. Beginning in the mid-1970s, the United States began deregulating its financial industry. Japan joined the American deregulation bandwagon by signing the Yen-Dollar Agreement of 1984. The agreement reduced Tokyo's role in setting domestic interest rates, created short-term money markets in Japan, and opened the Tokyo Stock Exchange to membership by foreign financial institutions. That same year, West Germany lifted the withholding tax on foreign buyers of Deutschmark bonds, the first move in a mountain of deregulatory changes. Finally, on October 27, 1986, deregulation spanned the financial world when the United Kingdom opened up Exchange membership to foreign institutions and ended the distinctions between stock brokering, market making, and banking.

Deregulation is by no means complete, but the trend is inevitable. Banking in Bonn, via home computer, is actually simpler than driving two blocks to the branch bank in Santa Monica, California. The technology is not only available and cost effective, but it is itching for implementation. Controlling currency is one thing, regulating electronically supported consumer impulses is another. Globalization, driven by Star Trek-like computerization, is certain to fuel the fires of continued deregulation.

Common currency should not be confused with competitive capital. The ECU serves simply as legal tender that enables consumers to buy products from various countries. To achieve status as a competitive commodity, the ECU must establish itself as a rival to the dollar and the yen. In order to do that, the EC must institute a central banking mechanism that can control monetary policy and, in turn, the ECU's competitive strength.

Next to taxes, central banking heats up the economic emotions more than any other unification issue. Take away a nation's ability to tax and to print money and, in effect, a nation is dismantled. For this reason, earlier unification efforts focused on the barriers to internal trade. These efforts skirted the specter of an EC central bank on the assumption that EC members might drop border barriers to products, services, and even people, but would draw the line at relinquishing the reins of national economy to the hands of central control. Fiat CEO Giovanni Agnelli is adamant that a common currency "is an inevitable development" that will ultimately lead to the "establishment of a federal system of central banks." The fact that all EC members, except one, have keyed their currencies to the ECU lends credence to Agnelli's speculation. But Britain, the sole exception, is a powerful contrary force. Pierre Beregovoy, the French Finance Minister, puts it bluntly: "A common monetary policy cannot work effectively as long as Great Britain remains outside the EMS (European Monetary System) exchange mechanism."

The British resistance to a single currency and central bank is led by Prime Minister Margaret Thatcher. Committing sterling to the EMS would be perceived as a compromise of national independence. The politically sensitive Thatcher is not blind to the importance of symbols to national pride. She did not hesitate to commit the British war machine to the defense of worthless islands off the coast of South America. But Thatcher's concern goes beyond national pride to the heart of national interests. Discussion about common currencies and central banks almost always begins with British resistance but ends in Bonn. The Deutschmark, backed by a strong central German bank, is the benchmark for European currencies. While London is an international trading center, the pound generally does not trade as strongly as the mark on international markets. The fear that common currencies and central banks will divert financial attention away from Britain toward West Germany is well founded, but not strong enough to keep Britain sterling independent. In June 1988, *The Economist* commented on the sterling's absence from the EMS: "Imagine that New York State had stalwartly maintained that it could keep its own independently floating currency as the rest of America's great dollar-based market evolved around it: a currency [the pound] which cost 9 percent in commission to buy and which harassed businessmen had to queue up for before boarding the shuttle to New York. The vision sounds absurd, because it is: sterling will stick out just as absurdly in a financially freer Europe." The projected outcome of the currency and banking debate varies across Europe. The EC cannot expect to stand on equal footing with Japan and the United States if it lacks one of the hottest trading commodities, capital. Despite the problems, central EC coordination of capital seems irresistibly inviting. Couple the United Kingdom's clout as a center for international stock exchange and investment banking with the power and stability of the West German Deutschmark, and the ECU is quickly on a par with the dollar and yen.

Trade Coordination. This aspect of coordination enjoys the most widespread consensus among EC members and perhaps strikes the most fear into EC trading partners. Recalling our discussion of reciprocity in Chapter 1, the fear is well founded. The EC demand for trade reciprocity—basically equal flow in both directions—takes on significance when the trading partner is no longer just France, Italy, or Spain considered separately. Twelve formerly separate traders, now functioning as a single unit, clearly means bad news for all of Europe's trading partners, but especially for Japan.

In the past, the Japanese have turned European national sovereignty to tremendous advantage. First, by concentrating on key EC countries, the Japanese have managed to establish an effective base of operation. Japanese banks, for instance, have centered in London but conduct business all over Europe. Second, the Japanese have used one EC member to gain access to another member's market. For example, Japanese cars, assembled in England, are exported to France supposedly as European-manufactured products, but in reality, the cars are only *assembled* not manufactured there. France is protesting and pushing for legislation that looks beyond where a car is assembled. Joined by Italy, the French proposal favors requiring that a car consist of 80 percent European parts to qualify as a European-manufactured, or assembled product.

Banking best exemplifies why EC92 will prevent the Japanese and other global trading partners from using one European country as a front for competition in another. If the EC acts as one trade market, then Japanese banks could presumably establish operations in any part of the EC. While some EC members who have traditionally resisted Japanese incursion will be forced to open their markets, any member of the EC should gain the reciprocal freedom to bank in Japan. The Japanese balk at that idea, arguing that Japan's banking presence predates unification. Therefore, any pre-existing banking agreements that restrict the entry of European banks into Japan remain inviolate. The weak argument does little to mask Japan's fear of a united European trade front.

The power of trade coordination also affects automobiles. When Japan exports cars to Portugal, Spain and Belgium, it need not fear that these countries will demand equal opportunity to export cars to Japan, since these EC members lack substantial auto industries. If the European auto industry functions as a single trade entity, however, then Europe may offset a Nissan sold in the Netherlands with a French Citroen or Italian Fiat sold in Osaka. The prospect unnerves a Japanese auto industry that marks up its domestic prices in order to effectively compete abroad.

Coordination of industrial, financial, and trade policy must occur if the EC expects to emerge as a serious global challenge to the United States and Japan. The importance of coordination to EC trade power is underscored by Japan's efforts to delay any attempts by the EC to unify its industrial, financial, and trade policy. A typical example are the minutes of an exclusive luncheon held in Tokyo for European business and political leaders. Despite the friendly air, the remarks were pointed. Eishiro Saito, Chairman of the Keidanren (the Japanese version of the Business Round Table) warns "the EC to arrest any tendency toward economic regionalism." The statement is odd in light of the Japanese import restrictions, which give new meaning to the concept of regionalism. But the Japanese are undaunted in lashing out at the EC. Foreign Minister Sosuke Uno demands that the community "dismantle discriminatory import restrictions on 130 Japanese products." Finally, Noboru Okamura, advisor to Honda Motor Company (the term advisor is often used by the Japanese to mean a retired company officer), expressed a hope on behalf of the Japanese auto industry that the "EC use local content regulations prudently to avoid discrimination among non-EC corporations." Okamura's comment was aimed directly at French efforts to mandate that cars having less than 80 percent European parts be considered imports.

As with dismantling the barriers that stand in the way of internal trade, any compromise must account for passionate national sovereignty. Would EC members rather retain full independence from one another and remain internationally impotent? Or would they rather run on an equal footing with Japan and the United States, even if doing so required unification beyond the mere movement of goods and services across intra-European borders and a consequent loss of individual sovereign integrity? The answers will unfold far beyond 1992.

EC THE WORLD POWER

In October, 1987, Soviet leader Mikhail Gorbachev offered the West a plan that would partially demilitarize the seas in the Nordic region. At the seaside resort of Nyborg in Denmark, European foreign ministers discussed and dismissed the gesture on the grounds that the "new plan" merely reiterated "a long-standing Soviet proposal." Soviet and NATO submarine activity in Northern Europe has always prompted diplomatic debate. The Soviet proposal and subsequent European rejection would hardly have deserved front page headlines, except for one small detail: the Soviet plan was submitted not to NATO, but to the foreign ministers representing the EC. In a world where diplomatic protocol is given high priority, the Soviet submission of a political-military issue to the EC, which many consider to be restricted to border and tariff issues, may be a glimpse of what the EC is becoming. Economic forces, the incident seemed to argue, now outweigh the old primacy of military forces. Bread and butter overrule guns and missiles.

The reality of economic and trade unification poses perhaps the most sensitive and significant question of all. Can military and foreign policy unification lag far behind?

Foreign Policy. If the mechanics of foreign policy connect directly to the motivation of national security, then in reality, the EC already follows a unified foreign policy in the form of global trade agreements.

If global trade, particularly when it involves Japan, represents a form of new-age warfare, then, in the continued absence of all-out nuclear war or more conventional regional confrontations, trade battles will rock every nation in the world. For weapons, the warriors will not rely on bombs and bullets, but rather on policies and procedures. For instance, Japanese-owned Fujitsu attempted to acquire 80 percent of Fairchild Semiconductor, located in California's Silicon Valley. The U.S. Department of Defense killed the deal on the grounds that since Fairchild represented a "strategic provider" to the military, its sale to the Japanese would compromise American "national security." Interestingly, Fairchild was not owned by American interests, but rather by Schlumberger, a French oil services firm. The Fujitsu-Fairchild transaction attracted less scrutiny in terms of price-earnings ratios and market share than it did in terms of foreign policy choices. France worried the Pentagon less than Japan.

Tokyo's global trade dependency makes it extremely vulnerable to the trade policies of competing nations. The simple, but unrealistic, demand that Japan completely open its domestic market or totally lose its access to the EC would literally cripple the Japanese economy. The severe consequences of this type of action, in both international economic and political terms, pushes the decision beyond trade imbalances into the realm of global power balances. Likewise, given the increasing flow of foreign investment into the United States, Washington would not sit idly back and watch foreign investors limit or even destroy American economic growth by calling in their loans or withdrawing vast amounts of their American assets. In the 21st century, the line between trade or economic policy and foreign policy will all but disappear.

In 1969, the EC asked Viscount Davignon of the Belgium Foreign Ministry to assemble a committee that would report on ways of increasing EC coordination in foreign policy matters. The resulting Davignon Report, published in 1970, recommended the "harmonization of foreign policy views and—where possible—joint decisions on matters affecting the foreign policy interests of Europe as a whole." Like most early EC initiatives, the recommendations lay fallow until they received the breath of life in the form of the EPC, or European Political Co-operation Group. This ministry-level committee shoulders responsibility to facilitate "closer co-operation on questions of European security." Of course, security cannot be discussed without talking about armies.

Military Unification.   Just how likely is a single European military? Understandably, the EC avoids the subject, preferring to concentrate on the mechanical, less sensitive decisions surrounding unification. Nevertheless, strong hints about the inevitability of a common European defense force have already begun to circulate. Their source? Not the EC, but the WEU.

Founded in 1948, the Western European Union is a European defense organization. Almost from its inception, the group has deferred to NATO, but recent changes in NATO have begun thrusting the WEU to the forefront of military thinking. First, NATO's European members have been carrying an increasing share of the military price tag. Europe contributes over 90 percent of NATO's personnel and the same percentage of tanks, artillery, and aircraft. Second, the perception of tension between Western Europe and the Eastern Bloc has been declining rapidly. For example, only 8 percent of West Germans in 1988 perceived Russia as a threatening influence on their daily lives, contrasted with 80 percent of West Germans who felt that way only a decade earlier. Finally, the United States has been rethinking its military commitment to the NATO alliance. The high cost of domestic programs in the United States has caused some Washington politicians to question the tradition of providing military "protection" for Japan and Western Europe while these "allies" literally wage a trade war against the United States. America's offshore military reluctance matches Europe's concern over United States dominance of NATO. David Greenwood, Director of Defense

Studies at Aberdeen University, suggested in the June, 1988, issue of the *NATO Review* that the alliance is "unhealthy, unequal and breeds European resentment" at the same time that defending Western Europe fosters "American disenchantment." Greenwood argues for three immediate steps: first, coordination of policy; second, cooperation in arms procurement; and third, collaboration in defense industry production.

The transition of allegiance from NATO to the WEU would not be that difficult to accomplish. Eleven of the 12 EC members also participate in NATO (Ireland does not), and 9 of those 11 belong to the WEU. In essence, the only significant difference between NATO and the WEU would be the elimination of the United States. Can the WEU defend Europe as well as NATO? The WEU's answer came in a 1987 statement: "We recall our commitment to build a European Union in accordance with the Single European Act, which we all signed as members of the European Community. We are convinced that the construction of an integrated Europe will remain incomplete as long as it does not include security and defence. . ."

In the same statement the WEU discusses Europe's need to respond to crises outside Europe whenever those crises may affect the continent's well being. The words seem to imply, at least on the WEU's part, that action will be taken when and if necessary to protect European interests. Crises originating outside of Europe seem destined for a European, rather than a French, British, or West German response. It may also come sooner rather than later. When Iraq and Iran terrorized oil shipping lanes in the Gulf of Hormuz, British, Dutch, and Belgian mine-sweeping efforts came under the control not of NATO, but of the WEU.

The post-1992 emergence of the EC as a United States of Europe, complete with a single foreign policy and the united military muscle to back it up, requires a long stretch of imagination under current world conditions. But these conditions are changing quickly, and the linking of trade, foreign policy, and military power also stirs the imagination of Japan as it wrestles with its own domestic and international adjustments.

CHAPTER SIX

The Setting Sun: The Japanese Decline to Equality

The EC financial market
might become highly protectionist,
depending on how reciprocity is implemented.

YOH KUROSAWA
Chairman of the Committee
Japan-EC Relations, Keidanren

MISREADING JAPAN

The Japanese look forward to EC92 with the same anticipation nations reserve for urban blight, drug abuse, natural disasters, and AIDS. Japan is worried about European unity and for good reason. The EC will be a huge market, 320 million consumers that cannot be ignored. According to Koichi Hori, author of *Kaware Nihonjin* (*Japanese, Change your Ways*), if the EC "gates slam shut" on the Japanese, "even their ability to compete in the massive markets of Japan and the United States might eventually be placed in jeopardy." Japan is so export reliant that denied access to Europe would force the redirection of Japanese products to the United States or back to Japan. Where else could they go? For Japan, the United States and Europe are the world's biggest consuming blocks.

But how threatening is the EC to Japan? After all, the chairman of UNICE (The Conference of Industries of the European Communities), in remarks delivered to the Japanese Foreign Minister in 1989, made the prospect of EC trade policy sound downright neighborly: "Every house has its own fences, but friends will be free to join." It is the emphasis on friendship that scares the Japanese. The terms *powerful, productive, superior, stubborn,* and *subtle* have all been used at various times to describe Japan, but friendly or fair? The Japanese, particularly over the last ten years, have proven to be neither. They understand that EC92 is not an invitation to a neighborhood open house, but rather is an act of trade war.

The EC is not ripping their way through national taxes and traditions to make trading with Europe easier for Japan or the United States. On the contrary, they hope to make it more competitive, albeit friendly. True friends, the EC reasons, give and take. Winning some, losing some, but somehow coming out roughly even at the end. Europeans do not like U.S. hormone-enhanced beef, so the United States slaps a tariff on European canned tomatoes. The fight may last a day or even a year, but when it's over everyone is still friends. What is $100 million in beef and tomatoes compared to billions of trade in other products? But the Japanese are different. They have to win all the time, in every category. When it is all over, they want all the points, and they will manipulate every rule to ensure victory. This is the Japanese version of friendship, which leads Europe to the inevitable cliche, "with friends like these, who needs enemies?"

Oddly, the Japanese are slow to respond to their fear, perhaps hoping that unification will die a premature death. Yoh Kurosawa laments that the Keidanren (Japan Federation of Economic Organizations) did not send its first EC investment mission to Germany until May of 1988. By that time, ten U.S. missions had already made the same visit, with the same intent—build closer ties with Europe. Nomura, Japan's largest securities company, did not take 1992 seriously until June, 1988, when it initiated its efforts toward *dochakuka*—going native. The Nomura approach, as explained by executive vice president Morimasa Yamada, is to "do more rather than less regional fine-tuning of our marketing strategies . . . as a form of preparation for 1992." The question is, why did it take Nomura until 1988 to realize the importance of Europe to Japan? A partial explanation may be that the Japanese are having domestic problems.

The Japanese miracle of post-World War II resurrection, like most miracles, eventually becomes a lot less mystical when awe gives way to hard analysis. Lately, a good deal of objective and persistent probing has helped replace the myths with a more accurate view of the subtle forces that have fueled the fires of Japanese expansion. Clearer vision will help us project an accurate picture of a post EC92.

Ironically, most perception of "Japan Inc." originates with Western, not Japanese, sources, each representing special interests. For example, American labor unions stress Japan's lifetime employment programs and quality circles, while their bosses tend to pay more attention to the Japanese emphasis on company loyalty and longer work weeks. The Democrats point to the unusual success of Japan's government-business alliance, while the Republicans boast that Japan clearly proves the triumph of the free market system. Simply put, *gaijin* (non-Japanese) tend to see in Japan what they find lacking in their own lives and faltering systems.

Another factor clouding the Western understanding of Japan centers on the fact that books by Japanese authors almost never appear in English translations, particularly when they touch sensitive subjects such as economic domination. The few translated books sometimes provide a shocking slant on the Japanese mind set. One such book, *A Japan That Can Say No*, is a runaway bestseller in Tokyo, but no English translation is planned. Attempts to publish the book in the United States have been stonewalled by co-author Akio Morita, Sony chairman. The book is a compilation of comments by Morita, particularly aimed at the shortcomings of American business. The lack of long-term thinking and commitment, and the stubborn refusal of U.S. industry to tailor products for Japan (for example, cars with steering wheels on the right rather than the left), form the basis of Morita's criticisms. These are the same ones he has been touting in speeches across the United States for the last ten years. So why has a bootlegged English translation of the book become an underground best-seller in Washington, DC? Because co-author, Shintaro Ishihara, a political leader in Japan's ruling Liberal Democratic Party, lacks Morita's balanced objectivity and expresses a more militant and less globally sensitive attitude than the seasoned Sony founder. Ishihara goes so far as to suggest that Japan could bring the United States to its knees by denying Japanese technology to America. He writes: "If, for example, Japan sold chips to the Soviet Union and stopped selling them to the U.S., this would upset the entire military balance. In reality, Japanese technology has advanced so much that America gets hysterical, an indication of the tremendous value of that card—perhaps our ace. My frustration stems from the fact that Japan has not, so far, utilized that powerful card in the arena of international relations." Not surprisingly, Ishihara greatly respects Japanese Admiral Minoru Genda, a mastermind behind the surprise attack on Pearl Harbor.

While the Morita-Ishihara book may provoke many Americans and some Japanese, it does open the door for a reappraisal of the Japanese miracle based on motives and methods rather than myths. Ishihara's reference to Admiral Genda suggests the third and perhaps most critical obstacle to a better understanding of Japan: the world's reluctance to take into account Japanese history from 1930 through the 1960s. In fairness, some of the reluctance comes from tact and sensitivity, which prevents the diplomatic world and even Japan's fiercest adversaries from pouring salt into the wound of World War II. By overlooking the immediate pre- and post-war periods, however, events that provide key insights into the Japanese mind set are overlooked.

For instance, history clearly documents that the surprise attack on Pearl Harbor proceeded, despite the realization that Japan could never win a prolonged war against the United States. It did not take a rocket scientist to compute the mathematics that proved America's productive capacity could, during a prolonged conflict, pulverize Japan. To their ultimate chagrin, Japan falsely assumed that the United States lacked the will for an all-out conflict and would eventually accept Japan's new geopolitical expansion in exchange for peace. Reasoning that it could survive a quick, vicious, and contained conflict, Japan hoped it could push the United States to its diplomatic limits and keep its military gains through hard negotiating. The plan, complete with its underestimation of U.S. resolve, more than vaguely parallels today's economic confrontations.

Of course, history does not consist only of warfare, and a cold look of post-war industrial Japan also shatters some myths that form perceptions of Japan. For instance, on May 25, 1953, negotiations between labor and management collapsed and Japanese workers of Nissan walked off the job. But what began as a strike, quickly became a war. Management hired several hundred *yakuza*—Japanese gangsters—to bully the workers. Yakuza were noted for their love of elaborate body tatoos, heroin abuse, and violence. Nissan managers shared executive restrooms with yakuza thugs, readying needles to get high for the day's agenda of breaking heads. For their part, the union matched the cruelty of management-supported yakuza, blow for blow. Wives and children of suspected management sympathizers were harassed and denied access to bathrooms and kitchens. Most workers lived in company dormitories and apartment buildings with shared facilities, and denied access was the same as eviction. Union leaders broke into the apartment of one suspected pro-management family during dinner and sat in the middle of the apartment, completely silent. Four hours later, one of the union leaders said, "Do you think he gets the idea?" Then they left.

By August 10, the harassing on both sides gave way to full-scale violence. The union crashed the barricades and hand-to-hand combat went on for days. Union members occupied the factory, like an invading army, until they were evicted by the ironic alliance of police and yakuza. The 1953 strike at Nissan is rarely brought up by those seeking to make a model out of seeming ideal management labor relationships in Japan.

Ironically, while the West has not easily gained a true historical perspective, the Japanese do not shrink from trotting out their own painful history when it suits their designs. Since 1986, the yen gained in strength against the dollar. This had the effect of making Japanese products more expensive to American consumers and thus a threat to Japan's export superiority. In 1987, the *Sankei Shimbun* (the Japanese version of *Barrons* or the *Wall Street Journal*) ran an article comparing the yen's dollar to Japanese defeats in World War II. "In a few months the yen [fell] from 245 to 200. This was the equivalent of Japan's loss of four aircraft carriers at Midway. . . . Washington's final objective is probably an exchange rate of Y100 to $1. That represents Japan's total defeat and Gen. Douglas MacArthur's triumphant entry into Tokyo. . . . We must not lose the Pacific War twice."

Somewhere along the road to unification in 1992, the EC will set its policy toward Japan. The question that must be addressed by the EC before its Japan perceptions become policy is just what kind of "friends" the Japanese will be. As pointed out earlier, superficial stereotypes may not provide the most accurate portrait of the Japan of the future.

As 12 countries strive to solidify into a single Europe, one might wonder if the homogenous nature of Japan looks inviting to EC leaders. One language instead of eight, one set of laws, rather than 12 and one binding set of customs as opposed to a rich array of cultural differences. But Japan may not be as united as it appears.

Along with the new Europe evolves a new Japan. The signs are evident. Boiling below the surface of the Japanese calm are domestic conflicts that threaten to change Japan more radically than the harshest American or European trade retaliation. The conflicts are best recognized as pieces of an intriguing paradox raised by Karen House, writing for the *Wall Street Journal*. She reports that Japan has the "richest of people and the poorest of people; the strongest of global competitors and the most fragile of global powers." While the paradox may confuse most Westerners, it offers not only a valuable insight into the nature of Japanese progress, but also signals that Japan has already begun her decline to equality.

THE POWER OF PARADOX

Paradox, by its very nature, confuses the mind with its seemingly conflicting messages, forcing the search for that elusive point where opposite forces integrate and finally make sense. Although Japan virtually pulses with paradoxes, three in particular relate to this discussion.

First Paradox: The Richest and the Poorest. Of all the characteristics attributed to the economic success of Japan, extortion receives almost no attention. Yet domestic extortion, growth at the expense of its own people, provides Japanese leaders with the most effective "soft management" tool in the country's economic armory. The "harder" techniques, lifetime employment, just-in-time inventory, quality circles, and company songs, contribute relatively little compared to the impact of what James Fallows, author of *More Like Us*, sees as the "Japanese public's astonishing apathy about the system of organized extortion that is Japan's consumer economy."

As the world's number-two economic power, Japan has the lowest percentage of paved roads of any developed country, the lowest ratio of public parks and recreation facilities to population, and a municipal sewage system that serves less than 40 percent of the nation's homes. For the most part, a Japanese camera or computer can be purchased for fewer dollars in New York City than in Tokyo, where an acre of land can sell for almost $1 billion. Ownership of a mere 800 square foot house within two hours of Tokyo eludes even the most diligent and loyal Japanese workers. Many people are forced to rent.

While Japanese capital and trade threaten to dominate the world, domestic Japanese purchasing power lags near the middle of the pack. One recent survey indicated that of the world's major cities, Tokyo ranked 28th in purchasing power per capita. The cost of living in Tokyo runs roughly 30 percent higher than New York and 40 percent higher than Frankfurt. A small melon, just enough for two, can cost close to $60, and a single sirloin steak in a Tokyo market costs $20. Not long ago, an American business traveler staying at Tokyo's Imperial Hotel sent two children to one of the hotel restaurants for a quick dinner. *Shabu-shabu* (thinly sliced meat) and vegetables cooked in a boiling broth came to $93 per child. The taxi fare from Narita International Airport to the hotel runs $125. No wonder that one Japanese executive, recently transferred to Nigeria, considered the move an improvement to his standard of living!

As it did in the now-extinct Aztec empire of Central America, human sacrifice forms a cornerstone of Japan's economic prosperity. In the case of Japan, though, money, not blood, flows down the temple steps.

The period of *endaka*, or high yen, provides a chilling insight into the domestic sacrifices consumers make to ensure their country's industrial success. In the early 1980s, 250 yen roughly equaled one dollar. This yen-to-dollar relationship provided an excellent competitive edge to Japanese companies exporting to the United States. The superior strength of the dollar effectively made goods produced by a yen-based economy more competitive than those produced by a dollar-based one. However, in the period from the beginning of 1985 to the beginning of 1988, the value of the yen almost doubled against the dollar. American competitors celebrated the event, reasoning that Japanese companies must now increase product prices to reflect the higher costs of production brought on by the higher yen-to-dollar ratio. To their embarrassment, those same U.S. competitors soon discovered that they had overlooked the extent to which Japanese business and government would force Japanese consumers to ensure that a few companies would maintain their competitive pricing overseas.

Toyota, for example, only raised prices on exports slightly more than 2 percent against the 10 percent price hike predicted by Detroit. At home, however, Toyota significantly raised prices to compensate for those held artificially low in the United States. Not surprisingly, other Japanese automakers matched the price hikes. Further, the Japanese government, in an effort to keep consumers from balking against the monopolistic higher prices, introduced a strict personal automobile inspection standard that forced consumers into buying new cars every four to five years. What could have spelled a major Japanese setback at the hands of a revenge-relishing Detroit, instead turned into a minor coup as American automobile manufacturers raised prices in anticipation of Japan's problems with endaka. The winners: Toyota and Japanese automobile establishments. The losers: General Motors, Ford, Chrysler, and Japanese consumers.

Such consumer extortion does not stop with big-ticket items like cars, but continues throughout the range of Japanese products by means of the famed Japanese distribution system. Most products sold in Japan must run the gauntlet of 8 to 21 intermediary agents before winding up at the cash register. While appearing almost absurdly inefficient to Western observers, the system works in the sense that it provides the most number of jobs per product. Twenty-one distribution layers between the factory and the department store floor for a hair dryer translates into at least 21 different jobs, an important consideration for a country with almost half the population of the United States crammed into a land mass slightly larger than California. The distribution system also serves as a curious financing device, with each layer practicing slightly different credit and return policies, which make a product even more expensive as it flows down the distribution channel. As expected, the cost burden of maintaining the cumbersome distribution network does not ride on the shoulders of banks and manufacturers, but on the backs and bank accounts of consumers. As long as all products must follow the same path to market, consumers will not be able to shop for alternatives to overpriced goods.

The phenomenon of consumer extortion underscores the homogenous nature of Japanese society wherein the lack of racial diversity creates the sort of unification and focus that can result in competitive advantage. The issue of race touches a very sensitive nerve in the Japanese, some of whom, like Shintaro Ishihara, even suggest that "Racial Prejudice Is at the Root of Japan-Bashing." Ironically, consumer extortion functions as a refined system of discrimination, separating Japanese consumers from the benefits of world consumption, in effect making them second-class world citizens. Contrary to Ishihara's accusation of racism against Japan, the most penetrating prejudice seems not to come from outside, but from inside the land of the rising sun.

Second Paradox: So United Yet So Divided. The Japanese government would define the consumer sacrifice that funds and fuels

Japan's economic expansion as self sacrifice, a willing consumer concession to the greater goal of national economic superiority. But when forming policy, the EC must cut through the rhetoric about the romance between Japanese consumers and Japan's industrial community to suggest a radically different view of the situation. To begin, examine a confrontation between consumers and Japan Air Lines (JAL).

A round trip JAL ticket between Tokyo and New York City, purchased in Tokyo, cost Japanese consumers 33 percent more than a similar ticket cost Chinese travelers for a Hong Kong-Tokyo-New York trip aboard JAL. Consequently, some Japanese travel agents were purchasing the Hong Kong-Tokyo-New York City tickets in Hong Kong, tearing off the Hong Kong leg, and selling them to Japanese travelers in Tokyo at considerably less than the established JAL price. This gambit saved Japanese consumers slightly under $2.4 million per month, but when news of it became public, *The Japan Times*, Tokyo's main English-language paper denounced it as a "tragic loss," inflicted not on the Japanese consumer but on Japan Air Lines.

The seeming misplaced sympathy of *The Japan Times* can be traced to the informal alliances among government bureaucracies and private companies called *zoku*. Somewhat similar to special interest groups in the United States and Western Europe, these alliances do far more than influence policy. For all practical purposes, they shape policy within their spheres of influence.

Bill Emmott, author of *The Sun Also Sets*, observes that "since the end of the American occupation in 1952, ministries rather than parties have run the country, initiating as well as executing policy." The power of an individual ministry depends on the financial clout of the industries it regulates, a relationship that results in a tightly knit symbiosis between government and industry. Bureaucrats maintain power by virtue of their ability to create law, while the private sector flexes its muscle by ensuring that its governing ministry remain strong vis-à-vis other ministries. For example, during the rapid export expansion of the

1960s and 1970s, the Ministry of International Trade and Industry (MITI) exercised more power than any other ministry. Since then, however, the world dominance of Japanese capital has boosted the clout of the Ministry of Finance. The rising and falling fortunes of ministries and industries can ignite fierce rivalries because the ministries share no love for one another and would clearly prefer, if possible, to dominate and dictate to all others. What appears on the surface to Western observers as an almost impossible level of government-business coordination and unity, turns out upon closer scrutiny to be a ruthless and competitive struggle for survival.

The business-government liaisons also seem at first glance to not differ all that much from those found in the United States and Britain. In those countries, however, the ministries do not adopt as adversarial a stance toward the general public. More often, Japanese ministers view consumers as simply the means to achieve ministry goals. That explains why the Ministry of Transportation will worry more about Japan Air Lines' loss of revenue than about consumer price gouging. It all sounds suspiciously akin to General Motors pronouncement in the 1960s that "what is good for G.M. is good for America." In Japan, that translates into "what is good for my ministry is good for Japan."

How long can Japan get away with treating its body and soul, its consumers, this way? Karel van Wolferen, the Dutch author of *The Enigma of Japanese Power*, frames the question this way: "The USA stresses that Japan itself stands to gain from free trade and open markets, but what it means by this—greater choices for the Japanese consumers—is not at all what Japanese administrators understand by gain. A truly open market would undermine the domestic order, so how, in their eyes, could this ever be considered a gain for Japan?"

Of course, Japanese administrators can get away with their self-serving logic only so long as relative peace exists among the ministries and no consumer revolt breaks out, both conditions which hinge on the national perception of external threat. In other words, it behooves the government-industry alliances to foster a single mentality. In a satellite Tokyo-New York City show, along the lines of the "Phil Donahue Show," participants from both countries voiced their opinions and concerns about the future of United States-Japan relationships. A middle-aged Japanese fellow began his remarks by addressing the American audience as his "older brothers and sisters" in an economic sense, as if Japan were not whipping the United States across the competitive board. The Americans responded with scorn at the condescension and hypocrisy, but the Japanese meant his remarks sincerely, a testament to his country's success at keeping the consumer thinking that, in economic terms, Japan's very life is on the line.

Third Paradox: So Long-term Yet So Shortsighted.   In a peaceful temple, on the outskirts of Kyoto, a simple inscription is found: "plant a tree for another to see." Sitting amidst trees, ponds, and delicate buildings constructed before the United States separated itself from Great Britain in 1776, it is easy to share the Japanese passion for the long term perspective. Nor can its power as an industrial tool be doubted. In 1948, Douglas MacArthur tapped two gurus, Homer Sarasohn and Charles Protzman, to instill American principles of production in the Japanese. Their pupils included Matsushita Electric's Masaharu Matsushita; Mitsubishi Electric's Takeo Kato; Fujitsu's Hanzou Omi; Sumitomo Electric's Bunzaemon Inoue; and Akio Morita and Masaru Ibuka, the founders of what became Sony Corporation. Forty years later these students command mighty armies in the war of global competition, proof positive that patience does indeed pay off.

The idea of translating patience into action itself has become a key Japanese maneuver, as David Halberstam described in detail in his book *The Reckoning*. "First they would study the Americans and the Europeans, adopting what suited them. Next they would go all over the world buying the most modern technology available for their factories, or buying single machines which they would then copy and make themselves. At this juncture, profit would not be important . . . the Japanese would base their critical decisions not on profit but on share of market. They would sacrifice everything for market share. Market share was essential; if a company gained it, all else would follow."

So entrenched in the Japanese psyche are patience and a passion for the long-term that Japanese CEOs in *Japan Business, Obstacles and Opportunities* suggest that foreign management seeking a toehold in Tokyo must "exhibit a strong degree of commitment, as reflected in patience and a long-term investment view."

When coming to grips with that sort of perspective, the world must look beyond the method and peer deeply into the motive. Careful scrutiny reveals Japanese patience less as a trait carved deeply into the national character, and more as a ruthless dedication to vision. A popular Eastern proverb asks, "Why does the river run slower than the stream?" The Japanese answer by observing that the river knows where it is going, while the stream lacks clear direction.

Japan possesses a clear vision of the future, which David Halberstam sees flowing from "each company's desire to conquer the world." So intensely have the Japanese dedicated themselves to this common goal that Halberstam labels the phenomenon "economic Darwinism," a sort of tooth-and-claw battle for survival of the fittest.

The attitude begins at home. Japanese companies, in general, compete against themselves with the same ferocity as they do against their global adversaries. Through such fierce fighting, a company becomes strong enough to venture beyond Japanese borders, all its "baby fat" worked off in the domestic ring, its competitive teeth sharpened on domestic sparring partners. At the heart of Japan Inc., then, there beats the brutal pulse of Japan versus Japan.

Like most champions who have battled their way through ranks of contenders, Japanese executives exude a confidence that borders on arrogance, and to a visitor, this arrogance contrasts sharply with the docile humility of citizens outside of Tokyo. While the executive class seems to feel close to the climax of world domination, the average Japanese citizen sincerely believes that Japan must literally keep fighting the post-war battle for mere economic stability, never mind world domination.

Since world events will not permit such an illusion to last forever, the Japanese strategy for the future becomes, ironically, rather shortsighted and suggests the lack of any real strategy at all. Instead, there exist only limited visions of self interest, largely unchecked by any balances. It is in this world where competing ministries, with close ties to the industries they regulate, waste little effort on policy integration for the good of the nation, but rather concentrate on enhancing their own power relative to other ministries. Then the current lack of global threat impedes Japan's future power. Barring cataclysmic events that force a unity of policy into a national consensus, individual industrial sectors will continue vigorously pursuing goals and visions that ultimately alienate Japan from the world.

The FSX fighter provides a stunning example of the effects of such shortsightedness. Under an agreement with the United States, Japan maintains a "self-defense" force that recently sought to upgrade its hardware with new fighter jets. Naturally, it turned to the cheapest and most politically advantageous alternative, the United States, the world leader in the aviation industry. The purchase of U.S. planes would improve the trade imbalance, at least perceptually, and contribute toward the softening of rising trade tensions; but certain interests in Japan saw the situation as a gilt-edged invitation to open new markets. These particular *zoku* insisted that the planes be licensed for production in Japan, at a much higher cost. The United States balked, fearing Japanese duplication of the many technological advancements that accompany the aircraft. Even Japanese observers agree that plenty of precedents support the American position. Still, *The Japan Times*, fresh from chiding Japanese consumers for desiring lower prices from Japan Air Lines, claimed that buying the planes from the Unites States would be "tantamount to eventual abandonment of that [aircraft] industrial sector." The paper made no allusion to the higher costs that the Japanese people would ultimately bear to support the interests of a domestic aircraft industry. Nor did it discuss how the FSX incident sparked suspicion throughout the U.S. military establishment about Japan's possible future militarization plans. Suspicion was already running high, as shown by the fact that the Pentagon protested the sale of Fairchild (an American manufacturer of semi-conductor chips) to a Japanese buyer.

Japan's current unchecked tide of technological and manufacturing expansion invites an inevitable confrontation with the United States and Europe. Despite the fact that the global community desperately needs a balanced approach to world trade, Japan lacks a national mechanism for determining which industries should restrain themselves for the overall future well being of the country. The entrenched self interests that dominate Japan will not easily abandon their shortsighted pursuit of the entire economic pie.

The existence in Japan of these and other powerful, interlocking paradoxes makes it exceptionally vulnerable to the forces of change that can upset the balance. Japan should expect renewed external pressure from a revitalized United States and a newly unified Europe. This will reflect the world's reappraisal of Japan in light of its international arrogance and lack of sensitivity to global concerns such as the environment, hunger, and third-world development. Those pressures will be joined by tremendous internal ones already sweeping the country.

MERGING MEGATRENDS

The natural law that all living things grow older applies to countries as well. Beginning in the 1960s, the United States aged rapidly under the full gaze of an unsympathetic world audience. Social change in the 1960s, political change in the 1970s, followed by business and institutional change in the 1980s, racked America as it struggled to cope with age and prosperity.

Japan ages, too, but at a greatly accelerated pace. Starting from scratch, the Japanese transcended the absolute failure of World War II to the seeming equally absolute victory of 1990 trade war, in a mere 40 years. This type of compression extends to the coping process that took so long in America. While the United States has burned up three decades adjusting to the realities of middle age, Japan will most likely do so in a very tumultuous ten-year period. What the 1960s visited on the United States, the 1990s will thrust on the tightly controlled and manipulated Japanese heartland as an unsympathetic world watches. Japanese energy that once sought the destruction of global competitors will turn its force to the task of simply holding the country together. Among the myriad internal trends crisscrossing Japan, three stand out.

Trend One: Gold for Silver. The aging of Japan is a quite literal development because the people are getting older. The trend, labeled "silver" in Japan, was discussed by Shiro Terakawa, a director of the Shinagawa Fuel Company in Tokyo and Superintendent of Shinagawa's Central Research Institute. He made these crucial points.

First, the birthrate has fallen sharply. Japanese prosperity has made parents less concerned than their ancestors about producing offspring to foot the costs of growing old. Second, the Japanese lifespan has increased, in fact, to the longest of any country in the world. The average life span of the Japanese overtook that of the Americans in 1982, and the Nordics in 1986. Finally, Japan experienced a baby boom from 1947 to 1951. Of the 11.3 million births during this five-year period, over 60 percent occurred in a single 24-month period. This startling statistic resulted in an unusually large bloc of people all due to retire at the same time.

Because of Japan's peculiar demography, almost one-fourth of the population will have reached age 65 or older by the year 2020. This projection exceeds the percentages anticipated for the United States and West Germany. Certainly, 2020 lies far in the future, and projections rarely turn out to be precise, but the current aging process is a cold, hard reality. What Americans sometimes call "the pig in the python," a population bulge moving steadily toward old age, has already begun taking an immediate toll in Japan.

To begin with, it is causing Japan to lose the competitive advantage of a relatively young population. When Japan broke through the barriers of international trade, less than 6 percent of the population was over 65, a far smaller percentage than found in the United States or Europe at the time. This fact translated to lower wages, but more important, a smaller pension and tax bill required to support an aging population. Now, with over 10 percent of the population having passed the retirement mark, younger workers must pay to provide social security protection for their elders. With the birthrate declining, however, the base for paying larger sums has shrunk. The bottom line is less savings to fuel the machinery of economic conquest.

Most observers agree that the relatively high level of savings per capita provides a cheap source of capital for Japanese industry. The current savings surplus breaks down to roughly $135,000 in liquid or short-term assets per individual. As the population ages, the savings surplus and the rate of continued savings must decline, not just because of a shrinking base of taxpayers, but because more older Japanese will tap their savings just to survive in the most expensive consumer economy in the developed world.

Finally, the aging population will challenge the government as Japanese "gray power" pursues the privileges expected by a group which helped conquer the world economically. More health care, better retirement homes, enhanced and tailored recreation facilities, but, more important, a reduction in the cost of living, will become major issues.

Consider health care alone. In October, 1989, the U.S. Congress withdrew legislation that would have offset the costs of catastrophic health care by assessing a health-care tax on the older population that most uses the system. By doing so, the government had hoped to prevent taxing the entire population to support the aged. When the plan failed, the nation lost its means to pay the medical bills for older patients whose hospital stays average six to eight days per patient. In Japan, such hospital stays average 28--30 days per patient, which means that any Japanese solution to the problem will cost three to four times as much as the American plan. The already worried Japanese actually contemplated a scheme to export senior Japanese citizens to whatever countries would have them, preferably in warmer climates. News of the project, codenamed Silver-Columbia, ignited hot domestic and global responses. After sacrificing their productive lives for Japan's current prosperity, the aging population hated the idea of being dumped offshore, far from the society they had helped create. Internationally, few developed countries liked the idea of easing the Japanese aging problem so that Japan could maintain its competitive advantage in the global marketplace. The plan seems doomed to failure, and the prospects seem inevitable that the Japanese gold will spend a lot more supporting silver.

CONSUMER REVOLUTION

The public's docile disregard for domestic material prosperity, which has allowed Japan to focus so doggedly on international competition, has begun to awaken. The *zoku* propaganda about self sacrifice in favor of economic stability no longer falls on receptive ears. Suko Iwatare, a member of the Japanese Diet, ventures that "Japanese workers, who have made many sacrifices over the years, believed that once the nation reached the economic superpower status it has now achieved, their efforts would be rewarded." To the contrary, the exploitation escalated.

The pressures of an aging population and the cries for domestic improvement are taxing the coffers of Japanese government an additional $30 to $40 billion needed to meet spending
priorities. If these funds come from industry or a reduction in
ministry budgets, the *zoku* will find themselves no longer able
to wage as vicious and profitable a global economic war. In a
sense, the current funding requirement presage the long-term
issues that will restrict Japanese expansion. As Paul Kennedy
suggests in *The Rise and Fall of the Great Powers*, the more powerful
a country becomes, the more it must pay to maintain that power.
In Japan's case, as global economic dominance escalates geo-
metrically, so do the costs of maintaining that dominance.

True to form, Japan displays little interest in restraining its
global quest. Consequently, the domestic population continues
to pay the price for industrial self interests, most recently in the
form of a 3 percent tax on consumption of all things. Now, not
only do Japanese consumers pay the highest prices in the world,
but they must also kick in a tax for the privilege. Again, true to
form, the government sells the tax to the public as absolutely
essential to Japan's survival. Prime Minister Toshiki Kaifu put it
plainly, "The consumption tax is essential . . . for Japan's future."
However, consumers have begun to take that line with a grain
of salt.

For all Japan's speed in spanning the globe with trade, it
moves toward internal change at an almost snail's pace. Nevertheless, revolution has become a reality, especially when two
issues sacred to the Japanese are inspected: rice and land.

Since *sakana* and *gohan*, or fish and rice, respectively, are the
meat and potatoes of Japan, the public's tolerance of government
control of rice mirrors its tolerance of exploitation in general.
The Japanese government pays rice farmers up to 1,000 percent
more than the world price for their crops. The rice then goes
into storage and eventually sells somewhere between five and
eight times the going global rate. In fact, Americans once gave
gifts of California rice to their friends in Japan, because the

Japanese appreciated rice that had not lain in a warehouse for one to two years before coming to market.

The origin of the government's rice policy extends back to the end of World War II, when it made sense. Currently, the policy does nothing but ensure the well being of special interests, particularly those that support the ruling Liberal Democratic Party. Nevertheless, in 1987 the government dropped the price of rice 6 percent. Another drop of 4.6 percent occurred the following year. Neither price change reflected a repentant government finally looking after the interests of its public. Rather, they marked a change in political demographics. Following the war, roughly 40 percent of the population worked in agriculture. By the 1980s, that number had declined to less than 10 percent. This shift from an agrarian population to an urban one not only decreased rice consumption by 40 percent compared to 1960 levels, but it also resulted in increased spending on consumer goods rather than on supporting the special interests that sought to keep rice prices artificially high. The price of rice, now tied more closely to the costs of production, reflects that the government has begun to see the consumer writing on the wall.

A look at the issue of land also reveals the creeping consumer revolt. The cost of real estate in major Japanese cities increased slightly more than 200 percent during 1987–1988. The abundance of capital and the inherent shortage of land in Japan combined for a classic case of free market land valuation. Or did it? The government's property tax system heavily favors farmers. While government estimates indicate that enough land is tied up in small farm plots in and around Tokyo to build over 3 million new condominiums, that land resists development because farmers, with special tax exceptions, pay only an average of $160 per year, compared to $11,500 a year for the same property not used for agricultural purposes. Further, the government's policy of subsidizing rice production provided little incentive to do anything other than keep Japan's farmland dedicated to agriculture rather than other uses, such as housing. Now, the decline in rice consumption coupled with the gradual changing of the government's rice control strategy may make it less attractive for farmers to hold onto their farms. Further, as the population ages, retirees may have little choice but to sell land held in the family for decades in order to finance a peaceful finish to a life of toil. Finally, consumers, few of which reap the advantages of high land prices, will certainly pressure the government to raise funds, not with more consumption taxes, but with higher property taxes, a large portion of which would flow from Tokyo real estate.

Runaway land prices have caused an interesting shift in Japanese mentality. Rather than saving for the dream of home or land ownership, they are spending their yen in other directions, having assumed that land or home ownership lies beyond their wildest dreams. Having experienced the exhilaration of mounds of disposable income, the urban Japanese population has begun to understand that high consumer prices maintained by *zoku* interests have made them second-class world consumers. The more they travel outside of Japan, the more they see dramatic confirmation of the discrimination.

In 1987, Japan saw 2.2 million foreign travelers. That same year, 6.7 million Japanese toured the world, mostly on shopping sprees. Cheaper food, cheaper clothes, and, most depressingly, cheaper Japanese products, greeted Japanese travelers everywhere. Returning home after comparing prices and witnessing first-hand Japanese world economic dominance, the travelers began raising questions about the necessity of their domestic sacrifice. To suffer for the economic survival of the homeland is one thing, but to do without for the increased profits of a few special interests is another. The questions, much to the government's chagrin, will only grow more strident as Japanese, who traveled abroad 25 percent more in 1988 than in 1977, spend more time immersed in the realities beyond their borders.

Significantly, foreign travel abroad by Japanese women grew at a much faster rate than for men. In 1987, men accounted for 55 percent of foreign travel, women for 45 percent, a higher ratio than anyone expected given the tradition of the home and duty-bound *mama-san*. The number of women traveling abroad, exacerbates the problem of keeping the domestic population politically docile, because Japanese women, like women the world over, pay attention to domestic prices, and women in Japan generally control the family purse.

The issues of rice and land only hint at the turbulence swimming just beneath the surface in Japan. Other challenges beckon. When will the worker join the consumer in questioning the demands of self-interested *zoku*? Today in Japan, less than 30 percent of the working population enjoy two-day weekends, compared to over 90 percent of Japan's Western trading partners. The issue of gender also promises to boil over. The last Prime Minister, Sosuke Uno, stepped down amidst *geisha* girl sex revelations. Seasoned Japan watchers note that the incident itself did not topple the man, because sex outside marriage is a traditional perk of the Japanese power elite in both business and government. What undid him, though, was the fact that the usually discreet press jumped on the story, perhaps reflecting a growing political force, symbolized by Takako Doi, predicted to become the first female Prime Minister of Japan.

ONLY FOOLS FAIL TWICE

At Dawn We Slept, the award-winning history of the Japanese attack on Pearl Harbor, documents that although the best and the brightest minds of the Japanese high command knew that Japan could never succeed in the military domination of the United States, Japan pursued the course anyway. Fifty years later, the sages could provide the same advice. Although Japan will not succeed in economically dominating the United States or the newly united Europe forever, the Japanese continue to trod that path anyway.

Similar foolhardiness abounds elsewhere. Again, from *At Dawn We Slept* it is revealed that the United States and Western Europe consistently underestimated the Japanese, and, embarrassingly, even considered them racially inferior. The error added two-and-a-half years to the Pacific War, as the United States and Britain chewed up unexpected resources battling the talented and far-from-inferior Japanese war machine. Fifty years later, the United States and Europe are making the same mistake. American and European policy toward Japan grows out of the misinformation that has tried to explain the sudden economic rise of Japan.

In the first place, until recently, the West never understood the true source of Japanese power, because supposed experts shifted scrutiny from the core issues that drive Japan to the superficial, flashier industrial gimmicks such as inventory control and quality circles. Many of these originated in the United States. Twenty years into the economic war, these supposed miracle methods, taken back and recopied by the originators, have not given the West a noticeable edge in performance. The survival instincts and consumer exploitation that lie beneath the visible layer of just-in-time inventory and consensus building cannot be copied.

In the second place, the West has consistently underestimated the rudimentary differences between Westerners and the Japanese. James Fallows, arguing against the dream of a U.S.-Japan marriage, paints a vivid portrait of those differences. Consider, for example, that such simple words as *fair* and *free* mean something entirely different in Tokyo than they do in London, Washington, D.C., or Bonn. The Judaic-Christian heritage, however distant at times, colors Western language and meaning in a way that totally confuses the Shinto-influenced Japanese. To the former, *fair* and *free* suggest an ideal that should guide the activities of men and women. To the latter, a people whose national religion Shintoism relates to the tribe, words embodying an abstract concept of morality (another word foreign to the Japanese) take a backseat to the impact of actions on the group itself. For example, while Western governments often justify their actions in terms of "right or wrong," the Japanese talk about "good or bad" for Japan.

Given the sophistication of modern politics and diplomatic relations, it amuses those who comprehend such differences to watch the West attempt to shame Japan by suggesting that restricting imports into the Japanese market is "unfair" and that the domestic Japanese community would benefit from "free" trade. To hear former Prime Minister Nakasone complain, it would be "unfair" for Americans to expect the Japanese to accelerate domestic consumption of foreign products at a faster rate. Nakasone would use such a word only in a speech aimed at American, not Japanese, ears. The Japanese people would not understand the word *fair*, particularly after years of exploitation at the hands of their own industrialists.

THE NEW LOOK

While Japan insulates against the shock of internal changes, the EC must respond with a fresh attitude toward trade. This new mind set must be hardened by the lessons of past failures and must bear a more accurate understanding of Japan's success and, more importantly, its motives.

Beyond the shock of internal changes, Japan faces a new Western attitude about trade policy. The United States and the newly united Europe now realize that Japan will not slow down once it has gotten its need to rebound out of its system. The reality that the drive for world domination never went away and will not easily go away must be accepted. No longer is that drive springing from a national consensus, but from the selfish interests of selected *zoku*. These realizations must bring about important changes in Western thinking.

First, the West must bypass the Japanese political system and concentrate attention directly on the *zoku*. How fitting, considering that the Japanese penetration of the American market initially bypassed the political process and zeroed in on American strongholds (steel and automobiles at the time). They paid attention to politics only when they realized that the American *zoku* wield far less power than their counterparts in Tokyo and much less than American politicians. Borrowing a lesson from that book, European industrialists must move the economic battleground away from endless meetings with Japanese politicians, who function as little more than the messengers to the interest groups, directly to the companies responsible for Japan's expansion. Negotiating global concessions directly with Honda before agreeing to another U.S. factory will accomplish more than beating down the price of domestic rice with the Ministry of Agriculture. A demand for Sony's assistance in lowering Japanese trade barriers erected by the zoku should precede permission for the further Japanese acquisition of American entertainment assets.

Second, the West must learn not to let verbiage derail its negotiations. James Fallows, in *Atlantic* (May, 1989) cites an instructive example. When the British were negotiating for seats on the Tokyo stock exchange, they promoted the position "that, in principle [a moral world, like fair and free], any company that met the financial and other standards should be allowed to enter the market." The Japanese, totally unfamiliar with the Western concept of "in principle" stalled the British with endless negotiations. Finally, the British simply demanded two seats, hinted of economic retaliation if they did not get them, and totally ignored the "principle" behind the demand. The negotiations then shifted from the abstract debate about the appropriateness of the request to the request itself. The British got two seats.

In current negotiations with the United States and Europe, Japan claims that it is doing all that it can do to accelerate domestic spending without forcing "unfair" consequences on the population. Behind that verbiage sits the real logic: that opening the domestic Japanese market will severely curtail the offshore competitive edge of Japan's industries. The consumer, as usual, rides in the backseat.

During earlier negotiations, Westerners would often get side-tracked by the "fairness" of their demands, but they must take a new track. The United States and Europe, for instance, should present conditions for cooperative trade and refuse to get into a fruitless debate over the domestic impact of any changes, because that is a Japanese problem of no concern to the United States of Europe. This approach would, in effect, force the Japanese to stick to the substantive issues surrounding world trade.

Finally, the United States and Europe, recognizing Japanese economic expansion as akin to war, must employ a language more appropriate to that arena, that of power. As Fallows points out, "The lack of interest in principle makes sheer power the main test of what is "fair" in the minds of the Japanese." History suggests that the Japanese will fight to the death for the ruling military clan or just as quickly push for higher productivity at the hands of another dictator, Douglas MacArthur.

By and large, Japanese policy will follow the dictates and dreams of the most powerful *zoku*, the landowners and indus-trialists. That is, until greater powers come along: Japanese con-sumers and the global trading partners Japan needs. Enter Europe 1992.

WHAT GOES AROUND COMES AROUND

The Japanese possess no magic management methodology, at least nothing that those willing to pay the price in the form of money and corporate change cannot duplicate. The real magic behind Japan's success is its consumers or, more correctly, its level of consumer sacrifice. This the United States and Europe cannot duplicate without demanding massive changes from their citizens. EC92 does the next best thing, introduce into the trade equation the power of the "consumption block."

With the unification of Europe into one economic zone, the world consumption map consists of three developed markets: Japan, the United States, and Europe. Whereas the Japanese have focused on dominating the American market with its 250 million consumers, it must now turn its attention to the combined European market of 320 million. No longer can the Japanese economically divide and conquer one country at a time.

Although the final pan-European trade policy remains unclear, the power behind the policy stands firm: reciprocity. Of any concept concerning global trade, the Japanese fear this one the most. The basis for the fear is that reciprocity sheds light on Japan's darkest vulnerability. The EC and the United States combine for just under 600 million consumers against 120 million Japanese. If, in fact, consumers are the latest weapons in the trade war arsenal, Japan is hopelessly outgunned. Consumers are the raw material that feed industrial growth. Not in the Marxist sense of exploited labor, but in the trade war role as exploited buyers. The more buyers an industry or collection of industries (called a country) has at its disposal, the greater coverage there is for mere profit and the means to fund the never-ending quest for technological competitive advantage. In Japan's case, American and European consumers are literally funding Japanese trade dominance. There are not enough Japanese consumers to foot the bill. If the demand for reciprocity is not met, the United States and Europe will ultimately cut off Japan from its most precious commodity, U.S. and EC consumers.

The various forms of reciprocity were discussed in Chapter 2, but at the heart of each lies the goal that countries become roughly equal when the final scores are tallied. In whatever form, the implementation of reciprocity, likely to occur over a 20-year span, will even out Japan's competitive edge. In the area of banking, for example, in exchange for the privilege of banking in the EC after 1992, Japan must allow all 12 countries that comprise the EC the same right to bank in Japan. But this means more than mere permission. Allowing Europeans the privilege of banking in Japan means nothing if social pressure and political blacklisting keep Japanese corporations and consumers away. In a very real sense, Tokyo must actually encourage the use of EC financial services if it hopes to preserve its banking presence in Europe. The *zoku* can already see the Japanese domestic market, its main resource, slipping away. Further, reciprocity shifts trade tensions from tariffs and restrictions to actual sales. For example, the West wants free access to the Japanese consumer, but under pure reciprocity, access alone does not matter unless Japanese consumers actually buy Western cars. If that does not happen, Japanese automakers will find their access to European consumers reciprocally restricted.

Nobody believes that pure reciprocity will take effect product by product. One hundred twenty million Japanese will never be able to buy the same number of cars as 250 million Americans or 320 million Europeans. But what the Japanese lack in automotive purchasing power, they can make up for by buying American rice, Spanish peaches, and Greek tomatoes.

The Japanese and their apologists claim that reciprocity will inflict "unfair" damage on Japan. Even accusations of racism have cropped up. But the cries will fall on deaf ears. The tide of Japanese domination has forced Europe into a massive set of internal changes over a relatively short period of time. Entire cultures are changing their way of thinking in order to form a united European group, comprised of countries many of which have fought bitterly in recent years. The Japanese must now deal with a Europe long on trade strategy and short on sympathy.

Imagine a reciprocal war in which American manufacturers sell only to Americans, European companies only to Europeans, and *zoku* only to Japanese. Simple mathematics indicates that such a turn of events would not only disrupt the world, it would crush Japan. Already overcharged by their own industries, 120 million consumers could never absorb all the Toyotas, Sonys,

Toshibas, and Sanyos that now flood the world market. Japan would sink under the weight of its own industrial power.

European motives, unlike those of Japan, do not drift toward domination. Rather, Europeans envision a balanced global trading game, eventually including even less developed countries, as far more conducive to world peace. A decimated Japan will not enhance post-1992 European trade, but an equal Japan, importing as well as exporting, would benefit Europe and the rest of the world, even the Japanese. Hishahiko Okazaki, Japanese Ambassador to Thailand, warns that the two greatest periods of Japanese economic prosperity occurred in 1902–1921 and 1945–1989. Both were periods of "cooperation with the Anglo-American world."

"Carrying out this sort of cooperation is the best way for Japan to achieve security for itself," adds Okazaki. The statement suggests that Japan might consider crash courses in international friendship, or at least a Dale Carnegie seminar. In addition to EC92, Tokyo must build better relationships with an emerging, revitalized United States.

CHAPTER SEVEN

The New America

You can always count on the American people
to do the right thing,
but only after they have tried
damn near every other solution.

WINSTON CHURCHILL

THE AMERICAN PHOENIX

The year 1992 not only promises the birth of a new Europe, but it is also the 500th anniversary of the discovery of America. That both events are marked by the same date is, of course, coincidental. But the symbolic unity, wrapped up in a date, is not necessarily shallow. Japanese tourists visiting Italy do not venture in quaint Sicilian graveyards, looking for headstones bearing the family name. Nor do they consume the beer and bratwurst of Germany's Octoberfest and reminisce to their grandchildren about the "old country." The point is that the origins of modern Japan go back to 4500 B.C. to the Jomon, an early culture that fished, hunted, and made pottery decorated with rope-like designs on the islands that now make up Japan. But Americans, even Japanese, Pakistani, and Hispanic-Americans historically trace their national origin to Europe.

Five hundred years after Christopher Columbus, the United States is clearly America, not Europe. "But it is equally clear, and a matter of great consequence for the future of the world, that the United States, though not a European nation geographically, is in truth the next thing to it," suggests Dennis Bark, Senior Fellow at the Hoover Institute. Bark's observation is based on the reality that trade war is as much dependent on alliances for victory as military war. The implication being that an EC-American relationship is bound to be deeper than that between the new Europe and Japan. Seeded even deeper in the implication is the hint that U.S.-EC cooperation may be the actual mechanism that reduces Japan's trade superiority to a level of relative equality with America and Europe.

It might strike readers odd that cultural ties would affect the cold and seemingly culturally indifferent flow of goods and services that are the weapons of trade war. But there is more to the observation than cultural comfort zones. Another reason, according to Nigel B. Christie, Managing Director of European Mergers and Acquisitions for Kidder Peabody, is economic history. "I think Fortress Europe is going to be more of an impediment in terms of European acceptance to the Japanese," he says, "because, historically, there has been clear reciprocity between Europe and the U.S., where there hasn't been with Japan." The tone of Christie's comment recalls the discussion of reciprocity and friendship that ended the last chapter. Who has been and will be a better trade friend to the EC, the United States or Japan?

There are two factors that make American friendship with the EC far more plausible than Japanese comradery: consumer connections and consortia combinations. These are given detailed attention at the end of the chapter. A brief scrutiny of the United States similar to that of Japan is provided first. Predicting the future relationship of the EC with Japan required knowledge of what is happening in Japan itself. Similar knowledge is needed about the United States.

The analysis of Japan suggested that the nation would grapple with serious domestic issues, which would in turn, partially divert focus away from the battle for international trade dominance. For example, yen diverted to improve the Japanese highway system would not be available as surplus funds in the form of savings.

The shifting of national focus intrigues historians like Arthur Schlesinger, Jr. In his book, *The Cycles of American History*, Schlesinger directs attention to the "patterns of alternation, of ebb and flow, in human history." He is intrigued by the cyclical nature of the shifts themselves, the timing with which nations alter their focus. Of particular importance to Schlesinger are the shifts between public purpose and private interest.

A period of public purpose is when a nation reaches out to affect the world outside of itself. Periods of private interest are introspective. While the outside world is not and cannot be completely ignored, these periods are when a nation settles in to solve its own problems, preferring to be left alone for a while. The concept of cycles concerns itself with the motives or momentum that lead to periods of public purpose versus private interest. But the key issue in understanding cycles is focus. Where is the nation's concentration, on matters external or on domestic details?

Within the framework of cycles, Japan would be positioned as heading toward a period of private interest. Remember, motive is inconsequential. Japan may be dragged, kicking and screaming to the point where at least some focus must be shifted from economically conquering the world to making life more pleasant for its people. An aging population, a less work-oriented rising generation, and scores of corporate drones that question the value of team loyalty all point to the fact that deep introspection may be in order. But the reverse is true of America.

It could be argued that the 1960s, 1970s, and 1980s were periods of intense introspection—that the United States, while not dropping out of world affairs, dropped in to tackle its own unique set of domestic challenges. The position is debated by C.W. Kegley and P.J. McGowan in *Cyclical Trends in American Foreign Policy Moods: The Unfolding of America's World Role*. The authors cite for color, not predictive value, the thinking of political analyst Frank L. Klingberg. In 1952, Frank L. Klingberg wrote about what he called "the historical alternation of moods" in America, whereby he saw the nation swinging between introversion (private interest) and extroversion (public purpose). Klingberg suggested seven cycles since 1776:

Periods of Introversion	Periods of Extroversion
1776–1798	1798–1824
1824–1844	1844–1871
1871–1891	1891–1918
1918–1940	1940–

The Klingberg cycle shows four introvert phases, averaging 21 years each, and three extrovert phases, averaging 27 years each. Though his own analysis did not go beyond the beginning of the 1940 extrovert phase, a projection of phases beyond 1940, using the average number of years consumed by the earlier phases, would continue as follows:

Periods of Introversion	Periods of Extroversion
	1940–1967
1968–1989	1990–2017

A political historian with no crystal ball on the future, Klingberg could not have anticipated that the next introvert phase would begin with the 1968 assassinations of Robert Kennedy and Martin Luther King, Jr., the political riots in Chicago, Woodstock, and the beginning of the end of the war in Viet Nam. That these events kicked off, rather dramatically, what Klingberg would suggest was the eve of a wave of national introspection, makes it tempting to use the theory as a means of prediction. But, Schlesinger warns that "there is no mathematical determinism in history." Cycles should excite imaginations, position perceptions, and increase sensitivity to trends, but they should not be used to predict specific events. Instead, cycles should provide some warning, that sweeping change is in the wind, at least as far as history is concerned.

Like 1968, the last three decades of American life hint of introspection. The 1960s, 1970s, and early to mid-1980s brought turbulence and tests of limits to nearly all facets of American life. In hindsight, historians agree that no one predominant issue set the match to the nation's morals, mores, and institutions, but the coming together of a whole set of sparks at one time. Providing a summary of each decade would require a literary bonfire, more appropriate for a history textbook. But a few random matches out of memory can be recalled, from periods where America's inward gaze grew so great and the response so radical that Paul Johnson, author of *Modern Times,* called the period "America's suicide attempt."

The Sixties.   If the major topics that competed for American attention were listed in order of importance, the Viet Nam War screams for center stage, though quite a few other issues bunch near the top of the agenda. For example, the quest for civil rights included the struggle for minority rights, gay rights, senior citizens' rights, students' rights, silent majority rights, and women's rights. Each group shouted for attention, energy, and money, and together they raised a deafening cry for dramatic change in the American way.

To sense the scope of that change, simply scan the literature of the times. *The Affluent Society* by Galbraith attacked conventional economic wisdom, while Harrington's best-seller, *The Other America*, lamented the failure of economics to help the American poor. Daniel Moynihan, then Assistant Secretary of Labor, argued in the *Moynihan Report* that the black population suffered from a "social pathology" caused by underemployment and the disintegration of the family unit. In 1965 Ralph Nader kicked off consumer activism with his automobile expose, *Unsafe At Any Speed.*

Throughout the 1960s, the American population searched for a framework that would best guide the country into the future. Unfortunately, the search often turned violent. In 1968 alone, The National Student Association tallied 221 major student demonstrations in America, the most effective being the march on the Democratic Convention in August of 1968, where 11,900 police, 7,500 National Guardsmen, and 1,000 FBI agents fought pitched battles with students, all on prime-time national television. By then, the student unrest had become a national pastime. According to John Bunzel, some observers prior to 1968 thought that the history of social change "started in Athens and ended in California."

The Seventies.   While Viet Nam may have symbolized the social upheaval of the 1960s, Watergate epitomized the political changes of the 1970s. In 1972, Richard Nixon, fresh from the euphoria of re-election, established his own "intelligence unit." Financed by State Department "special emergency" money, the staff of 11 was responsible only to Nixon. The paranoid president used the FBI and the Justice Department to harass and tap the phones of his enemies, especially the press. Paul Johnson reported, again in the *Modern Times*, that Nixon even "used the intelligence service to bug his wife's hotel room." In May 1972, and again on June 17, 1972, the Nixon unit broke into the Democratic Party headquarters located in the Watergate building in Washington D.C. On the second break-in, the highly secret team of "plumbers" were caught.

The significance of Watergate lay not in the dirty tricks to which the Presidency had stooped. Indeed, a well-known precedent occurred during the 1964 presidential elections when Lyndon Johnson supporters "bugged" Barry Goldwater. Even NBC-TV eavesdropped illegally on Republican Party headquarters in 1968. Just as Viet Nam touched a nerve in the American people, Watergate set ablaze the moral outrage of the American public. On the heels of the social revolution of the 1960s, America was primed for a change in political conscience.

From the arrests at Watergate in June, 1972, to Nixon's resignation from the presidency in August, 1974, the nation discussed, debated, and defined the faults of Nixon's "imperial presidency." In the end, all the scrutiny led to a shift in power from the executive branch to Congress. Unfortunately, Congress, itself ravaged by self interests and bipartisan animosity, was woefully ill-suited to rule. Into the vacuum of leadership rolled a new self-interest group that the *Washington Monthly* in November of 1976 labeled the "imperial press."

The media, both printed and electronic, became the conscience of America. Its networks left no stone unturned, no scandal unexposed as it displayed and flayed the nation's political and business institutions. The reign of the media continued throughout the 1970s until the nation's first "media president," Ronald Reagan, brought his masterful manipulation to bear. What Reagan started, presidential candidate George Bush finished. During a national news broadcast in the midst of the 1988 campaign, network anchorman and symbol of media power Dan Rather tried to bait Bush over the so-called Iran-Contra affair. The usually polite and proper Bush counterattacked by recalling that Rather had walked off the set during a news telecast. Bush's assault left Rather stuttering in retreat, an image that symbolically signaled the shift of power from the press and back to the presidency.

The Eighties. Purged socially and politically, America's revolutionary attention turned toward business as debt-financed leveraged buy-outs and junk bonds turned Wall Street into a dangerous jungle. Everyone watched as the business sector proceeded to cannibalize itself. For the first time in the history of American business, investors listened to the sylvan song of corporate raiders rather than the traditional tune sung by management. In a sense, the investing rank and file revolted against the corporate version of the "imperial presidency," where CEOs and their management teams, more often than not lacking strong ownership positions, reaped undue rewards from the corporate system and became just as arrogant and secretive as their political predecessors. When the opportunity to sell the companies right out from under the offending management presented itself, the stockholders seized the moment.

American enterprise found itself besieged by a seven-year run on operating companies by assorted raiders, investment bankers, and competitors. Raiders with little equity and lots of debt snatched up entire companies and then sold them piecemeal, leaving only memories and astronomical fees in their wake. Two events put the brakes on runaway LBOs. First, the Justice Department charged or convicted the very core of the LBO movement for a variety of offenses linked to financial manipulation. Second, the stock market sent two strong signals that the system could no longer go unchecked: the Black Monday price plunge of October 1987 and the Son-of-Monday setback of October 1989. Both market crashes sent raiders and junk bond dealers scurrying to protect fragile debt to equity ratios.

All these mini-revolutions—the social upheaval of the 1960s, the political realignment of the 1970s, and the business re-orientation of the 1980s—suggest, but certainly do not prove a preoccupation with introversion. As stated before, the entire introversion-extroversion concept merely excites thinking in the direction of trend. In fact, just the task of labeling a period as one of national introspection requires comparison. Future American actions will determine whether the past 30 years was more a period of private interest rather than public purpose.

In terms of the future, however, the United States may have jump-started into a period of involvement beyond its borders. The transition from one decade to another finds American troops invading Panama, American ships pondering a blockade of Columbia, and an American president traveling to South America to arm-twist Latin leaders into stemming the flow of drugs to the United States. Admittedly, all these actions are related to domestic drug abuse in the United States, itself a cause for national introspection. But, despite comparisons to America's failure in Viet Nam and fears of another land war on foreign soil, the American military not only engaged in, but started, an offshore conflict.

EC92 and the political and economic revolution occurring in Eastern Europe and the Soviet Union will be another test of the American will to get involved in matters of public purpose. Will the Unites States take the lead role in rebuilding Eastern Europe? Can Gorbachev count on American economic and technological assistance to push *peristroika*? At this time, the answers to these questions cannot be predicted. But a feel for the level of power that a more internationally involved United States would wield can be obtained. In order to do this, the myths that have tainted the American economic image must be attacked. Also, at least two of the problems that threaten to hamstring the future of American economic muscle must be pointed out.

DECLINE NOT FAILURE

To better understand the potential international impact of a more extroverted America, its current position in world rankings must be accurately assessed. That is not such an easy task. To begin with, just as many myths have sprung up about America's global failure to compete as have attended the Japanese management miracle. Five of these axe-grinding myths deserve special attention.

Myth #1: The United States Has Failed Economically. This myth, which results from confusing decline with failure, grows out of the fact that the economic dominance of the United States has declined since the end of World War II. This decline, however, must be put in perspective. The American share of the world's combined gross national product reached a record-setting 40 percent in the 1940s. The world has never seen, nor will likely see again, so great a level of dominance. By contrast, the British Empire, at its peak, possessed 25 percent of the world's wealth. By the mid-1960s and continuing into the 1980s, the United States has declined to roughly that same percentage. While multiple factors account for the decline, two merit discussion. First, the greatest decline occurred between the end of World War II and the mid-1960s. During this period, Japan was just emerging as a serious global contender and had not even begun to contribute toward the decline. In fact, the United States' economy had already dropped 12 points as a percentage of world GNP before it incurred its first trade deficit in 1972, a fact that leads to the second point. The United States *voluntarily* vacated its position of dominance, knowing the economic imbalance, though good for the nation in the short term, would harm world growth in the future. Japan watcher James Fallows drives home this point when he suggests that Tokyo has not recognized the value of voluntarily reducing dominance. "A historical comparison illustrates how little the Japanese have done to redirect their economy.

The last time one nation had such an unbalanced position in world trade was in the late 1940s, when the U.S. economy represented half the economic activity in the entire war-battered world. With its own industries newly expanded during the war, and everyone else's blown up, the United States could have completely swamped all competitors in an outright production contest. Instead, the United States rapidly and deliberately opened its markets to imports, and through the Marshall Plan, it helped rebuild foreign factories so that they could produce something for Americans to buy. In 1947, the U.S. trade surplus represented 4.5 percent of GNP. By 1950, it had been driven down to .05 percent. At the time, that was regarded as a great accomplishment—and it was, because the opened American market gave Europeans, Asians, and other producers a place to sell their goods."

Given fluctuations in currency values, a nation's output against a world standard cannot easily be computed. Many economists, therefore, like to look at "purchasing power equivalent," an approach that would place America's share of world GNP at 26 percent in 1987 compared to 22 percent for the countries comprising the EC, and 11 percent for Japan. Regardless of the method used, the United States still boasts the largest share of the world's combined output. Yes, it has declined from the 40 percent imbalance in the 1940s, but it has by no means "failed."

Myth #2: America's Lagging Productivity. This myth has gained credence by mistaking productivity in a specific sector for national productivity as a whole. What about the record? American productivity in all sectors (industrial, agricultural, services, etc.) cannot be matched anywhere in the world, and it is growing. The problem comes when analysis concentrates on productivity in one sector, such as the steel industry, and completely ignores another sector, such as American agriculture, where executives like Jim Saras quietly lead a productivity re-evaluation.

Jim Saras is a Stanford-educated peach farmer and Chairman and CEO of TriValley, the largest private-label food company in the United States. TriValley processes 50 percent of the U.S. market share of peaches, almost 30 percent of the U.S. olive market, and 40 percent of the tomato market. With a lean administrative staff of 300 crammed into three floors of a downtown San Francisco building, TriValley alone can fill Japan's entire demand for processed fruit and vegetables.

In agriculture, which has become a globally competitive and technologically advanced industry, the United States exercises absolute dominance. Although international competition has speeded up, no single nation, including a united Europe, can come close to the growing, processing, and marketing capabilities of U.S. agribusiness. Over 33 percent of the food and fiber produced in America goes overseas, and that despite programs to restrict production. American agriculture may shine, but American manufacturing has not been a bust, either.

Since 1985, U.S. manufacturing productivity has been increasing at over 4 percent a year. The Japanese and European manufacturing gains appear to be greater because both increased manufacturing from near-zero levels following the destruction of World War II. Still, Japanese manufacturing productivity comes in at only 93 percent of American productivity, with Western Europe even lower at 85 percent. The relative gaps have not narrowed since 1984.

Myth #3: The United States Has Lost the Trade War. This myth results from confusing trade deficits with trade volume. In fact, both the United States and Europe have run up trade deficits with Japan. In terms of sheer volume, however, the United States exports 18 percent of the world total, compared to 13 percent for West Germany and only 12 percent for Japan. The United States clearly leads the world in exports alone, at least until 1992. When EC unification becomes reality, West Germany's exports will be combined with those of eleven other EC members to take the world lead with a whopping 40 percent share of exports.

Many Americans fail to appreciate the export volume of the United States, because they enjoy importing as much as they relish exporting. The reasons behind the behavior further underscore United States economic superiority. First, Americans can afford to buy virtually anything their hearts desire. Second, U.S. prices for goods and services are the most competitive in the world. Third, the American government does not discourage or restrict consumption.

The perception of declining American trade also receives reinforcement from even a cursory comparison of Japanese success in America with American failure in Japan. According to Peter Drucker, the comparison should not be misleading. American-brand products, he points out, enjoy a much higher share of the Japanese market than most people realize—"about twice as much per capita than goods made by Japanese companies have of the American market." IBM, Coke, Johnson & Johnson, Apple, and Procter & Gamble are household words in Japan.

Myth #4: The United States Has Fallen Behind in the Technowar. Like all myths, this one contains some truth. In September, 1989, *Fortune* listed the latest technological salvos fired by the Japanese:

- A tape recorder the size of a matchbox, without cassettes or moving parts
- High definition television with 21-foot screens that have movie theater clarity
- Flat TV screens that hang on your living room wall
- Translation telephones, with simple vocabularies at first, that handle multilingual conversations almost instantaneously
- Semiconductor chips the size of silver dollars that act as electrical transformers
- Air conditioners that use one-third less power than today's
- Micro-miniaturized personal computers a fraction the size of the IBM PS/2 and Apple MacIntosh

o   Robots that sew, smooth concrete floors, hoist slabs into
     place, or wash windows better and faster than people

Add to these advancements the near destruction of the American semiconductor industry by the Japanese and no wonder
Americans think they have begun to lag behind technologically.
In a field where the United States once ruled, only a handful of
firms, such as Intel, still compete. In view of that situation, some
U.S. legislators, linking American national security with the ability to design and manufacture chips, panicked. But Japanese chip-
victory may not warrant any great excitement. George Gilder,
in his book *Microcosm: The Quantum Revolution in Economics and
Technology*, argues that chips signify the leftovers of computer
technology, with the real breakthroughs coming in software,
where Japan remains in the dark ages compared to the United
States. In fact, Mitz Kurobe, Mitsui's Harvard-educated computer
wizard, suggests that American software development "is probably 10 to 20 years ahead of Japan." The gap looks even more
impressive when it is realized that the computer industry re-
invents itself almost every 18 months. Gilder further minimizes
the importance of chip dominance by suggesting that software
such as Lotus 1-2-3 and WordPerfect, not the IBM PC, kicked
off the personal computer revolution.

The chip–software situation points to a major weakness of
Japanese technology: its totally linear nature. Sure, the Japanese
can make it smaller, prettier, less expensive, and more functional,
but in the final analysis all that activity simply refines something
that already exists. After all, high-resolution television is still
television. The Japanese have certainly pushed existing and evolving technology to the limits of practicality, but they cannot claim
much progress in breakthrough technology. Susumu Tonegawa,
a Japanese scientist who won the 1987 Nobel Prize in Medicine,
put the Japanese shortfall in breakthrough technology in perspective. In an interview with the *Kiplinger Newsletter,* Tonegawa
admitted that he was not able to accomplish his work in Japan

because of the demand for consensus-based research that stifles innovation. Consequently, Tonegawa's breakthroughs did not occur at a Japanese university, but at the Massachusetts Institute of Technology. In sheer numbers, the United States employs more techworkers than any other country: 3.5 million scientists and engineers, compared to 1.5 million Japanese counterparts. Further, the annual research and development outlay of the United States triples that of Japan. However, because the Japanese emphasize consumer technology and excel in getting enhanced products to the market, the steady stream of new products creates the illusion that great technological change originates in Japan. On the other hand, the United States, which focuses far more on breakthrough technologies with longer developmental cycles, seems to be lagging behind.

It is dangerous to overgeneralize. Seeing that the Japanese have seized the technological lead in electronics, robotics, and heavy industrial manufacturing, some observers feel tempted to extend such dominance to all products and services. Doing so fosters a huge illusion. The Japanese actually lag behind technologically in agriculture, genetics, aircraft design, optic fibers, prescription drugs, food service, weapons, and medical technology, just to cite a few examples. Given the gap in these areas, Japanese technological dominance will almost certainly remain limited to consumer electronics and cameras. It is not that the Japanese lack the ability or the creativity to compete, they just cannot depend on the United States repeating its error of handing technology over to future competitors or stagnating long enough for others to catch up. Once burned, twice shy.

As the weight of facts shatter these and other myths, the true competitive strength of the United States becomes more and more evident.

A FEW CHANGES TO COME

Despite the economic dominance, the United States still faces some serious problems that stand between it and a sustained competitive advantage vis-à-vis the other global players. As the United States makes the apparent transition from introvert to extrovert, it carries some old problems with it. Health care, the aging population, AIDS, drug use, and the homeless all persist with no hint of resolution in sight.

Two particularly stubborn problems, however, make all other challenges seem almost insignificant. In order for the United States to peak during its extrovert phase, it must completely overhaul its education system and eliminate the federal deficit. Otherwise, America can never realize its full potential.

So much has been written about both these subjects, it may seem pointless to talk about them here, but they do deserve a fresh look because no other factors will affect the American future more. Despite all the hullabaloo surrounding them, neither has received radical action yet. Without action, the potential offered by 1992 will slip away as surely as the tide.

EDUCATION: THE NEW FRONTIER

H.G. Wells defined modern history as "a race between education and catastrophe." President Lyndon Johnson said that "the answer for all our national problems comes in a single word. That word is education." While improved education will not solve every problem, the lack of a good educational system will inhibit progress in every other area. Unfortunately, each special interest group that seizes this issue taints the definition of the problem and the design of solutions with dangerous preconceptions. To get beyond such limitations, the broader strategic issues must be considered and the battle over specific alternatives must be avoided.

In the present information era, a country needs skilled, knowledgeable workers. Otherwise, a nation will lose any chance of sustaining a competitive edge with technologically driven innovation. It all begins with education, and at the starting gun the United States looks shaky. In 1982, American eighth-graders taking a standardized math test answered only 46 percent of the questions correctly, placing them in the bottom half of the eleven nations competing. That same year, the top 5 percent of high school seniors from nine developed countries took standardized tests of algebra and calculus. The American seniors came in dead last. Educators were quick to suggest that the computer revolution and the widespread use of calculators contributed toward the math deficiency, but unfortunately, the Americans came up short in other subjects as well.

Studies, such as *A Nation at Risk: The Imperative for Educational Reform* (sponsored by the U.S. Department of Health, Education and Welfare), have shown that one high school junior in five can write a comprehensible note applying for a summer job. Among high school seniors, fewer than one-third know to within 50 years when the Civil War took place, one in three do not know that Columbus discovered America before 1740, and barely half know that during the Second World War, Russia did not invade the yet-to-be founded nation of Israel. Well under 40 percent of graduating seniors can understand an average article in the *New York Times* or decipher a straightforward bus schedule. These deficiencies affect *students*, not dropouts.

Roughly 30 percent of American high school students drop out each year—nearly 1 million soldiers who will not engage in the knowledge wars. At some inner-city schools, the drop-out rate exceeds 50 percent. Of those who stick it out, some 700,000 graduate but cannot read their own diplomas. At the present rate, the literacy rate in America will drop 30 percent by the year 2000. All these alarming statistics are manufactured by an education model that has not changed in any meaningful way for over 100 years. Somehow, when most of America went through gut-wrenching change during the 1960s and 1970s, the educational system just moseyed along at its usual turtle's pace.

Meanwhile, the pressure on the educational system has been increasing steadily, especially from critics concerned about the greatest victims of the crisis, poor and minority students. In the next 12 years, over 5 million Black and Hispanic students under the age of 14 will enter the school system, and by the year 2000, minorities will dominate the school populations of over 50 major cities. On top of that, the United States continues to accept more immigrants than the rest of the world combined. If a chain is as strong as its weakest links, then the U.S. work force in the next century will be forged from a majority of weak links.

If education is a vital factor in the war for trade, then it must be put in some perspective. How does American education stack up against that of Japan or Europe? For the sake of sparing the reader a litany of international test scores, citing some qualitative, but perhaps lesser known facts is preferred. A Japanese or Western European student graduates from secondary school on the same academic level as American students with two years of college. In the case of Japan, raw numbers contribute to the gap. Japanese students attend school 240 days a year in contrast to American students who attend only 180 days. Over the span of twelve grades (first grade to senior in high school) that is four more years of school than the average American student.

$$\left[\frac{(240 \text{ days} - 180 \text{ days}) \times 12 \text{ years}}{180 \text{ days}}\right] = 4 \text{ years}$$

But at high school graduation, the numbers take an interesting turn.

Forty-four percent of American high school graduates attend college—only 39 percent do in Japan, 30 percent in France, 26 percent in Italy, 18 percent in West Germany, 17 percent in the Netherlands, and 7 percent in the United Kingdom. In addition to the differences in attendance, there also exists a quality gap. Julia Ericksen, Vice-Provost of Philadelphia's Temple University, the first American college to establish a branch in Tokyo, suggests that "the American higher education system is the best in the world . . . and the Japanese recognize that." There have been 188 Noble Prizes claimed by Americans against only five for

Japan. However, while the higher education system in the United States outperforms any other in the world, the eroding quality of the students being fed into the system by the secondary schools keeps higher education from pushing to new heights. The University of Utah estimates that almost one out of every two entering freshmen fails or drops out of school. Further, the dismal performance of high school seniors has spilled over to college seniors. According to a 1989 *Wall Street Journal* article, a test given to a nationwide sample of 696 college seniors revealed that: 60 percent could not identify the Reconstruction period as having followed the Civil War; 58 percent could not identify Plato as the author of *The Republic*; 54 percent did not know that *The Federalist Papers* were written to promote the ratification of the U.S. Constitution; 44 percent did not know that Herman Melville wrote *Moby Dick*; and 42 percent could not identify the Koran as the sacred scriptures of Islam. Ironically, on the same test, 23 percent said that Karl Marx's phrase "from each according to his ability, to each according to his need" appeared in the U.S. Constitution.

As the United States enters its next extrovert phase, it must radically restructure its educational system or risk the one decline it cannot afford. That restructuring must include four basic changes.

Teachers Must Be Paid More. Given the materialistic nature of developed countries money, more than any other indicator, establishes value. Using this yardstick as a measure of worth, it becomes obvious that America does not value education. In 1987, the average starting salary for accountants hovered around $21,200, beginning salaries in data-processing around $26,170, and starting engineers $28,500. The average starting salary for a teacher was $17,500. In 40 out of 50 states, an apprentice garbage collector makes more money than a new teacher. Astonishingly, in 1983 after the National Commission on Excellence published its damning report, *A Nation at Risk*, the Reagan administration attempted to *cut* the national education budget by $10 billion!

On the bright side, salaries have begun to rise, and the average teacher makes 26 percent more than in 1985. That improvement, however, will not ensure an adequate supply of talented teachers in the future. In 1970, one high school senior in five went on to major in education. By 1987, the number had plummeted to less than one in eight. By 1989, less than one in ten college freshmen considered teaching as a career. Eventually, only half of that 10 percent will actually become teachers, and half of them will abandon the classroom within seven years. Without tomorrow's teachers, from where will tomorrow's accountants, data processors, and engineers come?

The ability of the system to attract quality teachers depends to a great extent on the profession's material rewards. To remain competitive in a realigned technoglobe, the teaching profession must offer rewards commensurate with its contribution to society. This is no easy task in a culture where investment bankers make millions of dollars performing functions that add zero value to the national worth.

The Unions Must Go.   No educational system can attract quality teachers if it must indiscriminately pay its teachers the same, regardless of talent, potential, or performance. Yet unionism creates just such a predicament, and long after workers in most industries have abandoned the unions as a means of improving their lots.

Over 90 percent of the nation's teachers belong to unions, a fact that has, ironically, kept teachers' salaries down. In order to preserve near total membership, the unions must wring periodic salary gains for all members. While this may benefit some teachers, it hurts any teacher who performs above and beyond the rest.

Like other professions, the teaching profession includes three general groups: the excellent, the good, and the bad. Since unions bargain for pay increases as if all teachers performed at peak levels, excellent teachers become consistently underpaid while poor teachers become consistently overpaid. The cost of carrying poor teachers falls on the backs of the large middle group of good teachers. If the unions supported a merit pay structure, they would lose their clout overnight. More fairly rewarded excellent teachers would not need a union, poor teachers would despise the union for failing to win them increases, and the good or average teachers, seeing modest gains in salary, would question their continued financial support of the union. Although unions have staunchly opposed any form of pay differentiation for these very reasons, hard facts have been budging union resolve and letting in limited forms of incentive pay for a small percentage of teachers. Still, the incentives, delivered under such programs as master teacher and career ladders, generally range between $2,000 and $6,000 per year and do not adequately reflect the true differences in contribution between an excellent and a poor teacher.

The idea of merit-based pay makes the unions shudder. They argue that since teaching is a subjective art that cannot be accurately measured, a merit system could not possibly work. No performance criteria could account for the tremendous diversity of conditions that confront teachers. The argument may be sound, logical, and fair, but it completely misses the point. All institutions, both public and private, in a free market system evaluate performance on subjective as well as objective bases. Politicians win elections, executives capture promotions, and consumers buy goods and services, not just because they meet strictly measurable standards, but because people vote, work, and spend their money by whim and perception as much as by fact. Periodically, the education process itself looks pretty darned subjective from the students' point of view. Grades, test scores, and references all reflect subjective criteria to some degree or another. Critics have even challenged the seemingly standardized and objective SAT test for subjectively penalizing nonwhites and the poor.

In order to reach the 30 to 50 percent increases that must occur before the system can hope to keep the excellent and good teachers in the classroom, the system must ruthlessly expel all teachers who do not perform up to certain standards. Doing so will traumatize a system that has long protected and promoted its incompetent labor force, but in the long run, such paring of the inferior will better prepare the system, its teachers, and students to compete in an age of global knowledge networks.

Education Must Reflect the New American Family.   Allan Bloom, in his book *The Closing of the American Mind*, observes that "Europeans got most of the culture they were going to get from their homes and their public schools . . ." The same holds true for American students, but what sort of culture can be obtained from schools under siege? Exactly what do American homes have to offer?

The home has been in trouble lately. In 1987, the average household contained 2.66 people, compared with 3.67 in 1940, but the average 1987 American household is poorer than its 1940 counterpart. The middle class—those with incomes between $20,000 and $50,000—accounted for 53 percent of the population in 1973, but only 47 percent in 1986. Of all Americans, 13.5 percent live below the poverty level ($11,611 for a family of four), an increase of 3.3 million people since 1970. In 1987, 5.3 percent of American families earned less than $5,000 against 3.3 percent in 1970.

The percentage of two-income married couples increased from 28.5 in 1960 to over 50 in 1989, and may well reach 75 percent by the year 1992. In 1989, almost 60 percent of American women worked outside the home, a significant portion of them serving as the sole income source for their families. The traditional American family, with a working father and a mother who stays home to tend two or more children, accounts for less than 8 percent of American families today.

These changes suggest less parental interaction in the education process. When both parents work, often just to make ends meet, they find little time or energy left for participating in homework or other school-related activities. Those living below or near the poverty level can be expected to provide almost no parental support. In such a climate, students will alternate between the classroom and the street, where the educational process sometimes takes a brutal turn to violence and drugs.

The American educational system, designed in another era, has not evolved alongside society itself. The concept of 9:00 A.M. to 3:00 P.M. school hours, with full summers off, worked well when kids had somewhere to go, more often than not with adult guidance, and where they enjoyed enough food and pleasant surroundings. But that time is long gone from the American landscape.

Class Size Must Diminish and Facilities Improve. The most talented and dedicated teacher cannot provide individual attention for up to five classes of 30 to 40 students per day. In most schools, education has turned into a hands-off experience, with overworked teachers unable to spend even token time with bright, average, or failing students. Beyond the issue of instruction itself, the lack of personal contact particularly hurts students who live in poverty or other stressful situations. More parents expect teachers to fulfill parenting roles. Carole Bogue, Dean of Students at Fairfax High School in Los Angeles, says that most "kids today look to the teachers for support that they don't get at home."

In addition to overcrowded classrooms, teachers must cope with working conditions that doctors, lawyers, and management consultants would never tolerate. *Time* (November 14, 1988), in a cover story about frustrated teachers, reported: "Copiers, ditto machines, lab glassware and even books, the basic tools of the trade, are battered or non-existent in many school systems. Teachers are frequently left to fill the gap from their own pockets." Crowded classrooms and the lack of proper facilities and equipment make an atmosphere of learning nigh on impossible. Until all that changes, students will feel little motivation to buckle down and rise above the conditions, especially in the inner cities, that surround them.

The single most important change in educational facilities that confront American schools is technology. In Vail, Colorado, an exclusive, internationally recognized, and very expensive ski resort, schools are collecting receipts from the local grocery store that can be redeemed for Apple computers. According to the posters placed throughout the store, the goal of the local school district is to add four computers during the 1989–1990 school year. The well-intentioned program between Apple computers and the local businesses poses a pointed question. Why are computers and education consigned a relationship contingent on grocery purchases, much like the toys on the back of cereal boxes? Perhaps Americans are not adequately aware of the influence that computers, in tandem with traditional education, can have on students.

WICAT (the World Institute for Computer-Assisted Teaching), a pioneer in computer-aided learning, conducted research involving 18,000 students from 12 schools in 7 states. In 7 of the schools, over 90 percent of the students were minorities. Two were private, mostly white schools, and the balance were schools with a mixed white and minority student body. Students at the test schools were provided 20 to 60 minutes of computer-assisted learning per day, under the supervision of at least two instructors, a computer professional and a traditional teacher. Based on the nationally administered Iowa Test of Basic Skills and state tests from California and Texas, students in the test programs increased their test scores by an average of 55 percent. WICAT is careful to point out that the most significant gains in test scores occurred in the most economically disadvantaged schools. The caution is commendable, but are these not the very students that needed technology-assisted learning the most—students that the traditional educational approach is letting down?

Can the United States turn the escalating crisis around? One effort to do so suggests that it can. Waterford School, a new, small private institution in Utah, has responded creatively to the pressures on today's education system. Ranked by the U.S. Office of Education as one of the twelve best American schools in 1986, Waterford has addressed the issues of compensation technology and the new American family in ways that offer hope for an embattled system.

The faculty reviews compensation according to a carefully applied range of subjective measures. Students take national tests twice a year, once at the beginning of the school year and once at the end. Teachers must account for test score performance. This new regard for value and accountability has attracted faculty trained at Harvard and Cornell, as well as teachers with experience running educational programs in Saudi Arabia and the Bahamas. On the other hand, the school does not keep teachers who do not measure up. Since Waterford realizes that it cannot measure certain elements of teacher performance before hiring, the school closely watches performance in the classroom and quickly and quietly releases poor teachers.

On the surface, Waterford would pass for just another school, with two noticeable exceptions. First, it maintains small class sizes, never more than 24 students to a class. By Grade IV, students begin selecting elective courses with lower enrollments, and some classes, such as computers, enjoy two teachers. Second, its facilities also differ from most schools. Waterford began in 1980 as an experimental learning center in an abandoned school building. WICAT, capitalizing on over $100 million dollars in research and development, recruited approximately 500 students from the public school system in Utah and absorbed the costs of educating these students full time, combining the latest in WICAT computer technology with the most traditional liberal arts training. Within five years, the "learning experiment" stimulated a waiting list of students trying to get into the school. Middle-class schools in Texas and inner-city schools in New York City and Chicago soon snatched up the WICAT computer systems. In 1986, WICAT began gradually phasing out the learning center and transplanted its approach to new facilities that now comprise the Waterford School.

The school operates over 150 computer workstations for a student body of just under 300, or one computer for every two students. The computer center remains active throughout the day, helping eighth graders learn programming and teaching first graders how to read. In addition to the computer center, the school runs a photography lab, an art room complete with kiln for firing ceramics, a music lab with a full complement of band instruments, and a science lab where ten-year-olds begin by dissecting chicken wings and ninth graders progress to whole pigs. On their way to and from classes, the lower school students walk by a 30-by-30-foot rabbit farm and a functioning honey bee hive which they can watch on a daily basis. Although other schools across America may enjoy similar facilities, Waterford's are totally operational, fully equipped, and used intensively by students in all grades.

Remarkably, the school functions as an education ecosystem that daily reflects the world for which its students are being prepared. The faculty do more than teach; they provide role models for students searching for skills and interests. For example, the science teacher, who participated in a national study on eagle and hawk migration, led thirteen students on an overnight expedition up to the 9,000-foot elevation to trap and tag hawks. Student enthusiasm for the project and their subsequent sensitivity to pollution's effect on bird migration proved that a project in the wild is worth ten in the lab. The history teacher injects color and life into the ancient world of the Greeks and Romans by relating personal experiences of his own frequent trips to the ruins. During summer, students will tag along. The German teacher and soccer coach, once a resident of Munich, also prepares his charges for a trip to Europe, where they will study culture and play German Youth soccer clubs. Another teacher, a former member of Cornell's NCAA Champion Lacrosse squad, plans to introduce Waterford students to the game, all on his own time and initiative. Still another teacher took interested students to Yellowstone National Park for a three-day outing.

Teacher-student involvement includes social issues. Thirteen Waterford ninth graders donated food and time to help feed over 300 transients one Sunday morning, and the entire school collects newspapers and recyclable cans to raise money to plant trees in depleted areas. The school itself responds to the changing American family by offering a full preschool program and an extended day program for children whose parents work long hours.

The Waterford experience could be duplicated across America, if the nation will only replace talk about educational reform with action.

Some observers would discount the Waterford example, pointing out that the financial differences between a private school and a public institution make the comparison unfair and unrealistic. They would suggest that similar funding of a public school would yield the same results as Waterford. However, the numbers do not support such a contention. In the 1987–1988 school year, the average national cost (per year) of educating a student in the public school system totaled nearly $5,000. In 1989, the beginning tuition for a full time student at Waterford stood at $3,875. The problem is not merely money, it is the system that determines how and where the money is spent that needs a radical overhaul. Critics should not underestimate just how quickly the system can get back on its feet.

DEFICIT AND DEBT: DECLINE OR DELAY?

The monument to American soldiers killed in the Viet Nam War differs from all others in two regards. First, it rose under pressure by veterans' groups rather than as a national government undertaking. The government felt reluctant to erect a permanent reminder of the only war the United States had fought and lost, an adventure historian Barbara Tuchman labeled a *March of Folly*. Second, no other war monument lists by name each and every American casualty. This individualizing of personal sacrifice stands as a unique contribution to the art of national monuments; but then again, Viet Nam was unique in the annals of war.

Unlike World War II, the last so-called "good" war, dissidents from every segment of the population refused to fight in Viet Nam. History mistakenly singles out students as the primary source of protest, but dissatisfaction ran much broader than university halls. Many other citizens, particularly middle-aged and middle-class Americans, protested by generally ignoring the conflict, merely tuning into prime-time newscasts to catch the latest score. The so-called "silent majority" did not lie about their ages and rush to military service as they had done in World War II. Even the usually gung-ho National Guard, the nation's "weekend warriors," preferred to practice rather than participate in the conflict, making the Guard a haven for noncombatants in uniform. Instead, the young, mostly poor and often minority draftees waded into jungle combat, while an older generation watched events on the six o'clock news. For most of America, the prime-time spectacle did not symbolize national sacrifice. It took a stark black wall with the names of 58,000 dead and missing chiseled in the marble to do that.

In fact, the nation could not bear sacrifice in any sector, demanding that the government add billions of dollars of domestic spending to the billions being spent on warfare. Two programs in particular, the 1964 War on Poverty and the 1966 advent of Medicare, sapped the nation's resources. The cost of both programs, just like the cost of the war, escalated beyond original expectations. But unlike war expenditures, domestic spending never stopped.

By the early 1980s, the beginning of the Reagan years, overall government spending totaled roughly $100 billion more per year than revenues through taxes and fees. Though conservative Reagan, having campaigned on a promise to do so, actually held the line on taxes and reduced the cost of social programs, it was too little too late. By 1986, the national deficit had ballooned to $221 billion.

The habit of spending more than one makes leaves government with two options: literally print more money, which results in inflation, or hold down the value of currency and borrow to cover the gap between spending and revenues. As a rule, the United States prefers to borrow.

During its last introvert phase, the United States became a debtor nation for the first time since its beginnings in 1776. The country swung from creditor status with approximately $141 billion owed it in 1979 to a position of owing $3 trillion in 1989. Foreign creditors stand in line for much of this debt. In 1988, foreign sources earned $30 billion on U.S. notes, double the amount the government spent on housing for the poor. If the current growth rate of the national debt goes unchecked, it will reach $13 trillion by the year 2000, with annual interest payments of $1.5 trillion or one-half the entire 1989 national debt. Positions on the impact of the national debt on the well being of the United States fall into three categories: no problem at all; imprudent, but not overly destructive; and a crisis that will destroy the country sooner or later.

Those who say not to worry about the debt point to the obvious size and health of the American economy, often citing Herbert Stein's position that the budget deficit, and thus the debt, "reflects a collective lack of will, not U.S. economic weakness." According to that logic, the debt must be analyzed in terms of the nation's ability to eventually pay it back. The debt does not seem so menacing if one believes the nation can pay it. At its current growth rate of 2.5 percent, the United States could turn the century with a GNP of $5 trillion, excluding the estimated billions that flow through illegal activities. To the optimists' way of thinking then, deficit spending can be curtailed whenever the national will decides to bite the bullet. Until then, the United States enjoys a buffer or unused capacity of economic resources it can deploy when necessary.

The industrial experience of World War II certainly supports this line of reasoning. To win the battle at Midway, American willpower reduced the time for scheduled repairs on the carrier *Yorktown* from three months to 48 hours. The Pentagon, current headquarters of the American military with its 600,000 square feet of office space, took a mere 14 months, rather than the projected 7 years, to open for business. However, the most remarkable example of America's reserve strength combined with the national will came from Henry J. Kaiser, Henry Morrison, and John McCone, who cut the construction time of a "Liberty Ship" from 196 to 27 days, and by 1943, turned one out every 10.3 hours. America won the war by harnessing powerful capitalistic methods to the unprecedented production of firepower, something the optimists say can happen again.

The less-optimistic stance, that the escalating national debt is imprudent but not overly dangerous, has been adopted by most mainstream economists. They point out that the United States has always been a nation of "firsts" and that insufficient precedent exists to declare the rising debt a catastrophe waiting to happen. The only other example of a developed nation increasing its indebtedness to such relative levels in peacetime was France in the 1780s, but that hardly provides a useful comparison. The supporters of the middle position, preferring to avoid scenarios of ultimate consequences, bemoan the more immediate imprudence. The interest paid on the debt, they say shaking their heads, should be funding those areas that will most influence future well-being, such as education or research and development. At the same time, they complain that the lion's share of the deficit, and thus the debt, results from social programs, which may provide immediate relief, but really do not solve long-range problems. Finally, this faction sees the combination of valueless interest costs and social program costs as directly detrimental to the international competitiveness of the United States. Not only should the United States avoid deficits, they argue, but the country should direct more money away from domestic maintenance and toward areas that can fuel international competitiveness.

The pessimists cry doom, basing their warning on pure common sense: what is borrowed must eventually be paid back. The pay-back scenario usually follows two tracks. One track details the doom in terms of runaway inflation caused by the overprinting of money to repay the debt. This scenario always harkens back to the crash of 1929 and the subsequent depression, and it points to prevailing images, wheelbarrows crammed with worthless dollars and bread priced in terms of precious gold. The second scenario suggests that foreign lenders, particularly the Japanese, might call in all their loans at once. When the United States government failed to meet its obligations, it would forfeit assets to foreign owners. According to both scenarios, the towers of Wall Street come crashing down in complete and final destruction. The stock market plunge of October 1987 and the scare of October 1988 panicked the doomsayers who feared that the debt had finally achieved the critical mass to set off a chain reaction of economic destruction.

Of the three positions, the middle one probably makes the most sense, but not for the reasons cited. The deep involvement of the United States in the global village links the health of the world with the wealth of America. Any real catastrophe in the U.S. economy would drag yen, Deutschmarks, and pounds down the same route to destruction. Any fear of a global conspiracy to call in all loans to the United States ignores the question of just how Japan would take physical possession of its collateral or what it would do with the cash if the United States returned the principle. Regardless of one's attitude toward the debt, a great part of the world's discretionary income ends up in the United States, which still shines as the safest, most stable, and profitable place to invest in the world.

Although the various camps of economists debate the impact of deficits and debt, they all agree on the concept that less is better. No one denies that the nation would achieve greater well being and become more competitive without the current hemorrhage-level spending. Beyond that consensus, however, the debate revolves from economic to political.

Deficit spending is pure politics in motion: Everyone agrees on what needs to be done, but no one wants to sacrifice anything to do it. Former President Reagan, while holding the line on taxes and social programs, escalated the deficit with unprecedented peacetime defense spending. Congress pays lip service to a balanced budget but steers clear of slicing the big-ticket items, Social Security and Medicaid programs. Surprisingly, a balanced budget lies within reach. Consider, for example, the gasoline tax.

Since American drivers burn up 100 billion gallons of gas each year, a 40 cents per gallon increase in the federal gas tax would generate more than $40 billion per year, a windfall that would cut deeply into the deficit. The increased tax would not even raise the price of gas in the United States beyond what European and Japanese drivers already pay. However, Americans hold their cars sacred and no politician wants to risk re-election promoting an obviously unpopular notion. As a result, the Bush Administration raised the gas tax six cents on a gallon. Why not higher? Poor people spend more of their income on gasoline than the wealthy do, so a tax would hit them harder. A higher gas tax, interpreted by voters as taxing the poor, would hand the presidency to a Democrat on a silver platter next time around. Pure politics in motion. American vices enjoy a certain amount of protection, too. The federal tax on beer and wine in the United States has not gone up since 1955, and tax on hard liquor has not risen since 1951. Merely adjusting these tax rates for inflation, not raising them at all, would kick in an extra $20 billion in revenue per year.

Peter Drucker, in his book *The New Realities*, suggests reforming the entire concept of government services. Back in 1969, Drucker, as usual, marched ahead of the pack when he coined the term "privatization" for the divestiture by government of nationalized companies and services. Drucker recalls that "when the *Economist* reviewed the book, it derided the very thought [of privatization] as perfect nonsense and as something that could not possibly happen." Eight years later, Margaret Thatcher, freshly elected Prime Minister of Great Britain, immediately started to privatize.

Although privatization has caught on slowly in the United States, it has begun to gather momentum. In 1987, the Department of Defense contracted with Foundation Health Corporation of Sacramento, California, to provide health care for military dependents. The CHAMPUS contract shifted more than $3 billion in government spending to the private sector. Terry McGann, the nation's leading health care lobbyist, cites CHAMPUS as "a window into the future of government health care." In Florida, certain criminals are transferred from government responsibility into the care of the Salvation Army. So far, more than 25,000 have successfully completed the experiment. Some states have become completely reliant on privately run prisons that charge the government a fee per prisoner. A whole host of other services are now being considered on a state-by-state basis for transfer of public responsibility to the private sector, among them, garbage disposal, snow removal, park upkeep, fire departments, ambulance services, municipal transportation, drivers licensing, and road repairs.

CONSUMER CONNECTIONS AND CONSORTIA COMBINATIONS

From the trading partner perspective, EC92 raises questions of Fortress Europe and reciprocity. Like Japan, the United States is a competitor, and American trade dominance is as much a catalyst toward a united Europe as is the Japanese export machine. John Yochelson and Robert Hunter, both from the Center for Strategic and International Studies in the United Kingdom, suggest that "Europe's declining competitiveness in world markets relative to the United States and Japan—especially in technology—generated increasing pressures for a Community-wide response." On the surface, a defensive EC trade posture would be aimed as much toward America as it would be toward Japan. But a slightly deeper look at U.S.–EC and Japan–EC relationships, particularly in those areas that economists consider "insignificant," hint of two intriguing possibilities. The first is that the resulting trade policy of EC92 will be more favorable toward the United States than Japan. This possibility hinges on the analysis surrounding reciprocity. The main issue is whether American trade with Europe is perceived as being as one-sided as Japanese trade. Another way of phrasing the issue is, what kind of friends have the Americans been to Europe, compared to Japan? The second possibility, which will be discussed in Chapter 9, suggests that U.S.–EC relations will rise above trade friendship into an outright trade alliance against Japan. This scenario sees a combined transatlantic effort, aimed at making Japan a more equal trading power.

Both possibilities are speculative and perhaps contrary to conventional hard economics. But before they are dismissed, two soft links between the United States and the EC should be considered: consumer connections and consortia combinations.

Consumer Connections.   In a world where consumer power is growing, just how much do American, Japanese, and European consumers interact? If fortress walls are erected and reciprocity takes shape as official trade policy, will it make a difference in daily lives, a reality often overlooked by traditional economic theory?

Begin by looking at trade itself. In 1988, total trade between Japan and the EC was just under $43 billion. That same year, over $164 billion of trade passed between the EC and the United States. American and European corporate and individual consumers had four times as much trade contact with each other than did Japanese and European consumers. In addition, the trade contact between the EC and the United States was far more balanced. Of the trade totals tallied in 1988 between Japan and the EC, 73 percent of the products were Japanese headed toward Europe, while only 27 percent were headed the other way, toward

Japan. In contrast, roughly 44 percent of U.S.–EC trade made its way to Europe. The remaining 56 percent were European products destined for American consumption. Not only was dollar-for-dollar trade contact more frequent between European and American buyers, but in a given year, European consumers buy almost as much American goods and services as Americans would European.

Hard numbers, however, do not tell the entire story. Not only is trade with Europe imbalanced when comparing the United States with Japan, but the product mix is also interesting. Fifty-six percent of Japan's trade with the United States and the EC consists of three products, automobiles and trucks, machinery, and electric machinery. In contrast, West German exports in the same categories amount to only 43 percent of the total, 30 percent for France, 29 percent for the United Kingdom and 35 percent for the United States. The different percentages suggest that Japan's interaction with European and American consumers is concentrated in more expensive products, what U.S. consumers call big-ticket purchases. U.S. and European trade, in contrast, has less concentration in more expensive products, touching consumers on a broader scale. For instance, how often will an American or European consumer purchase a Toyota or Nissan car, a Toshiba or Sharp computer, a Nikon camera or a Sony Walkman? This is compared to a Coke or Evian, a Big Mac or a slice of prosciutto ham with Spanish melon, a stay in an American Holiday Inn (British owned) or one dozen disposable diapers in Denmark (Johnson & Johnson). On any given day, in any given American state or EC member country, consumers are more likely to buy transatlantic products than they will reach for those made in Japan.

But trade consists not only of goods, but also of services. In a way, services come closer to connecting consumers than do products. Goods are relatively lifeless and impersonal after the point of sale, but services almost always involve interaction between people. Whether the service is financial in nature, such as banking or life insurance; hospitality-oriented, like hotels and restaurants; or transportation-focused, as in the airline industry, the person-to-person interaction is high and readily visible for all to see. The United States is the world's largest importer and exporter of services. In 1988, U.S. imports and exports of services almost doubled the nearest competitor. Six of the top ten service importers were EC-member countries, and seven of the ten highest-ranked exporters were also from the EC. Japan placed only fourth in service imports and dropped to fifth in exports. Again, what consumers are likely to contact in the daily consumption quest is an American or European service delivery approach.

The extent that consumer connections will influence trade relationships remains to be seen. But two current consumer indicators, not often discussed, provide some clue as to how consumers view the competing hemispheres. The first is consumer perception.

Japanese products have become synonymous with quality, particularly in cars, computers, cameras, and consumer electronics. The association, not lost on the Japanese, has become the core of marketing to Western consumers. It has also become the shop-worn scapegoat of Japanese attempts to explain away one-sided trade. Yet, while Japan has succeeded in taking verbal possession of the term *quality,* it has failed in its search for status.

Consuming societies have icons, goods, and services that escalate beyond the sum of their parts to become symbols of the elite, the top of the consumption ladder. Oddly, for the trade superiority of Japan and its emergence as a world power, its goods and services are conspicuously absent from the Western perception of status. This argument is completely subjective and insupportable, but fascinating, nonetheless. In cars, status suggests Rolls Royce, Mercedes Benz, BMW, and Jaguar. Younger, more adventurous seekers of status migrate toward Porsche, Ferrari, and Lotus. Nissans, Toyotas, and Hondas are not even close. Sensing the gap, Tokyo is responding with new models like Infinity and Lexus. But once again, the byline is quality, not status.

They are different. Mercedes, BMW, Jaguar, and Porsche rarely make the top five in terms of cost-efficient transportation. The fact is they have little to do with getting from place to place and much more to do with announcing an arrival. At least in cars, achieving quality does not necessarily deliver a ticket to status.

In clothes, the names are Gucci, Pierre Cardin, Ralph Lauran, Laura Ashley, Bally, Polo, and Benetton. There is not a Sato, Nishihara or Suzaki in the lot. Certainly, some avant-garde Japanese designers are making their mark, but they are not yet icons, symbols of refined taste, or at least the need to provide the perception of refined taste.

American business executives value Swiss watches, German pens, Italian attachés, French wines and mineral water, Norwegian salmon, British marmalade, Liechtenstein and Luxembourg bank accounts, Scotch whiskey, *The Economist*, Monte Carlo, and the French Riviera.

Admittedly, listing icons is subjective and the importance attached to them is shallow. But they do point to the qualitative rather than the mere quantitative perception of trading regions in the eyes of consumers. How the perception might affect the numbers can be seen in tourism. Given a choice, where are consumers drawn in their spare time? Are Europeans and Americans fascinated by Japan, eager to drink in the culture of a country they confront almost daily in their national newspapers? Travel statistics suggest not. In 1988, slightly more than 2 million visitors from all countries headed toward Japan. Just under 2 million Americans stopped in Italy alone, and 9 million Europeans visited the United States. Ranked in order, eight European countries were among the ten most visited in the world in 1988. The United States and Canada were the other two on the list. Japan was ranked 32nd, behind Romania, Bulgaria, Yugoslavia, Ireland, Tunisia, and Thailand. Even considering that a portion of the travel reported was business in nature, Japan does not appear to be a popular destination of choice.

The factors discussed only serve to suggest that the level of consumer interaction between the United States and Europe is far greater and more personal than exists between the EC and Japan. How this might affect trade policy cannot be effectively measured, yet it does suggest an interesting question. In the event of full-scale protectionism, is denied access to Japanese products the same as denied access to American products on the part of EC consumers? If planning to buy a car, camera, or computer, the answer is yes. But if the shopping list calls for disposable diapers, two steaks, a box of breakfast cereal, soft drinks, and frozen french fries, the answer might be different.

Consortia Combinations. Japan has been successful in denying American and EC access to its domestic market. But the success may also be a contributing factor to the eventual decline of its trade edge. To the extent that business influences policy decisions in trade, the formation of a strong transatlantic bond, linked by consortia, can be expected.

In the beginning of the 1960s, 88 percent of the world's 50 largest multinationals, as reported by *Fortune* (August 1959), were American, the remaining 12 percent were from Western Europe. By 1988, only 40 percent were American, 40 percent were Western European, 8 percent were Japanese, and 2 percent hailed from the rest of the world. By Japan's own admission, until very recently its domestic economy has been essentially off limits to foreign growth, except to a handful of joint ventures between non-Japanese and Japanese companies. This means that the changing membership of consortia among the top 50 have sustained their growth off European and American consumers. It is unlikely that consortia leaders will support any turn of events that deny them access to the very markets that have fueled their growth. The head start that consortia have in cementing transatlantic interaction is illustrated by Ford.

Murray Reichenstein, Ford Vice-President for Europe, believes that Ford "did 1992 in 1967, though we didn't realize it at the time." The Capri was Ford's first European car built for America, followed by the Fiesta. Plants were built in the United

Kingdom, West Germany, Spain, France, Belgium, and Portugal. In contrast, Nissan has the only Japanese assembly plant in the EC.

Ford's European strategy paid off. By 1989, Ford held a 12 percent market share in Europe, which as a single market, is the most evenly matched competitive arena in the world. On a corporate basis, Fiat, Volkswagen-Audi, and Peugeot-Citroen exceed Ford's penetration, but no single company beats Ford's market share by more than 5 percentage points.

In anticipation of 1992, Ford is pursuing two directions in Europe. The first is a European purchasing system that will buy commodities like shock absorbers or wiper blades on a Europe-wide basis. This approach equates Greece and the United Kingdom to California and New York, miles apart, but the same market. The second trend flows from the first. Ford hopes that a Europe-wide purchasing system will persuade a West German supplier to shift production, say to Spain, where labor costs are lower. Obviously, the second trend requires that supplier decisions be made on economic, not political or nationalistic grounds.

The value of the Ford example lies in the fact that "Ford has an advantage over all its competitors in Europe: it is the only truly international company," notes Bud Coughlan, Vice-President for Sales, Ford Europe. In 1979, Ford Europe made 104 percent of the parent's new earnings, and without the European contribution, the parent Ford's $3 billion worldwide losses in the three years from 1980 would have been one-third higher. Since 1984, Ford Europe has almost doubled its profits each year.

The suggested international nature of Ford makes keeping the flow of trade international very important to management. A retreat to regionalism that cuts off the United States and Europe would be a brick wall to Ford's consortia evolution.

Going in the other direction, European companies had an American acquisition love feast in the 1980s. Shell, BASF, Hoechst, and ICI heavily participated in the petrochemical boom that shook the United States in the early 1980s. Activity was particularly noticeable in Louisiana and Texas because European chemical companies needed to locate near sources of ethylene, which is abundant in both states. The mid-1980s found European corporations making a run on the American food and household products industry. Unilever snatched up Cheseborough-Ponds, Nestle bought Carnation, and Grand Metropolitan picked up Pillsbury and Heublein. In fact, 62 percent of the largest foreign acquisitions in the United States between 1979 and 1988 were made by companies headquartered in Western Europe.

Ronald Freeman, head of European investment banking for Salomon Brothers, sees European acquisitions of American companies being "driven by corporate buyers." The observation is important in that the motivation behind the buying binge is consortia development by European corporations, not a quick turn of investment banking fees for financial speculators. This transatlantic development was discussed in terms of dollars in Chapter 2, but the actual number of transactions demonstrates that European interest in the United States exceeds even that of Japan. From 1978 to 1987, European buyers purchased 1,164 American companies against only 94 acquisitions by the Japanese. The European purchases break down to 640 by Britain, 150 by West Germany, 113 by France, 86 by Switzerland, 81 by the Netherlands, 63 by Sweden, and 31 by Italy.

This critical mass of consortia that span the Atlantic will sooner or later pressure both sides to form closer alliances. The primary resistance will come from companies that have resisted consortia tendencies and prefer to be the protected industries of single countries. The pending unification of Europe into a single trade zone and competitor make the latter strategy seem out of step.

SOKOJIKARA: THE AMERICAN WAY

How the United States will use its still-prevalent power, address its pressing problems, or react to a uniting Europe are questions without current answers. A poll by accounting firm Ernst and Young reports that the majority of U.S. executives surveyed "predict that the EC will demand reciprocity." If the prediction becomes reality, then assessing what reciprocity between the United States and the EC actually entails becomes important.

The EC as Fortress Europe amounts to a declaration of trade war, forcing the United States to see evolving Europe as an enemy. This scenario focuses attention on the actual economic strength that the United States can bring to bear in an international trade conflict. It also points out what competitors will be up against. Neither side can afford to be sidetracked by the myths that suggest widespread American economic decay.

Another possibility is that reciprocity does not cut off the world from Europe, but rather escalates into a global free-for-all—a first-come-first-serve survival of the fittest where maintaining competitive edge becomes a deciding factor. In this type of war, education and the American deficit could become prime issues, especially in a strategy that pits nation against nation in a quest for technology to sell to consumers and for consumers to offset the costs of developing technology. If Europe is forced into alliances, the transatlantic connection between the EC and the United States seems the most likely, at least in terms of "soft" indicators. But this outcome seems dependent on the EC assessment of the future economic role of the United States. If the EC becomes convinced that Japanese domination and the threat of American decline are permanent fixtures of a rapidly forming future, then the transatlantic connection may never materialize.

Regardless of the direction that EC92 spins the world, myths and problems should not detract from the unique position of the United States. Unlike such countries as Japan and the Soviet Union, the United States suffers from too much rather than too little: too much land, too many natural resources, too many people wanting to immigrate, too much foreign money searching for stable investments, and too many opportunities to remain the leading economic power in the world. The Japanese call this

American abundance and the power it produces, *sokojikara*. Authors Joel Kotkin and Yoriko Kishimnoto, in their book *The Third Century: America's Resurgence in the Asian Era*, warn Japan and other competitors not to underestimate this "reserve power" which makes economic dominance over the United States virtually impossible. A few widely held myths aside, the statistics shore up America's position of world dominance and suggest the power that re-emergence as a national extrovert can create.

The relationship between *sokojikara* and Klingberg's cycles, mentioned at the outset, come sharply into focus if two concepts are borrowed from sports: building and peaking. A building team works hard to mold and position itself for future wins with less emphasis on immediate performance. A peaking team combines all its past building activities to create immediate exceptional performance. The United States has begun to emerge from a long and difficult building period and has already embarked down the path to peak performance as a nation. Japan, Europe, and the Communist Bloc still face a lot of building ahead. In *The Rise and Fall of the Great Powers*, Yale historian Paul Kennedy summarizes the future implications of a building world running smack up against a peaking America: "The American position is a very special one. For all its economic and perhaps military decline, it remains the decisive actor in every type of balance and issue. Because it has so much power for good or evil, because it is the linchpin of the Western alliance system and the center of the existing global economy, what it does, or does not do, is so much more important than what any of the other powers decides to do."

CHAPTER EIGHT

Technowave: Riding the Technology Rollercoaster

I'll have my first Zambian astronaut on the Moon by 1965 . . . We are using my own firing system, derived from the catapult . . . I'm getting my astronauts . . . acclimatized to space travel by placing them in my space capsule every day. It's a 40-gallon oil drum in which they sit, and I then roll them down a hill. This gives them the feeling of rushing through space. I also make them swing from the end of a long rope. When they reach the highest point, I cut the rope— this produces the feeling of free fall.

EDWARD MUKAKA NKOLOSO, 1964
Director-General of the Zambia
National Academy of Space Research

BACK TO THE FUTURE

In 1985, the National Aeronautic and Space Administration invited France to include an experimental package in one of the space shuttle payloads. The French, ever so sensitive about national priorities, proposed to study the aging of wine in space. The Americans took the proposal as a joke until they discovered that French astronaut Patrick Baudry had smuggled a bottle of Bordeaux aboard the shuttle in his personal kitbag.

While the race for technology can have its lighter moments, the race toward 1992 promises to make technocompetition a harsh reality. As early as 1984, long before the world became aware of EC92, the cream of Europe's industrialists—the leaders of Siemans, Philips, Nestle, Olivetti, Thyssen, Ciba-Geigy, and other companies—met in Paris to map technological strategy. Those who attended the fourth meeting of the little-known G-22 Club pledged to keep the proceedings secret, but the opening remarks by Volvo Chairman Perh Gyllenhammer shed light on the industrialists' concerns. Gyllenhammer stressed the need for a "new and more dynamic industrial Europe, strong enough to develop without depending on technology from sources outside Europe." The recommendation flowed from Gyllenhammer's personal experience.

In the early 1970s, Volvo was in trouble. The world automobile market dropped from 30 million cars in 1973 to 25 million in 1975. At the time, the auto industry was predicting that only global manufacturers would survive. A minimum number of 1 million cars per year was being tossed around—Volvo was making slightly more than 200,000. To make matters worse, Volvo employees worked fewer hours than any other automaker and the company had the smallest home market of its competitors, 8 million Swedes, compared to 60 million West Germans, 120 million Japanese, and 240 million Americans. Boxed in by a shrinking market, growing competition, and an unproductive labor force (that year Swedes worked 1,640 hours per year against 1,930 hours in the United States and 2,100 hours in Japan), Gyllen-hammer saw technology as the only solution and began construction of a new plant in Kalmar, Sweden, which would scrap the traditional assembly line and use assembly teams. Each group of workers would build the entire car, rather than merely attach a fender or doorknob. Critics scoffed at the new plant, calling the approach academic experimentation. As expected, the plant opening had its share of bugs. But once fully operational, the Kalmar plant proved itself on three crucial issues. Turnover was less than 10 percent against 55 percent at Volvo's traditional assembly line in Torslanda. Cars built in Kalmar had 40 percent fewer defects than those in Torslanda. Most surprising was the fact that the labor-hours per car equaled that of the traditional plant. Fifteen years later, Gyllenhammer was suggesting the same type of technological turnaround for Europe. The suggestion may be just in time.

In 1980, futurist Alvin Toffler claimed in his book, *The Third Wave*, that "the human story, far from ending, has only just begun." In his mind, a powerful tide of change would surge across the world, creating startling new approaches to politics, families, workplaces, and environments. Toffler used the image of the "third wave" to shift emphasis from the "future shock" he had talked about in an earlier book to the great potential the future holds for humankind.

Seven years later, Alvin and Heidi Toffler spoke to a packed house of Brazilian business and political leaders. Fresh from a meeting with Mikhail Gorbachev and on their way to an audience with Deng Xiaoping, leader of the Chinese Communist Party, the Tofflers had been invited to São Paulo to lecture on the leading edges of world change. The most amazing aspect of their talk was not so much the future the two speakers described, but the history-making fact of their appearance itself. Unlike their predecessors, these two prognosticators were actually living to see their predictions, not just come to pass, but to do so even more outlandishly than they had ever imagined.

Lately, the world has been changing faster than the prophets of prediction can write their books, and this breathtaking pace of change has been increasing the gap between the emergence of new technology and subsequent consumer awareness. Like the Zambian Director-General for space research quoted at the opening of this chapter, most citizens of the world possess only a bare inkling of technological reality. Seen later in the chapter, this applies even to consumers in so-called advanced nations. European, American, and Japanese families could be living today in computer-controlled houses, built far less expensively and far more efficiently than traditional housing, yet most everyone continues to rely on housing technology that has scarcely changed in 100 years.

It takes time, of course, for technology to progress from the laboratory to the living room, but if the gap between technological innovation and consumer application can be shortened, then humans can be whisked more quickly into the future. An incredible stockpile of high-tech wizardry just sits there begging for a chance to change lifestyles.

Karlheinz Kaske, CEO of Siemans AG, warns that the stockpile of life-changing technology may actually increase before the application gap narrows, because "innovation cycles are getting shorter and shorter." In the past, he said, "10 to 15 years went by before old products were replaced by new ones . . . now, it takes only four or five years." This fast-forward effect creates an interesting problem of "half-life" for scientists and the applications industries that thrive on them.

Physicists use the concept of half-life to predict the deterioration of radioactive substances. For example, if plutonium 238 has a half-life of 50 years, it will take that long for one-half of the substance's atoms to disintegrate. In a world where products change every 14 years, a consumer product has a half-life of roughly seven years. At the half-life point, the product no longer represents an emerging technology, but has already started its decline to obsolescence.

In the field of information and information technology, the problem becomes even more acute. Richard Wurman, author of the book *Information Anxiety*, observes that the amount of information available to the world "doubles every four years." With a two-year half-life, information can quickly become obsolete if it does not get disseminated at the speed of light. The same applies to technology. Kaske's estimate of a four-year shelf life for emerging technologies allows a mere 24 months to get a product designed, produced, and distributed before the technology behind the product reaches its half-life and enters decline, after which it gets swept aside by the next wave. Computer technology provides a stunning example. During World War II, two University of Pennsylvania scientists, J. Presper Eckert and John W. Mauchly, built what historians recognize as the first electronic computer. Though the scientists originally developed ENIAC, or the Electronic Numerical Integrator Computer, to perform ballistic curve calculations for the U.S. Army, they eventually left the groves of academia and sold their experience and technologic wizardry to the private sector. Remington Rand delivered the first civilian computer to the U.S. Census Bureau in 1952. By 1960, eight major companies had jumped into the computer business. Nicknamed "Snow White and the Seven Dwarfs," they were IBM, Sperry Rand, Control Data, Honeywell, Burroughs, General Electric, RCA, and NCR. By 1970, over 340 computer companies had staked out claims in the field, and the number had crested 10,000 worldwide. Naturally, more computer companies meant more computers.

Fewer than 50,000 computers were in use in 1970. By 1989, the industry was pumping out more than 50,000 machines every day, but it made its real breakthrough in quality, not just quantity. From 1952 to 1989, computers went from the laboratory to the lap, with the cost of computing power plunging by a factor of 8,000. If the price of a Cadillac had depreciated at the same rate, a new Fleetwood would now carry a sticker price of under three dollars.

The rise of computer technology and the industry it spawned provides a sharp contrast between the incremental technological development of the auto and appliance industries and the explosive technological growth of the information and communication industries. Whereas better automotive gas mileage and less electricity consumption per wash load both exemplify technological fine tuning—fax machines and optic fiber transmission completely redefine how people work. Joe Cappo, futurist and author of *Future Scope*, suggests that people have seen "more mind-boggling innovations . . . in the past 90 years than in any other century in the history of mankind . . . and 10% of the century is still left!"

Before contemplating the phenomenon of stockpiled technology and the world conditions that continue to add up, the difficulty, even impossibility, of accurately predicting the integration of technology with human lifestyles must be accepted. In 1943, Thomas J. Watson, then Chairman of the Board of IBM, suggested that "there is a world market for about five computers" and as late as 1957, an editor in charge of business titles of book publisher Prentice-Hall predicted that "data processing is a fad and won't last out the year." Even as late as 1977, Ken Olson, President of Digital Equipment Corporation (DEC) saw "no reason for any individual to have a computer in their home." As a result of such myopia, DEC did not enter the personal computer market until 1982, by which time one million American homes already boasted a personal computer.

FANNING THE TECHNOLOGICAL FIRES

While individuals may climb mountains because they are there, institutions and organizations only do so for a reason: profit. Technological growth does not fuel itself. Rather, it feeds off a complex ecosystem of national paranoia, corporate interests, and consumer support.

There are two old standbys that continue to contribute toward technological expansion: military spending and space exploration. But they are joined by three phenomena that are linked directly to the shifts toward consumers, consortia, and capitalism.

The rise in consumption results from increased consumer sophistication. Buyers are no longer content with those advancements that make life easier; they want life to be more fun. Consumer technology is directed at the wants of consumers and is designed to meet the demand for instant gratification.

The evolution of multinationals to consortia enhances the technological horizon by bringing more yen, dollars, and Deutschemarks to bear on developing technology. Rather than an IBM or Nixdorf sponsoring isolated research and development, groups of 20 or 30 companies, crossing national borders, join forces to pursue the cutting edge of technological gadgetry.

Finally, the emergence of Eastern Europe and the Soviet Union as potential game players of capitalism promises a consumption surge as Communist citizens try to play commodity catch-up. The resulting expansion of consumers provides a larger base of buyers over which the cost of new-product development can be spread. The old standbys and the new forces—consumer technology, technical consortia, and expanding markets—propelled by consumers, consortia, and capitalism each require individual discussion.

The Military Balance.   Soviet involvement in Afghanistan theoretically ended in 1989, but the USSR continued to contribute over $300 million per year in military equipment. Not to be outdone, the American Central Intelligence Agency included in its 1990 budget $280 million in covert aid to Afghanistan, designed to balance the Soviet contribution.

Hot and cold wars bring out the technological best in the human race. From nuclear power to penicillin, the real or perceived threat of war has launched billions of dollars and rubles on the search for better ways to hurt and heal. The more comprehensive the specter of war (a worldwide conflict as opposed to a localized police action), the more it serves as a magnet for investment in science and technology.

Despite all the talk of *detente, glasnost,* and declining military buildup, the Soviet Union and the United States continue with record levels of military expenditures. Combined, these two superpowers budget just under $700 billion a year for defense of national security. Not only does such stupendous spending kick out mind-boggling technologies (albeit not always in the most efficient manner), but it also delights the hearts of entrepreneurs. For example, the Stealth Bomber, an aircraft supposedly capable of eluding Soviet radar, uses a plastic and graphite composite material in place of metal. The development of this composite technology attracted Australian interests, who developed a radar system that can detect composite aircraft. That little innovation could fetch a bundle in rubles. The technology of war is a big, and often ugly, business. The United States still upholds sanctions against Japanese products made by companies convicted of selling valuable submarine technology to the Soviet Union, and the biggest of American defense contractors have been accused of illegal activities in the pursuit of government contracts to develop state-of-the-art technologies.

Japan will surely engineer a technological leap, propelled by military spending, as Tokyo takes a new tack toward its national defense. Japan currently spends less than 1 percent of its gross national product on its military, but now there are movements within Japan, with possible support from the United States, which want the country to assume a greater military burden in the defense of the Pacific region. If these developments lead to the increased investment of yen in military spending, then technological output should increase proportionally.

Space Exploration. In 1959, the Soviet Union stunned the world when it successfully orbited the *Sputnik* satellite. President John F. Kennedy responded by commencing the "space race," a contest that not only culminated with men strolling the face of the moon, but also flooded the market with new products such as Teflon, digital watches, microwave ovens, mini-computers, and freeze-dried ice cream. Thirty years later, the nature of the race has changed a good deal, but continues running at full tilt.

Since 1986, the Soviets have launched scores of satellites, sent two scientific probes to Mars, and ferried teams of cosmonauts between Earth and space station Mir. Even Communist China negotiated a contract to launch two foreign communications satellites, a move that further increased competitive pressures in the space community. But the contest will escalate with the EC's entry into the space race.

"By the year 2000, you won't need an American or Soviet passport to go into space," predicted French Minister of Industry, Alain Madelin. Fortunately, the French enthusiasm is backed by programs, not mere words. France, Germany, and Italy are picking up 90 percent of the costs of building a European space shuttle (*Hermes*); a giant booster rocket (*Arian*-5); and a European space station (Columbus). The programs have their share of skeptics, but the European Space Agency is already putting payloads in space at bargain-basement prices, around $40 million per launch.

The European space program is rippling throughout the technological community. There are several hundred thousand Europeans employed in all facets of the quest for space, spread over 90 primary contractors. In Germany alone, over 300 companies are directly involved in design, production, or testing. How much will the effort affect European technology?

In the United States, NASA suggests that the Gemini, Apollo, and space shuttle programs have paid for themselves seven times over by the technology they have passed on to industry— 10,000 new products and processes in all. European studies by the University of Strasbourg put the value of commercial spin-offs at a more conservative 3.5 times the amount of space expenditure. Regardless of the exact relationship between costs and contributions, the spin-offs are already appearing in Europe.

French company Matra SA has applied technology developed by its space subsidiary to develop an automated subway transportation system, which it has sold to a number of cities in France and abroad, including Chicago. Germany's Dornier Company used the results of shock wave studies from space re-entry to invent the "lithotripter," a machine that shatters kidney stones using sonic waves. Brochier AS, another French company producing high-tech plastics, is applying its space technology to provide fabric for use in high-altitude balloons and sails for racing yachts.

There is more to the EC interest in space than profits generated by technological spin-offs. A report by representatives from Germany, France, Italy, the Netherlands, and Britain warns that unless Europe becomes "an autonomous space power," it will in effect "abdicate as a major actor in world politics." What might be prompting the link between global leadership and space is the Star Wars Defense System.

Former President Reagan's much-debated space defense scenario not only requires billions in development costs, but also adds to the general overhead of the space program. In order to make Star Wars fully operational, the program would need to launch the American space shuttle system 60 times over a five-year period. The costs of the program have been complicated by the in-flight disaster of the shuttle *Challenger* in 1986. The disaster prompted 400 design changes in the shuttle system at a cost of $2.4 billion, but of greater significance, it forced a reduction of scheduled flights from 25 to less than 10. As a result, the overhead associated with each launch has increased from an initially budgeted $10 million to well over $200 million. Implementing Star Wars—60 launches at $200 million each—will not only stimulate political concern, but also a steady stream of technological innovations. The ramifications of competition in space are so great that Jean-Paul Vautrey, space advisor to French minister Alain Madelin, stresses that Europe cannot stay on the sidelines of space "for cultural, technical, political and strategic reasons."

237

Consumer Technology. The Japanese have added a new dimension, marketing consumer technology the way Americans sell cars, the Italians clothes, and the French wines—two, three, or even four are better than one. The Sony Walkman, for example, comes in over 35 variations. While each model basically performs the same function, each sports color and other "fine-tuning" options. Consequently, Sony can sell the same technology to the same consumers, in a variety of styles, just like ties, shoes, and hats. Any consumer with the desire and the will can become the Imelda Marcos of personal stereos.

Gene Bylinsky, writing for *Fortune*, observed that the "Japanese are stuffing appliances, automobiles, commercial buildings and homes with all sorts of new electronics, devices and systems." Far from technological breakthroughs, the incremental innovations simply amplify market demand for a product that would normally last for years but gets stored in the closet in favor of the latest popular style. In the field of photo-technology, the Japanese have added elements of video, still, and video still (electronic pictures saved on computer disks instead of film), autofocus, and disposability (the film container doubles as a camera that the user throws away after snapping all the pictures), and big or small (the latest Sony camcorder fits in the palm of a hand). All these enhancements result in a broad range of products the Japanese can sell in multiple quantities to the same customer base.

Consumer technology emphasizes the quick transfer of laboratory innovations to the retail market in limited quantities. If the transfer occurs too slowly, the products lose their fad appeal. If too many flood the market, manufacturers will support the product until inventory declines, but by then, the technological edge has been dulled.

The Japanese have mastered the art of quick consumer technology transfer, paying three times as much to others for licenses, patents, and royalties as they earn from selling their own ideas abroad. Then they dump all the new products on foreign markets.

However, some indications suggest that the United States has begun bridging the gap. Between 1979 and 1986, American manufacturing employment fell 9 percent, while output rose 13 percent. This means that more output came from automation rather than human labor. The quick turnaround of consumer technologies demands automation. In 1980, the average age of an industrial machine in America was 20 years. By 1990, the average age had dropped to 14 years and should fall to 10 years by the mid-1990s.

While Japanese investment in and commitment to consumer technology, particularly electronics, will probably not decline for the rest of the century, the United States and Europe will be working feverishly to catch up, a likelihood that will drive the Japanese toward increased investment to defend their dominant position. As a result, an even greater stream of technological gadgets will be flowing into the hands of eager consumers around the world.

Technical Consortia. In recent years, Japan and other countries have proven that the coordination of research and development, and the subsequent sharing of findings and information among all stakeholders in an industry, can make it possible, not only to reduce the overall costs of technological advancement, but also to accelerate the introduction of new products to the marketplace. The lesson has not been lost on the United States or Europe.

More than 150 industry consortia involving 1,000 companies now operate in the United States. The biggest and best known is Sematech. Located in Austin, Texas, Sematech has engaged in the battle to regain United States dominance in the manufacturing, not just the development, of semiconductors. To help it win that battle, Bruce Merrifield, Assistant Secretary of Commerce for Productivity, Technology, and Innovations, predicts that antitrust barriers will lower, thus making it more attractive for former domestic rivals to combine resources into more internationally competitive consortia. In addition, Congress recently passed legislation mandating that American companies benefit from the "right of first refusal" to license university research developed with federal funding.

Such European consortia as ESPIRIT (European Strategic Programme for Research and Development in Information Technology) and EUREKA (European Programme for High-Technology Research and Development) have already risen to Gyllenhammer's challenge. ESPIRIT is an EC-wide research and development effort established to counter the invasion of foreign technology, such as computer software, over two million pieces of which flowed into Europe in 1987 from the United States alone. ESPIRIT not only aims at innovation, but also at standardization. Andy Lokes, Marketing Manager of Dowty Information Systems, Britain's leading modem manufacturer, says that the lack of standardization in Europe has driven the price of modem cards for personal computers to $250 in Europe, more than double the price in the United States. Without European standardization, a modem manufacturer in a given country can only recover development costs from its relatively small domestic population, while one in the United States can spread costs over a customer base of 250 million. Consequently, while one out of three personal computer users in the United States employs a modem card, only one out of 300 in Britain do. The ratio plunges even lower in other European countries.

The ESPIRIT program has already enabled new European manufacturing consortia to compete in the international market. Between 1983 and 1986, the number of consortia agreements increased 700 percent, an escalation that helped lower production costs and close the technology deficit in key areas, such as computer microchips.

Another technological consortium, EUREKA, reaches beyond the EC to include 19 European countries. Conceived by French President Francois Mitterand in 1985, this consortium formally commenced in December, 1986, and since then has spread to include over 600 industrial companies and research institutions, with a budget of about $5 billion spread across 165 projects. The endeavors include:

- ○ PROMETHEUS, a $68 million attempt to develop technologies for computer-aided automotive transportation. The system would use "intelligent" cars and electronic traffic flow controls. Twenty of Europe's leading car manufacturers, including Fiat, Volvo, Renault, and Daimler Benz have backed this project.
- ○ FAMOS, a $160 million initiative to integrate advanced technologies into a range of manufacturing and assembly systems. FAMOS has targeted the aerospace, textile, pharmaceutical, and composite materials industries for the first applications.
- ○ EUROLASER, a five-year, $47 million program to develop and evaluate the industrial uses of laser technology. This venture enjoys the backing of companies and institutes from five countries.
- ○ COSINE, a government project supported by all EUREKA members and aimed at establishing a pan-European communications network. Among other things, the system would link the largest research computers used in every country.

According to an internal study commissioned by U.S. electrical giant Westinghouse, $2 trillion will be spent worldwide on high-tech research and development between 1985 and the end of the century. This unprecedented amount of funding will certainly increase competition between consortia and spill scores of new product innovations into the consumer market.

Expanding Markets. When the East German government opened the Berlin Wall in October, 1989, 3 million East Germans, each clutching a 100-Deutschmarks (about $55) West German gift, engaged in a weekend capitalistic spending spree in West Berlin. The dazed East Berliners marveled at the range of goods and services offered by the capitalistic system. Sony Walkmen, Swiss chocolates, fresh fruit, Levi 501s, and cartons of Coca Cola drew their eyes like shiny magnets. That two-day consumption binge merely hints at the power of global retail when the combined populations of the USSR and Communist China become world consumers. That development will make EC92 look like a cake-walk in a dimestore.

With the addition of over one billion communist consumers, the developers of new technologies can tap a huge base with which to offset their development costs. Oleg Bogomolov, a senior advisor to Mikhail Gorbachev, estimates that Soviet citizens have hoarded some 100 billion rubles ($165 billion) that they would eagerly spend on the right products. The potential purchasing power packed in the Soviet Union, Eastern Europe, and Communist China not only means lower prices for new products and services, but also greater incentive for companies to increase research and development budgets as they recover their investments more quickly across a larger field of consumers. For example, in Chapter 3 it was estimated that it would take an additional 200 million cars for the Soviet Union to match the per-capita level of car ownership in the United States. This type of market growth would spur competition for building the most technologically efficient car to attract the new consumers. Again, this sort of pressure would stoke the fires of technology to the continued benefit of the world's consumers.

THE TECHNOWAVE
AND COMPARATIVE ADVANTAGE

There is more to the technowave than enhancing the quality of life or paving the way to more consortia profit. Technology is the major factor in maintaining trade advantage.

In the history of military conflict, technology—the cross bow, the machine gun, nuclear warheads, and Star Wars—has always been the source of creating a strategic edge. It was the means with which one side, for a period of time, exerted control (or influence) over the other. The final chapter suggests the reality of trade war, the evolution of conflict in the 21st century. In this global battle for consumers, technology, once again, provides a strategic edge. Only in a trade war the strategic edge is more appropriately called comparative advantage.

The quest for international markets comes down to two issues, protection or comparison. In France, sales of athletic shoes from Taiwan jumped from 5 million pairs in 1984 to over 15 million in 1989. This was not a case of dumping, or charging predatory prices below the cost of manufacturing and distribution. The shoes were simply cheaper, much too cheap to be ignored by French consumers. France had only two options, encourage its local industries to compete with better prices (comparison) or lock out the foreign competition (protection). They chose the latter solution, at least until 1992. Technology faces the same scenario.

If a nation cannot match technological enhancements in the product itself or in manufacturing and distribution techniques, then it will lose comparative advantage. Consumer assessment will find the product lacking in comparison to the other options available, requiring governments to either protect their industries or risk their destruction to competitors. Take telecommunications, for example. The current European market for telecommunications goods and services is about $25 billion annually. But government purchases alone are expected to reach a whopping $600 billion by the year 2010. Who will meet the demand? The EC clearly has a European preference for suppliers, but then reality sets in. While West Germany has relatively reliable telephone service, one of four international calls made from neighboring Austria fails to connect. The number of failed international calls soars in Portugal and Spain, assuming one even has a telephone line. Spain has a six-month waiting list of 430,000 people. The list is four-months long in Portugal, three months in Ireland, and averages six weeks for the balance of the EC. By comparison, the typical U.S. telephone company installs a new line in less than seven days. Once the line is in, only Danish customers know for what they are paying. Other European telephone services do not itemize call charges, not even for corporate customers. Finally, the quality of telephone service is too "dirty" to facilitate data transmission from one computer to another. Consequently, ordinary voice telephone calls still represent 90 percent of a typical Post Telephone and Telegraph authority's annual income within the EC.

As governments and corporations develop their telecommunication strategy to account for a shrinking "global village," will they buy European or turn to American and Japanese suppliers that demonstrate clear comparative advantage? The very question worries EC policymakers.

West German official Hans-Dietrich Genscher warns that the EC must "reduce its dependence on the United States for advanced technology" in order to "increase its voice in world affairs." The implication links technology to national security, a relationship underscored by the fact that Genscher is the foreign, rather than trade or industrial minister, of West Germany. George Krneta, Chairman of Landis & Gyr AG, a Swiss industrial equipment firm, is even more specific. "Today, information and know-how have superceded financing as the strategic resource," he argues. "Being one step ahead of your competition in technology doesn't represent the big advantage it used to because it has become so much easier to copy products."

The quest for comparative advantage relates to the opening paragraphs of this chapter. If the assessment of Perh Gyllenhammer and G-22 are accurate, that the EC lags technologically behind the United States and Japan, then the implications go beyond the EC. Trade war is rapidly resulting in a triad outlook, dividing world consumers into three regions. Nations or national alliances within each region are expected to play specific roles in triad evolution. The role of the EC is that of a competing technocenter to the United States and Japan. Within the EC's triad block, the latest in technological innovation must originate from within. As explained in the next chapter, Eastern Europe and the Soviet Union are counting on EC92 to meet their technological expectations. This fact forces the EC to create, not merely ride, the technowave of the 1990s.

CHAPTER NINE

Trade Wars:
The Triad Connection

If we don't move fast enough,
we risk being passed up by events.

FRENCH PRESIDENT FRANCOIS MITTERRAND

FREEDOM AND EMPTY SHELVES

Abbess Mother Alexandra knows by experience to keep a finger on the pulse of world events. The founder of the Orthodox Monastery of the Transfiguration, a monastery for women, 81-year-old Mother Alexandra once traveled under a different name, Princess Ileana. The great-granddaughter of England's Queen Victoria and Russia's Csar Alexander II, Princess Ileana is the last surviving child of Queen Marie of Romania. Global events—two world wars, occupation by both Germany and Russia, and finally Communist dictatorship—stripped the princess of the power of royalty, leaving her to live out her life in a mobile home in Pennsylvania. Romania's most recent dictator did not fare as well as the princess. The last earthly residence of Nicolae Ceausescu is a coffin, buried somewhere in Romania, not a trailer park, an hour north of Pittsburgh.

Three months before his trial and execution by a Romanian court, Ceausescu, in an interview with Kenneth Auchincloss, editor of *Newsweek International,* boldly claimed that Romania was "one of the first countries when it comes to consumption per capita . . . we have no empty shelves." But during the videotaped trial, prosecutors charged that Romanians had been starved of heat, light, and food while government warehouses bulged with meat, chocolate, and fruit for the private use of Communist officials. Sensing the momentum that was sweeping sister nations in Eastern Europe, Romanian citizens finally revolted, sending their dictator to his death on Christmas Day, 1989.

The events of Eastern Europe are moving fast enough to pass up even the most flexible and forward-thinking countries and companies. With the breach of the Berlin Wall in November 1989, virtually every Soviet satellite in Europe has either questioned, contained, or politically castrated the reign of the Communist Party. Heady words like freedom and democracy flowed freely while countries hasten to make sense and order of the chaos that is Eastern Europe.

During the 40 years following World War II, the global situation remained predictable, reliably divided, and partisan. No wonder that 1989's quakes of change in Eastern Europe alarmed, more than pleased, so many world leaders. They fret that the rate of change will make it more difficult to sustain the illusion that politicians determine, or at least manipulate, world events and their consequences.

For example, U.S. President George Bush warned against "uncalled for euphoria," basing his conclusion on the notion that the political changes in the Warsaw Pact countries of Eastern Europe may suffer a setback and not really gain the freedoms that would signal the end of the Cold War. Given President Bush's image as a peacemaker and conciliator rather than a right-wing warmonger, why would he dash cold water on the world-changing events in Eastern Europe? Precisely because they are changing the world. Within a week of the border opening between East and West Germany, the cry for a "peace dividend" arose in the United States. The dividend depends on transferring defense spending either to debt reduction or to increased support of social programs. Mr. Bush's concerns ran in two directions. Publicly, he worried that a premature reduction in defense spending could signal the United States' too hasty acceptance of the depth and motivation behind the communist world changes. Privately, of course, administration officials felt uneasy about the economic impact of a reduced U.S. defense industry, which has relied on the tensions of the old divisions for profit and growth. While these industries need a certain amount of time to effect a smooth transition, the lessening of Cold War tensions has been moving at a rate that spins the heads of defense establishment directors and managers, who have long profited from fear and suspicion. Ironically, but not surprisingly, Eastern Bloc freedom threatens to wreak havoc on American free enterprise.

Yesterday's primary target of fear and suspicion, Soviet Premier Gorbachev, faces the same change-driven difficulties as President Bush, but in a different form. While Gorbachev clearly "supports changes in the national leadership" of Eastern European countries, he cautions against the "drive to unify East and West Germany." Like Bush, Gorbachev holds public and private concerns. Publicly, he cites the historical specter of German dreams of ruling the world, a specter that stalked the continent a mere 40 years ago. This warning attracts strange bedfellows. The French joke that they like Germany so much, they are "glad there are two of them;" and Prime Minister Margaret Thatcher, with her customary subtlety, insists "absolutely not" when asked about the possibility of unification. Privately, the objections to unification hinge on the threat of future German economic dominance more than on the fear of German military power. A united Germany would weigh in second only to the United States in terms of economic clout. It would certainly dominate the newly unified Europe, and would be positioned most ideally to exploit the new drive to modernize communist Europe and the Soviet Union. At the moment, handing Germany such economic dominance does not top anyone's agenda.

This book began with a discussion of the transition from "ballistics to bananas." In the spring of 1989, when Chapter 1 was written, the old order, maintained by military technology and directed by political power, seemed firmly entrenched and unmutable. At the time, a shift in the wind was sensed, but the hurricane to come was hardly foreseen. It was known that the new order, unlike the old, would select winners and losers on the basis of global trade and an evolving consumer consensus, but the assumption was that the transition would take decades, not months.

Still, the world situation warrants some caution on the matter of timing because old orders die slowly. Specifically, those individuals and interests who have profited from the old order will not give up their power without a fight. Even after the execution of Romanian dictator Nicolae Ceausescu, the Securitate, Ceausescu's dreaded secret police, continue to wage guerilla warfare against the new government. In East Germany, citizens take to the streets in the thousands to protest the government's delay in disbanding their internal security police, and on the other side of the world, the crack of gunfire in Tiananmen Square is not far from the memory of those Chinese students who were fortunate enough to survive. Finally, Russian troops on hand to prevent revolution proves that ideological death certificates should not be hastily drawn up in Lithuania. Still, even if the old order suffers a lingering death, it seems clear now that it cannot forestall the birth of the new.

In the Western hemisphere, Cuban leader Fidel Castro, garbed in the green fatigues of insurrection, has made a heavy personal investment in the old order, and, as late as July of 1989, he still thundered for world revolution. But the world has passed Castro by, and its revolutionaries no longer sport green fatigues, but the navy blue pinstriped suits and "power" red ties of business negotiators. They are trained at Todai University, Harvard, and The London School of Economics, and pull the triggers of Hewlett-Packard calculators. This generation, like most others in history, wages a kind of war, and Fidel would not survive a day in the new conflict that focuses on consumers instead of casualties.

The Hof experience with East German shoppers, which was related in the first chapter, draws attention to the roughly 400 million communist consumers in Eastern Europe and the Soviet Union alone who may soon effect the transition from tanks and torpedoes to bananas and Big Macs. While the "banana" invasion may appear silly on the surface, deep down, bananas are serious business. For starters, bananas do not grow in Eastern Europe or in the USSR. Neither do state-of-the-art computers, sturdy cars, reliable telephone systems, fax machines, adequate housing, efficient transportation or decent tennis racquets. With 400 million citizens primed to play consumer catch-up, the market seems large enough for all interested parties. Wrong. Trade war, like nuclear war, supports the premise that more trade, like more warheads, will win the day. As a result, countries are rushing pell-mell for new markets, strengthened positions in old markets, and the unending quest for competitive advantage. "Peace with products" is just another slogan in a new kind of war.

TRANSITIONING TO TRADE WARS

"War is hell," applies to trade war as much as any other war, but the trade version makes hell attractive. While the seductive nature of trade war makes the battle seem enjoyable, once accurate score is kept, the brimstone can surface. For years, the world cowered under the shadow of nuclear destruction, then the missiles and bombs never came. Instead, the world got new fangled canned potato chips, microwave milkshakes, and the pet rock. However, as frivolous as these products may seem, they are like all goods and services, weapons of the trade war. And the object of this war, as with all wars, is to win.

The contemporary world did not invent trade war, nor did the Japanese, as some American politicians would like voters to believe. However, the Japanese, always and forever trade-dependent, have historically defined trade as a national weapon.

As early as the 1700s, Japanese philosopher Honda Rimei warned the ruling shoguns that "foreign trade is a war in which each party seeks to extract wealth from the other." The Japanese have always astutely valued the subtle destruction caused by a successful trade war, but Europe did not get the message until they confronted literal trade battles. One lighthearted example is found in what Steven Schlossstein, author of *Trade War: Greed, Power and Industrial Policy on Opposite Sides of the Pacific*, calls "The Chicken War" of the 1960s.

In 1929, FDR promised "two cars in every garage and a chicken in every pot." At the time, American poultry farmers produced 34 million pot fillers weighing an average of 3½ pounds each. Each bird consumed 12 pounds of feed during its 16-week trek from egg to pot. Since chicken farming hardly fires the

imagination, the world scarcely noticed when 20th century genetics came to roost. By 1955, a farmer could grow a 4-pound
chicken in 8 weeks on 8 pounds of food. Happy as roosters in a
hen house, the farmers brought 2.2 billion chickens to market.
The price of chicken dropped from 35 cents a pound in 1929 to
14 cents in 1955, with every breathing American eating 28 pounds
a year, 5 times more than they did in the 1930s. By the late 1950s,
America was up to its ears in poultry, and supply finally drenched
demand.

The chicken farmers panicked. A billion broilers cannot be
warehoused. In the nick of time, salvation came in the form of
a telex from an American agricultural representative in Rome:
"Italians don't like wings or legs—send only breasts and thighs."

In 1959, America sold Europe $19 million worth of chicken.
In 1960, sales exceeded $30 million, and in 1961, $50 million.
In 1962, when 150 million pounds rolled into Germany alone, it
was Europe's turn to panic. At the time, Europe had just begun
fiddling with the concept of unification, but chicken paranoia
forced the EC ministers into over 200 hours of marathon meetings. On January 14, 1962, after 45 meetings, 137 hours of plenary
discussion, 214 hours of drafting in subcommittees, 3 heart attacks
and 582,000 pages of documents, the ministers signed into law
their first chicken legislation, officially titled the Common Agriculture Policy of the Six.

American chicken sales in Europe immediately dropped by
$25 million. U.S. President Lyndon Johnson, incensed by the
European action and egged on by the American chicken lobby,
threatened to counter with a tariff on some European products
imported into the United States. Since Europe did not export
chicken to America, Johnson needed to find a substitute that
would teach Europe a lesson. On December 4, 1963, the President
slapped a tariff on a product that his advisors suggested had little
value or interest to Americans, but would send the right retaliatory message to Europe: Volkswagens.

The chicken skirmish provides light contrast to the very serious business of death and destruction by military conflict. Still,

Europe felt a legitimate fear. American chicken productivity would all but wipe out the more traditional European chicken industry, making Europe chicken-dependent on the United States. Would not the same logic apply to automobiles, aircraft, telephones, computers, and consumer electronics? What kind of free trade exists when one or two countries operate the only stores in town? Japanese dominance of the European office equipment market is a good example. Japan claims an 80 percent market share of copiers, typewriters, fax machines, and microcomputers sold in the EC. Recent legislation, aimed at eliminating predatory pricing (also referred to as dumping), is intended to lessen the Japanese stranglehold and balance the market with European products. In the last half of 1988, the EC slapped fines on over $3 billion worth of imported Japanese copiers and printers. The impact of the new legislation, measured by shifts in market share, may take years. But the EC is immediately impressed with how difficult it is to counterbalance an entrenched competitor, especially if the competitor is Japan.

While trade wars have been waged just as long as military wars, the 1990s will mark a period of great escalation. Just as the refinement of domestic nuclear power ironically forged a tool of mass destruction, so could global peace, igniting the fuse on a new era of vicious trade conflict. Waging peace presents three new problems global leaders must tackle.

The New Power.   Under the old order, and if possessing enough strength, if a country lacked something crucial, it merely took it. In 1868, with a population of 32 million, Japan cultivated 6 million acres of rice, each yielding 20 bushels. In the 1930s, Japanese policymakers estimated that the yield per acre would double by 1940 to 40 bushels, while the population would also jump to 73 million, with rice consumption per capita rising to almost 6 bushels. If so, Japan would incur a 65 billion bushel rice shortfall. The solution was to invade China. Fifty years later, Japan's problems remain the same: too many people, too little land, and virtually no natural resources, except water. The new solution is to buy China.

Just under 30 percent of all China's trade occurs with Japan. This compares to under 11 percent between China and the United States. Japanese-owned or affiliated companies represent the single largest source of private investment in China, and not even the brutality visited on Tiananmen Square in 1989 could dampen Japanese investment enthusiasm, particularly where that enthusiasm springs from national interests. In fact, while the Japanese government strove valiantly to play down the Chinese government's violent response to the demonstrating students, it did send a strongly worded protest when Chinese soldiers fired upon three Japanese businessmen playing golf in Beijing. The Japanese take their golf very seriously.

The development of nuclear weapons obviously renders a military solution, such as Japan's 1930 invasion of China, a very risky undertaking for any nation in the 1990s. The defensive response could strike like lightning, most likely in nuclear form, with the whole affair exacting a political cost that would make any gained resources seem like chicken feed. Still, even as the world is jubilant over the lessening of Cold War tensions, a few countries cling steadfastly to the military option. China still threatens to take Taiwan by force, numerous Arab nations still quest for the total destruction of Israel, and Iran still believes that it stands against an entire world enthralled by satanic verses. With nothing left to lose, in the face of an immanent Arab victory, even perennially logical Israel might opt for a nuclear response.

But most countries realize that they must find an alternative to military power as the means of imposing their interests on other countries. Global trade provides that means, endowing nations, even small ones like South Africa, with remarkable power.

For decades, the world has seethed over the apparent injustices of the South African apartheid system, but few nations have applied strong external pressure for change. The public justification insists that nations should not meddle in the internal affairs of others. Privately, however, the rationale relates directly to the fact that South Africa owns half the world reserves in gold and diamonds, 99 percent of the world's supply of chromite, and, with the Soviet Union, controls the global flow of manganese, platinum, and Vanadium. Since technologically dependent countries need all of these minerals to survive, they understand them as a defense mechanism for South African interests, every bit as effective as a standing army. Saber rattling and rhetoric regarding apartheid on the part of global partners does not really bother South African leaders, but an aggressive act, such as a real economic boycott, would result in swift retaliation, cutting aggressor nations from precious materials only South Africa can provide. Thus, the United States, easily taking a strong verbal stand on apartheid, always stops short of doing anything that would provoke a South Africa shutoff of scarce commodities. While small, and militarily insignificant, South Africa runs the only store in town.

Switzerland feels so confident that its unique financial services provide a similarly strong defense mechanism in the new environment of trade war, that its citizens went to the polls in 1989 to vote on dismantling the Swiss Army. While the Swiss government opposed the idea in a bitter national debate, the population narrowly voted to retain the army. Over 35 percent of the voters wanted to abolish the army, a figure that virtually ensures that the issue will come to a vote again.

Rising Productivity.   In 1986, employment in Western Europe began to surge at the fastest rate since the late 1970s. That same year, France created over 101,000 new companies, 20 percent more than the previous year. Across the Channel, Cambridge, the "Silicon Valley" of Britain, spawned 250 new high-tech companies in the first half of the 1980s.

While authors Ravi Batra (*The Great Depression of 1990*) and Paul Erdman (*The Panic of 89*) predict economic hellfire in their best-selling books, the world races in the opposite direction. In reality, the current drive for global market share propels the world toward what Stanley Feldman of Data Resources calls the "Third Industrial Revolution" of productivity, a revolution that operates on simple logic: raise productivity or perish.

The message has even reached the ears of such super producers as the United States and Japan, both of whom realize they must not rest on their laurels. Since 1982, U.S. productivity in the manufacturing sector has risen at an annual rate of 4.3 percent, one of the highest American productivity runs on record. According to merger consultant Charles Morris, writing for *The Atlantic Monthly* in December, 1989, for the first time in 20 years, American steel actually costs less than Japanese steel.

Predictably, the Japanese will not sit still. After experiencing an actual decline in productivity in 1986, Japan scrambled back to the head of the pack with a 5.9 percent growth rate in 1987.

Great Britain, once the prime example of how to dismantle a productive economy with socialism, now sits just behind Japan in the productivity race. In fact, British workers in 1988 literally put in more hours per employee than the Japanese, or any other country. The erosion of socialism in Britain also contributes to increased productivity. Since 1979, Britain has raised over $25 billion by privatizing government-owned companies such as British Aerospace, Britoil, and British Gas. The last sale constituted the single largest stock offering in the history of the United Kingdom. The British have engineered an impressive turnaround, but not nearly as dramatic as that taking place in southern Europe.

Europe's second fastest rate of productivity growth has been racked up not by West Germany, France, or the Netherlands, but by Italy. In fact, Italy just barely edges out the United States for the number-three position among developed countries. Amazingly, this is the same Italy historically associated with extended lunch hours and a penchant for style over substance. Given its resurgence, Italy serves as a warning that in the new order, the world's stereotypes can be shattered overnight. In 1987, while few European executives were even pondering the impact of a united Europe, Italian financier Carlo de Benedetti made a futile run on the largest conglomerate in Belgium. He felt that EC92 would call for a pan-European strategy, not one confined to Rome. When Eastern European political and economic barriers began to fall, de Benedetti was again leading the pack with a billion dollar venture capital fund to rebuild small business in Hungary. According to de Benedetti, "the most active part of Italian industry is well along the road to 1992."

Elsewhere in southern Europe, the leftist Portuguese government attempted in 1978 to nationalize SONAE, a diversified company headquartered in Oporto. SONAE workers sustained a four-month strike, not against management, but against attempted government interference. At the head stood CEO Belmiro de Azevedo, who realized even then, that "the new Europe would not survive, governed by old political ideologies and outmoded management practices." Since 1978, SONAE has evolved into the largest privately held conglomerate in Portugal, running chains of grocery stores, distributing Apple computers, merchant banking with London partners, and building Europe's second largest shopping mall in Lisbon. Like the new Portugal, de Azevedo smashed to smithereens the world's stereotype that performance automatically deteriorates in southern Europe.

Lining the walls of Oscar Fanjul's office in Madrid are rows of management books in various languages. The books are not surprising, but the fact that he has read them, and can discuss each one insightfully, is. Clearly, there is more to Spanish business style than sunshine and sangria. Fanjul is the young (39 years old) and agressive CEO of Repsol, Spain's largest petroleum company. An often overlooked result of Spain's string of 20th century political persecutions and uprisings is that the age of the country's political and managerial elite averages 40 years. The managing editor of the most widely read Spanish newspaper is 34. The second largest bank in Spain boasts a CEO who is just 39. Spain's President is a relatively young 46. As a rule, this youthful group shuns the villas and beaches, preferring instead the Paseo de la Castellana, the long broad boulevard in Madrid over which towers the tallest building in Europe. Not content with the highest economic growth rate in Europe, almost twice the EC average, aggressive Spanish executives put in long hours carefully carving out a top European and global position for their country. Clearly, the executive elite relish the challenge of *horizonte* (horizon) 92. The recent listing of Repsol on the New York Stock Exchange reflects Fanjul's comment that Spain is "ready to compete with anyone, anywhere in the world and we'll be ready when other companies come here."

Recent productivity increases in southern Europe, and the EC in general and the developed world at large stoke the fires of world trade, because productivity translates into a higher output of goods and services. Companies and countries have not poured billions into productivity improvement only to cut back on production when improvement actually occurs. Increases in productivity mean high-quality, lower-priced products, desperately competing for market share. Productivity, in the absence of available markets, would be like fielding the largest army in the world but with no war to fight: tremendous expense and no return.

The quest for markets will become even more vicious as the opponents become equal and the gap of competitive advantage narrows. Selling products in Spain and Portugal has always formed a key component of every European company's strategic plan, but selling against the likes of de Azevedo and Fanjul will make the game more competitive, if not more intricate.

Portugal, for example, experienced a 600 percent increase in investment from Brazil in 1988. Not to be dismissed lightly, the Brazilians account for 11 percent of all foreign investment in Portugal. Even stronger trade links were forged in a 1988 meeting between Portuguese Prime Minister Anibal Lavaco Silva and Brazilian President José Sarney. Both leaders promised lower tariffs and easier issuance of import licenses before 1992. Brazilian investors see Portugal, and the likes of Belmiro de Azevedo, as their link to EC92.

Defense Reduction.   The interests of nations run hot and cold, but as of this writing, every country seems interested in peace. How long the trend will last is anyone's guess, depending on some very shifty winds. Events in Eastern Europe, and the surprising noninterference of the USSR, has provided sorely needed proof of the sincerity behind Mikhail Gorbachev's sweeping vision— proof that applies strong pressure on U.S. and EC leaders to rethink defense expenditures.

The United States, the USSR, and the EC combined spend more than $1.5 trillion each year on defense. While no one with any knowledge of history really expects worldwide demilitarization, anyone with a modicum of mathematical ability can calculate that maintaining current levels of military buildup amounts to being all dressed up and having no place to go.

War, or its constant threat, creates big and easy business, so when the market for destruction declines, business gets a little harder. This forces the players to step back and look for avenues of diversification. One month after the Berlin Wall fell, the redirection began. IBM, a major defense contractor, announced that it would cut 10,000 jobs by the end of 1990, and Lockheed Corporation, another major contractor, reported that it planned to lay off 1,000 employees at its Watchung, New Jersey, electronics plant. At the same time, American Defense Secretary, Richard Cheney, ordered the Pentagon to draft plans to cut spending by $180 billion over a two year period. Almost overnight, the global market for destructive technology shrank, though in different ways in different countries.

Soviet Nobel Prize Laureate for Economics, V. Leontyev, welcomed the change and advised that the output of the military complex can and should be transferred to the private sector. Gorbachev got specific: each terminated military job should result in three civilian positions, the military economy should turn to production of consumer goods and services, and billions should go toward joint national efforts on technological and scientific projects, mostly with EC countries.

The Soviets, however, face a problem far different from that of the EC and the United States. In the USSR, consumer goods and services are so scarce that even the entire Soviet military complex, converted to consumer output, could not meet the demand. Just to meet existing needs, the country needs to build more than 2.5 million houses and apartments in 48 months. The waiting period for a new car is five years. In 1987, consumer goods accounted for 13 percent of Soviet imports, down from 18 percent in 1970. This sent prices soaring. Few Soviet workers, making an average of $300 a month, can afford a new car at $27,000, a foreign video cassette recorder at $9,000, or black-market Levi 501s for $500. The continued scarcity of these consumer commodities keeps prices up, out of reach for the rank and file, and the standard of living down. The USSR desperately needs imported consumer products as the domestic population gobbles up everything produced by a defense industry making the transition to retail.

When Soviet coal miners struck in the summer of 1989, one of their main demands was for more soap. In Moscow, two police officers were stabbed when they tried to break up a brawl over scarce bottles of shampoo. In contrast, European and American consumers enjoy a saturation of supply. A relatively small neighborhood grocery store in Milan, Italy, recently carried over 17 brands of soap and shampoo, each brand in full supply. In late 1989, the flood of East German refugees clogging up the autobahns with East German-manufactured Trabants provided a startling contrast to the Porsches, BMWs, and Mercedes driven by others. A West German tow truck operator in the process of separating 15 Trabants from an autobahn fender bender grumbled that "the East Germans are 40 years behind us." East Germany could certainly benefit from diverting defense production to build better cars, but the last thing West Germany needs from its defense establishment is another high-performance Mercedes.

In fact, like West Germany, the West as a whole does not need anything. Consequently a defense company making the transition to consumer goods and services will be hard pressed to come up with new products, leaving only two alternatives: compete with existing products by dropping the price, or compete by exporting. Both solutions fuel the trade war.

A rise in the quality of domestic goods and services puts the squeeze on imported foreign products, and those that do not match the new level of quality and price competitiveness will inevitably lose market share. While this illustrates pure competition at its best, the intricacies of global trade complicate matters. For example, a radical enhancement in American automobile production quality, in conjunction with an equally sharp drop in sticker price, could erode the sales of Japanese cars in the United States. But then as the volume of Japanese auto exports of America dropped, the Japanese government would almost certainly retaliate by limiting the import of some American products such as computers or telephone equipment. While General Motors prospered, IBM and Motorola would lose shares of the Japanese market. Trade competitiveness depends on flow not fairness; the rate and volume of goods moving from one trading partner to another overrides morality. Then something disrupts the flow, and governments must intercede to protect national interests.

The Japanese, for instance, are agitated over the EC crackdown on so-called "screwdriver plants." These are facilities located in European countries that serve as assembly points for products made in Europe but using mostly Japanese-produced components. This is similar to the General Motors-Toyota joint venture plant in Fremont, California. The operation uses American labor to produce American cars. On a tour of the plant, the Japanese production manager proudly points out that over 80 percent of the parts used in assembly originate in the United States and Canada. What he does not add is the fact that the 20 percent Japanese contribution includes the engine, chassis, and drive train. That this same situation exists in the EC has prompted a crackdown. A major Japanese target was Brother Incorporated. The EC claims that its European-manufactured typewriters are merely screwed together in Europe, but are essentially all-Japanese products. Fines were slapped on the Japanese company. Brother filed suit against the EC and in October 1988, the EC Court of Justice ruled against Japan. But the Japanese, having tried the European approach of due process and fairness, simply fell back on the Japanese approach. Kozo Oikawa, Counsel at the Japanese Mission to the EC, warned, "if Brussels gets too rough in its retaliatory measures, Japanese firms will not feel comfortable putting their money into Europe." Those accustomed to working with the Japanese are not deceived by the polite usage of the term *comfortable*. What is really being said is that the EC can and should expect retaliation.

TRIAD ECONOMICS

In 1978, two University of Texas economists, Robert Green and James Lutz, wrote a brilliant book on international trade. Based on exhaustive research, *The United States and World Trade: Changing Patterns and Dimensions* suggested that nations traded in "hierarchies" that tended to divide trading partners into clusters. Unfortunately for policymakers around the world, the idea did not get much further than the city limits of Austin until a similar conceptual seed independently sprouted from professor and consultant Peter Drucker and McKinsey partner Kenichi Ohmae in the mid-1980s. Drucker and Ohmae (working separately) simply enhanced the notion of hierarchies with the "triad concept."

The triad concept divides the world into three spheres of economic influence: America, Asia, and Europe. Both Drucker and Ohmae took pains to restrict the theory to economic ties that do not necessarily entail political unity. Clearly, the countries that make up the triad are exceptionally diverse and not at all inclined toward political integration.

The American third of the triad consists of the United States, Canada, and Central and South America. The Asian third joins together Japan, Communist China, Australia, New Zealand, and the Four Tigers (South Korea, Singapore, Hong Kong, and Taiwan). The European third includes the EC, the Eastern European Bloc, the USSR, and the EFTA (European Free Trade Area) countries, which are Sweden, Austria, Finland, Switzerland, Iceland, and Norway. Obviously, not all European countries belong to the EC, most notably, six remain aloof from unification efforts. Switzerland and Sweden, for example, will not figure into 1992, even though they and their EFTA comrades form the largest trading partner with the EC nations, generating a greater volume than the United States or Japan. It is important to bear in mind that projections of the unified power of the EC in terms of population, production and trade, although impressive, do not include the EFTA countries. As part of the triad, the EC and EFTA would create an even greater competitive economic zone or more impregnable Fortress Europe, depending on one's attitude toward unification.

Why does the triad concept apparently exclude such entities as India, the Middle East, and Africa? While these areas certainly do not lack in global influence, they do not yet fit neatly into a particular third of the triad. This fact is significant. As the triad develops into three competitive spheres, each will naturally fight for new markets and new members of their group. The quest for growth will focus on the fringe countries not yet securely aligned with one group or another. Seen later in this section, triad competition relies on new consumers, and India, Africa, and the Middle East represent a significant bloc of wealth in terms of population alone.

Triad economics maintains that trade and economic cooperation within a specific cluster, say Europe, will eventually become greater than transactions between one cluster and another, say Europe and America. Further, trade battles between individual countries will evolve into outright trade war between the combined triad spheres.

At first glance, this triad business may seem like little more than a pretty theory. In reality, Japan, the core of the Asian hierarchy, directs 37 percent of its exports to the United States, with only 22 percent reaching destinations within the Asian triad. Across the ocean, the United States desperately distances its "gringo growth" from Mexican economic stagnation, even though each day thousands of Mexicans illegally cross the border between the two countries, creating an invisible "linkage" between them. In Europe, billions of pounds, marks, and francs conduct a desperate search for American, not EC assets. Great Britain alone invested $32 billion, or almost 3 percent of its gross national product, in American operating companies in 1988. The odds that the world will fall neatly into the triad configuration by the middle of the next century equal the chances, in April of 1989, that the Berlin Wall would crumble before the year ended. The whole triad economic scenario looks utterly impossible—and inevitable.

A little common sense, a calculator, and *The World Almanac and Book of Facts: 1990* can combine to prove that the world has moved a lot closer to the triad arrangement of power than anyone imagined, and that the predicted divisions, America, Asia, and Europe, have already engaged in a highly competitive economic scramble. Consider these five factors:

Population. The demographics are compelling. Asia weighs in with a whopping 1.6 billion people (not counting India), followed by Europe with 807 million, and the Americas with 687 million. Communist China clearly tilts the scales in favor of Asia, accounting for 1.1 billion of the total. But if population is viewed in terms of consumers, not merely warm bodies, then the order reverses. Asia drops from number one to dead last in per-capita consumption, and the Americas pop up to number one. Europe stays sandwiched in the middle.

However, since triad theory suggests that consumers will drive a block's power, Asia will gain a strong competitive advantage when China's masses reach the per-capita consumption levels of American or European citizens. The only way that the American and European clusters could counter Asia's future consumer clout would be to join forces against Asia, equalizing the populations and, thus, consumer clout.

Gross National Product.   Asia's lead, gained in terms of sheer population, evaporates when the category changes to gross national products. The first position goes to Europe, with a combined GNP of just over $8 trillion. The American sphere takes second place with just under $6 trillion, and Asia trails along in distant third with $3 trillion. Again, Communist China's population provides the pivotal factor for increasing Asia's output. Sixty-eight percent of the Chinese now work in agriculture, against only 4 percent in Canada and 9 percent in France. As technology increases Chinese agricultural productivity, the population will shift to industrial production, which in turn will boost the Asian GNP.

Trade.   By definition, trade is the single most important variable affecting triad competitiveness, and the numbers reveal two important things. First, the trade volume for Asia, supposedly the global trade powerhouse, comes in dead last with slightly over $1 trillion in combined imports and exports. The American region, at roughly $1.4 trillion, moves into second place, leaving first place to Europe. And what a gap! The European countries import and export almost $2.9 trillion each year, double that of the Americas and triple that of Asia. Second, the direction of trade should surprise triad skeptics. The volume of imports and exports *between* countries making up the European block is greater than the volume of goods entering or leaving the block. In simpler terms, the sphere itself is its own largest trading partner. Interestingly, the same condition exists between countries forming the American sphere. The United States, Canada, and South America trade more with each other than the entire group trades with either Europe or Asia. So, in this sense, the global triad nearly exists already. Asia, the exception to the rule, demands a little scrutiny.

The countries making up the Asian sphere import and export more goods and services from the two other blocks than they do among themselves. The specific breakdown illuminates the issue. Imports are fairly evenly balanced: 22 percent from the Americas, 22 percent from the Middle East (not included in any triad sphere), 22 percent from Asia, and only 6 percent from Europe. Oddly, the balance does not continue through exports. The Americas account for roughly 37 percent of exports, Europe 12 percent, and the Asian countries only 21 percent. The numbers seem to suggest that while the Asian group can churn out and export massive amounts of goods and services, it lacks an economically advanced consumer base to absorb the majority of its own products. Thus, Asia remains completely trade dependent, whereas Americans and Europeans can consume the majority of their own products. This fact plays a king role in developing triad strategy.

TRIAD STRATEGY

Much more than a theoretical model, the triad concept has become a reality and will influence world events every bit as much as EC economic unification and Eastern European political disintegration. That influence becomes acutely apparent when three issues are examined: ranking, competition, and development.

Ranking. With so much attention focused on Japan, the world has overlooked the simple fact that the EC, in terms of gross national product and gross trade (imports plus exports) will be number one on January 1, 1993. The gap between number one and number two widens with every bit of economic cooperation between the EC, Eastern Europe, and the USSR, a trend already beginning to take shape.

In a personal letter to the Madrid Summit of EC members in 1989, Mikhail Gorbachev spoke of the future of Europe with deliberate references to "we." Within a month of the border opening between East and West Germany, West German Chancellor Helmut Kohn presented a ten-point plan for German reunification. At the heart of the plan lays the assumption that the EC and the USSR would link economically via a newly united East and West Germany. Irving Kristol, publisher of *The National Interest*, suggests that German reunification "has already happened where it counts the most—in the political and moral imagination of the German people. In that sense, it's over. Pronouncements from Moscow, Washington or the capitals of Western Europe that talk vaguely about possible reunification in the more distant future are hollow rhetoric. Germany already is a unified nation—one, however, whose Western and Eastern territories happen to be occupied by foreign troops."

On the business side, Percy Barnevik, CEO of Asea Brown Boveri, Europe's largest electronic products company, was negotiating in Poland six months before elections replaced the communist government. Barnevik expects "the USSR and East bloc countries to offer the biggest potential of all Europe's markets during the 1990s." His vision is shared by his counterpart, Jack Welsh of General Electric. Within weeks of Hungarian political and economic reforms, GE snatched up a majority stake in Tungsgram Company, the largest lighting manufacturer in Hungary. Barnevik and Welsh represent the rare breed of triad corporate leader who break from the pack and jump at least one step ahead of global change.

Of course, the old military dominance of the Soviet Union and the United States will not just disappear. Nor will Japan easily give up center stage in world trade. Further, the United States continues as the most balanced—military, economic, trade, natural resources, and quality of life—superpower in the world.

In 1993, however, an immediately competitive and powerful player will walk on to the court. Before the game concludes, the EC might well have evolved into a total European sphere, number one in almost every category of comparison.

Development.   By the end of 1988, foreign investment in the United States had crested $329 billion. Roughly 65 percent, or $216 billion came from Europe, and a mere $53 billion from Japan. The Europeans made a smart investment.

Given its political stability and economic power, the United States offers the safest place in the world to invest money. Ultimately, however, unification and triad evolution may cause a swing in investment strategy, with Europeans bringing their money back home. Combined with effective economic integration, the Eastern Bloc and the USSR, with a sustained period of Europe-wide political stability and peace between it, would make Europe as inviting an investment environment as the United States. The pendulum may have already begun its swing. For example, as Hungary lifted the suppression of its economic system in 1989, foreign capitalists shot off 650 proposals for investment in that country. Only 30 of these initiatives originated with American companies, another 20 came from Japan, and the remaining 600 reflected either EC or EFTA interest in doing business with Eastern Europe. These projects would absorb funds that might otherwise gravitate toward American assets.

If investment funds do begin circulating more within the triad spheres, the most surprising benefactors may be Central and South America. The press and the policy-makers may have ignored Europe in their preoccupation with Japan, but they seem to treat Central and South America as if they were on another planet. With the exception of a spectacular World War II nostalgia battle between Britain and Argentina, the last spasms of ideological proxy battle between communism and capitalism in El Salvador and Nicaragua; the U.S. invasion to depose Manuel Noriega; and the Columbian drug standoff, South America may as well have been on the other side of the galaxy during this period of history.

After the early European economic exploitation of the 1600s and 1700s, the entire region just dropped out of the picture of world influence. Aside from providing a haven for sitting out two world wars or wintering while the mother country froze, South America languished in the shadow of its giant northern sisters. Save for a brief period, the political instability of the region merely served as a distant arena while the United States and the Soviet Union fought battles wherein no Russian or American got hurt. South and Central America, for the 40 years after 1945, would provide the field where Fidel Castro could get all dressed up and play war, while the United States and the Soviet Union engaged in "meaningful" political discussion about peace. That all changed when, in the summer of 1989, the Soviet Union advised Cuba's Castro that though he could still dress up, the war game was over.

Triad evolution shines the spotlight back on South America, perhaps for the first time in 200 years, and the potential has not escaped its leaders and business executives. Lorenzo Zambrano, CEO of CEMEX, a giant Mexican cement company, believes that "the economic border between Mexico and the United States has disappeared . . . we are all North American companies." Zambrano's words do not express mere machismo. Since 1988, his company has spent over $1 billion on acquisitions, and by the beginning of the 1990s was not only the largest cement producer in the United States but the biggest in North America, and the fourth largest in the world. Remember, this is Mexico, a nation stereotyped as so economically laid back that American songwriter and pop-philosopher Jimmy Buffet refers to the entire country as "Margaritaville." That stereotype has begun to collapse. Japanese auto giant Nissan recently announced the construction of a $1 billion auto plant in Mexico, and a number of top American Fortune 500 companies assemble hundreds of products just across the border from Texas and California.

The 21st century clout of Central and South America will derive, in part, from their combined population of over 400 million. That is 400 million people to assemble and ship almost any Canadian and American products more cheaply than Canadian and American laborers. Even more importantly, that is 400 million consumers to buy Canadian and American products. As mentioned earlier, the trade volume within the American region already outstrips the trade volume that enters or exists in the triad sphere itself. This means a great deal when it is realized that the consumption of the Central and South American region, like that of China, still wallows in the embryonic stage, particularly when it comes to high-end consumer goods. A market three times the size of Japan and 80 million people more than the EC sits smack on the doorstep of the United States. For it to achieve its potential, each country must develop its economic prosperity to a point where it can function as a full-fledged global shopper, and that has already begun to happen.

In 1989, free Brazilian presidential elections took place for the first time in 29 years. In the small fishing community of Puerto Montt, Chilean shoppers can browse through stores stocked full of items banned by most other South American countries: outboard engines from the United States, clothes from Europe and knives from Brazil. Chilean presidential candidate Hernan Buchi believes that "Chile has a golden opportunity" for position and influence in a radically changing world, and he suggests that it only need create "a more open economy with genuine political freedom" to allow Chile to have a new future in world events. Since the same argument could apply to all of Central and South America, the United States and Canada must start valuing the economic rather than geopolitical value of the area, and make the long-term investments there that will ultimately increase the competitiveness of the entire American sphere.

The Asian sphere confronts its own South America in Communist China. The 1.1 billion Chinese also offer the simultaneous potential of low-cost laborers and eager consumers. The entire Asian triad needs the consumers desperately, since it produces more products than Asia can now consume, and the world has lost patience over the resulting trade gap. If harsher trade positions against Japan and the Four Tigers come from the American and European spheres, the Asian sphere will have no place to turn except inward for economic survival.

Competition.   In his book *The New Realities*, Peter Drucker warns that successful nations must "have a strong presence, if not a leadership position in all areas of the triad of North America, Western Europe, and Japan. The three do not constitute one market, but they do constitute one economy."

Competition in the triad environment will embody even more complexity than the present battles for trade superiority. It will be like playing three-dimensional chess, with a move in one dimension affecting pieces in every other dimension. Two changes in particular will make the game fascinating to watch: a new emphasis on imports over exports, and the transition from country versus country competition to triad gamesmanship.

Perhaps the least understood change in global competition involves the shift in emphasis from exports to imports. The prevailing logic holds that a country must focus on exporting the way Japan has and hold down the heavy importing that has burgeoned the United States trade deficit. The new game overturns that shortsighted logic.

The American and European spheres will not allow the Asian group to continue unloading its exports simply because its industries lack a prosperous population base for internal consumption. The overpriced and overburdened Japanese consumption base, and the low consumption levels of the rest of the Pacific Rim, place the entire Asia sphere in a position of grave vulnerability when the period of fierce triad competition begins. The American and European spheres will demand that Asia import as much as it exports. If Asia refuses, trade sanctions will surely follow. Those sanctions will not entail much sacrifice on the part of Americans and Europeans because Asian exports, particularly Japanese consumer goods are, for the most part, luxuries, not strategic necessities. The most viable option for Asia, of course, involves strengthening internal consumerism via capitalism and consortia. For China this means allowing its industries to become more capitalistic in terms of its management methodology. The special economic zones situated mostly along China's coast waive Communist restrictions on business practices in favor of attracting foreign investment. Motorola is considering a $100 million plant in Tianjin, and even the Wrigley chewing gum company is contemplating a $20 million dollar facility in Guangzhou. This type of Western involvement helped push China's industrial growth to a peak of 21 percent in 1988. The events on Tiananmen Square in 1989 may affect Western investment enthusiasm, but Hisai Kobayashi, Director of Dai-Ichi Kangyo's international planning division (the largest bank in the world), thinks otherwise. "We certainly cannot neglect what happened in June," says Kobayashi, "but China is forever, and we have to take the long-term view." The sentiment is also shared by Chase Manhattan and Bankers Trust, both of which syndicated loans to two large Chinese companies just after the massacre on Tiananmen Square.

To the Japanese, the emphasis needs to be on consortia. Claiming only eight of the world's 50 largest multinations, Japan needs to reassess its strategy of taking on the world trading game alone. Although some companies, like Hitachi (joint venture with Texas Instruments) and NBM Semiconductor (joint venture with Intel), are forming innovative cross-border relationships, most are plugging along with traditional investment expansion and product-specific ventures such as jointly producing automobiles with the likes of General Motors and Ford. But the clock is ticking. A major factor motivating EC unification in 1992 is self-defense against Japan. If faced with Fortress Europe, the only market left open to Asia will be itself and the United States. Here, if the trade imbalance does not improve by 1992, anti-Asian sentiment will be running high.

The import emphasis encourages each sphere to invest the imagination, energy, and resources to build up the most proximate consumption bases. For Japan that means China; for the United States and Canada, it means Central and South America; and for Europe, it means the Eastern Bloc and the USSR.

In 1989, Canada and the United States implemented a landmark trade agreement that, beneath the technical rhetoric, makes the two countries one economic zone. Following the purge of communism in the Eastern Bloc, the EC and EFTA rushed in with billions in aid, loans, and joint ventures. In December of 1989, the USSR announced a new five-year plan aimed at providing a freer economy and more consumer goods and services. The plan depends totally on generous access to Western technology and on industrial cooperation with Western nations. Each one of these changes not only serves respective national interests, but each also further cements countries into economic zones that would be very painful and expensive to dismantle. With the zones in place, interdependence becomes a "sink or swim together" reality. Canada cannot escape the impact of a U.S. economic downturn; all of the EC would suffer if the new freedoms in Poland and Hungary were rescinded; and the Soviet five-year plan would disintegrate if the EC failed to unite and left the USSR with the unwieldy task of dealing with 12 separate nations, each with a unique set of trading conditions.

As a natural and logical consequence of increased integration, the respective zones will begin to see their economic well being in a broader perspective that abolishes any old national narrowness. Japan, for all its trade insensitivity, has not single-handedly caused U.S. trade woes, nor can it alone solve them. If Japan as a trade power disappeared today, any one or all of the Four Tigers could claw their way into the vacancy. Interestingly, during World War II, the Japanese enlisted the Koreans to run their prisoner of war camps because they believed that the Koreans were less sympathetic and understanding of anglo-culture than the Japanese. Therefore, the Koreans made effective wardens.

THE IDEAL TRIAD SPHERE

The exercise of triad competition will cause spheres of nations to shape into the most effective competitors. The program demands three key ingredients for success: technocenters, price-competitive production, and consumers. Each triad sphere, the Americas, Asia, and Europe, has already begun the work.

Technocenters. Each sphere needs a constant internal source of technological products and services that frees it from the need to negotiate for technology from another sphere. The technocenters for each sphere already exist: Japan for Asia, the United States for the Americas, and the EC for Europe. These three locations accounted for 85 percent of the roughly 11,000 patents registered in the world. Japan has earned its stripes with quick technological transference to consumer applications, while the United States has won distinction for creating breakthrough technology. Only the EC has yet to prove its full mettle in this arena.

Technological development constantly dangles like a carrot before the European countries supporting unification. A union of twelve nations working on coordinated technological applications can surely outpace any one country's efforts. The acceleration of political reforms throughout the Eastern Bloc will pressure the EC to take a more aggressive approach to research and development. American Secretary of Commerce Robert Mosbacher said in November, 1989, that the "most favored nation status may be granted to the Soviet Union within five months." This would pave the way for greater technological transfer from the United States to the USSR. The EC would like to avoid a situation of supporting the Eastern Bloc and the Soviet Union with low-tech development, such as construction and manufacturing, only to see the United States, or possibly Japan, profit from the more lucrative high-technological trade.

The vital role of the technocenter in a triad sphere will be to provide coordinating nations with the information and invention to manufacture and assemble technological products rather than spend scarce resources on duplicated efforts. The importance of sophisticated high-technological output in an increasingly technological world suggests that the nation functioning as the technocenter for a sphere will most likely dominate that sphere to some extent.

Price Competitive Production.   In a technocenter nation, labor costs invariably run high, with those nations holding the monopoly on patents also leading the world in labor costs. While these countries have traditionally passed on those costs to consumers, the flood of competitive products, and consequent declining prices, makes the global consumer wary of paying to support a developed nation's excessive labor costs. Ironically, while the Japanese were clobbering American steel and autos, the Koreans were preparing an unpleasant surprise for the Japanese. In 1990, the Tokyo newspapers were crying over Korea's dumping of steel on the Japanese market. The reasons boil down to the state of factory equipment and the cost of labor.

After World War II, the United States resumed industrial competition with Japan and West Germany. For the most part, the United States competed with technologies and equipment developed during the war and not updated by the time global competition hit full speed in the 1970s. Japan and West Germany, on the other hand, enjoyed the relative luxury of starting from scratch. Since not one viable industry was left standing in either country in 1945, they both could reconstruct themselves with the latest industrial machines and methods. At the peak of competition, the aging American industrial complex was struggling to hold its own against fast, young rivals from overseas. Having finally gotten the message, however, the United States increased factory automation 150 percent between 1980 and 1985. Computer-aided engineering went up 531 percent, and communications increased 146 percent. This type of investment must continue unabated if a triad sphere hopes to maintain its competitive position.

But even with increased automation, production still requires hoards of human labor. As that labor gets more expensive, countries, particularly technocenters, cannot avoid concentrating their domestic work force on technology and shifting mundane manufacturing operations offshore. This trend has already unfolded in Japan, where more Japanese technology-based consumer products are manufactured in Korea, Singapore, Taiwan, and Malaysia. Each triad sphere needs a source of relatively low-cost labor that can manufacture and assemble goods carrying competitive price tags. In the Asian sphere, the source of low-cost labor could well be China, where literally millions of workers, currently tied to the land, can be shifted to factories. To lower its production costs, the American sphere must look to Central and South America, while in the immediate future, the European sphere will continue to rely on southern Europe for its lower labor costs. In the long run, the Eastern European Bloc and the Soviet Union may fulfill that function.

Consumers. In 1990, a joke circulated among sausage shoppers in Poland: One store advertises sausage for $3.00 a pound, while just across the street, a competitor sells the same product for only $1.25 per pound. A confused shopper asks the store owner selling the lower-priced sausage how he can do that. The fellow replies, "When we have sausage, it's $3.00 a pound, but when we're out, we drop the price to $1.25. Right now we're out."

When demand exceeds supply, the seller calls the shots. In the triad-driven world, though, supply will exceed demand, giving consumers the upper hand. The sphere with the most buyers will win, because more domestic consumers means more products sold locally and less dependence on exporting to other spheres. Japan's 120 million consumers have reached the limit of their patience with high prices at home and the lack of less expensive imported alternatives. However, Japanese industry lacks the EC or American population siphon that can absorb development and production costs.

More local consumers means a bigger base over which to spread research and development costs, thus facilitating a quicker infusion of new products as consortia reach profit levels more quickly. McKinsey consultant Kenichi Ohmae calls the process "triadian depreciation." Simply put, if a product costs a company $100 to develop, would that company rather spread the costs over 120 buyers or 2,000? The population of France approaches 55 million. When the united EC becomes reality, French companies will enjoy unrestricted access to another 265 million European consumers with which to offset development and production costs.

Finally, Japan's economic miracle has taught the world that a strong, cutthroat "local" economic system provides the best training ground for offshore trade competition. One of the biggest obstacles to 1992 unification is the very real fear that each nation comprising the EC will incur its share of corporate casualties as the floodgates of competition open. Still, the possible short-term will eliminate the weak and permit the strong to consolidate and compete more effectively against other spheres in the global triad. As mentioned in Chapter 5, the Italians have lamented the vulnerability of their pasta industry to Dutch and German imports. However, an elite circle of protected Italian pasta companies cannot hope to compete with the Koreans, Japanese, and Chinese who will soon realize that the difference between pasta and ramen noodles is in the name, not the flour. Domestic consumers within a triad sphere offer good practice targets for consortia, hoping to fire off global cannons. If a company cannot cut the competition in Milan, it certainly will not survive in Manhattan.

THE THREE C'S

In 1985, 1.8 million Poles requested telephone service, but the government only installed 131,000 lines. When Poland's communist government fell in 1989, a New York investment banking firm immediately grasped the opportunity, shocking the newly elected Polish leaders by offering to finance 250,000 new telephone lines each year, for the next ten years (at a handsome profit, of course). Welcome to the new world power game.

In the opening chapters, we suggested that students of world change keep a sharp eye peeled for the forces of consumers, consortia, and capitalism, which together will make the old globe obsolete. Millions of Eastern Europeans enjoy unprecedented freedom, but still face empty shelves. Previously sleepy southern Europe has joined the race for consortia at a full spring, under the direction of relatively unknown global CEOs such as Fanjul, de Azevedo, and Bennedetti. While a member of a Soviet mountain-climbing team visiting America sighs that "Communism is the most arduous route between capitalism and capitalism," Mikhail Gorbachev asks for an invitation to the EC92 party. Unfortunately, holdouts of the old order may also pick up on the significance of these trends and their impact on the world in the next century. Two days after German Chancellor Helmut Kohl unveiled a recovery plan for East Germany, a terrorist bomb murdered Deutsche Bank Chairman Alfred Herrhausen while he drove to an important meeting. The Red Army Faction, long labeled a group of psychopaths, claimed credit for Herrhausen's death.

The Red Army Faction, like Cuba's Castro and Libya's Khadaffi, stand as icons of past tensions and differences. These are giving way to new tensions and new differences, equally deadly but revolving more around trade than tanks. Ironically, the assassination of Alfred Herrhausen represented nothing more than a desperate act of a revolutionary group mired in the old ways and unable to accept the new order. Herrhausen, as chairman of one of the world's largest banks, was on his way to discuss the financing of a united German industrial nation. This new country would ply its products to customers all over the world.

Herrhausen was the very symbol of a new world and its political and executive elite, wise to the ways of consumers, consortia, and capitalism.

EPILOGUE

If you cannot speak Eurospeak,
you are out of business.

Sign Prominently Displayed
in the Office of a
Congressional Sub-Committee

THE RIGHT TO CONSUME

When hordes, rather than individual escapees, breached the Berlin Wall in November 1989, three million East German citizens saw firsthand what their leaders had propagandized as the degeneracy of the West. Interestingly, the first taste of real freedom since the end of World War II did not find liberated East Germans crowding the churches or scouring the libraries for banned books. Instead, they invaded the merchants of West Berlin. They went shopping.

To some observers, calling consumption a human right may downgrade the historical and universal quest for freedom. More than 20 million Soviet citizens died during World War II keeping Germany off the sacred soil of the "motherland." There was certainly much more to their total sacrifice than a steady supply of soap or shampoo. But what is freedom if it is not tied to the quality of life? Freedom to queue hours for a few cups of rationed sugar is somehow less attractive than the same freedoms enjoyed by a society trying to keep its children's consumption of candy, cakes, and cookies down to less than 50 pounds per year. Amidst the drama and debate that surrounds the liberation of Eastern Europe is a raw demonstration of how important the abundant life is to the everyday citizens behind the headlines. News clips beamed around the world of East German shoppers going home teary-eyed over ownership of a single banana dispel all doubts that Eastern Europe is anxious to trade the label comrade for a new designation: consumer.

The decline of communism in Eastern Europe has eclipsed the rise of the EC into a world power but the overshadowing of one significant event by another is shortlived. The liberation of Eastern Europe has diverted attention from the EC as a jumble of directives, legal challenges, and bickering countries to the EC as savior and initiator of the biggest economic reconstruction since the Marshall Plan. And 1992 is still two years off.

While the President of the United States and the American Congress politic over $800 million in aid to Poland, France and

West Germany combine for over $3 billion in funding, just in the form of development loans. The total value of EC assistance directed toward Eastern Europe will dwarf that of the United States and Japan combined. Is this sudden surge of charity on the part of Europe? Not at all. The reconstruction of the communist failure into a capitalist industrial center is a bold move of pure competition.

The world is engaged in a trade war, and new markets, like beachheads, signal the direction of the invading armies. Jan Carlzon the future-minded CEO of Scandinavian Airlines, likens Eastern Europe to the Four Asian Tigers. Skilled eager labor, wages destined for stocked store shelves, and an attitude of catch-up will fuel the fires of competition in East Germany, Poland, Hungary, Yugoslavia, Romania, and Czechoslovakia. In 20 years, these countries may be trade-threatening the EC like South Korea and Taiwan now stalk Japan. The quest to conquer new markets of consumers draws attention to the makers and breakers of the 1990s.

MAKERS AND BREAKERS

The makers are those countries or international alliances that have the power and economic reserves to transform new markets into trade powerhouses. The United States, Japan, and the EC are the elite in this category. Like IBM, these nations do not necessarily need to be the first in the market. IBM did not actually start the personal computer revolution. Rather, the strategy is to expand the market and then conquer, hoping, again like IBM, that they will emerge with the largest chunk of market share. For the time being, the EC is the leader in the redevelopment of Eastern Europe, but the United States and Japan will not be lagging far behind.

Breakers are those nations that have desperate needs and desires to play in the game of world trade, but cannot do so without help, particularly in the form of technology and capital. Besides Eastern Europe, add India, South America, Africa, and lesser-known Asian competitors like Thailand. The current economic vulnerability of these countries downplay the future trump that they hold over the makers. India is the most-populated democracy in the world. What would happen if India threw its trade weight in the direction of one or two makers, rather than all three? Distancing a maker from consumer markets in the 21st century is the equivalent of cutting a country off from natural resources in the 20th century. Japan went to war in anticipation of that kind of isolation. In a very real sense, developing countries will have the ability to break a maker's hold on the world market. However, in a trade war, countries cannot invade those that choose to see things differently.

Whatever the vocabulary, a discussion of breakers points positively to the Soviet Union and China. Both have massive populations of suppressed consumers, both hunger for developing technology and money, and both have a history of relishing the role of breaker. Either one of these lower-developed countries (in a trade sense) could swing the balance of trade power from one region of the world to another. If China formed closer economic ties with the United States and the EC than with Japan, 1.1 billion consumers could be snacking on Big Macs and Perrier rather than sushi. On the other hand, if Gorbachev swings Soviet friendship in the direction of Japan rather than Europe, EC trade expansion could end on the borders of Eastern Europe, a trade border carefully controlled by Russian customs officers riding in Toyotas and jotting notes in hand-held Toshiba computers.

The neighborhood is definitely changing. Some of the internal and external challenges that confront its three most prosperous citizens, the United States, Japan, and, of course, the EC, have been discussed. But there are new faces on the block and each publicly wants a seat on the city council. Privately, each wants to *be* the city council. How the neighborhood grows is in the hands of national and business leaders, who, if the fall of the

Berlin Wall is an indicator, will have a lot of change and little time to seek the details.

DECISION POINT: 1990

In Japan, Prime Minister Toshiki Kaifu and his party, the Liberal Democrats, must undergo ratification by the nation's voters. The Liberal Democrats have enjoyed 34 years of uninterrupted power, which they have used to fuel the business-dominated export machine. Much like the Republican Party in the United States, the Liberal Democrats are pro-business and favor a continuation of current Japanese trade policies. The major opposition comes from the Socialist party and its leader, Takako Doi. She hopes to put together a coalition of opposition parties to oust the Liberal Democrats and shift some focus to domestic issues and the consumer burdens heaped on the Japanese over the last 30 years. A Liberal Democrat victory means more of the same, perhaps with more enthusiasm. The Democrats would come away with a vote of citizens confident in their vision and methodology. Success by Doi and the Socialists signals a change in the current trade policy to exchange the vision of international dominance for one of mere world leadership that would make domestic life more abundant and less expensive. When the decade ended, one poll showed 41 percent favoring a change, 37 percent in favor of the Liberal Democrats, and the balance undecided.

Confronting the United States is Trade Bill 301, which can be either a polite warning or an outright declaration of war against those nations that are perceived by the United States to trade unfairly. The trade equivalent of a visa, the bill can declare products from offending countries as "persona non grata," or simply not welcome on American shores. The bill is law, but the interpretation of the law is up to the Bush Administration. The challenge of 1990 is to determine if the bill should be long on bark, but short on bite; a verbal warning that stops short of blocking products. The alternative interpretation is to bear some teeth and begin cutting off the U.S. market from offshore competition. While the bill is international in scope, Brazil being one of the listed offending nations, it is no secret that Japan and the Four Tigers have the honor of inspiring the legislation. A bark means a few more years before trade war escalates into a "hot landing zone." A bite, on the other hand, means the gloves are off and the hostilities have begun.

Finally, as it approaches 1992, the EC must decide whether it is constructing a twelve-nation theme park focused on trade, or whether it is going to exit 1992 as a global powerhouse. Relaxed borders and reduced tariffs do not make a trading champion. They simply make it easier to buy a German beer in Paris and Dutch pasta in Rome. Real trade power means reciprocal trade, common currency, and a central bank to back it all up. At a 1989 EC summit in Madrid, eleven of the twelve EC members came out in favor of all three. The lone holdout was the United Kingdom, led by Prime Minister Margaret Thatcher. For those that favor the EC as a global powerhouse, the summit was encouraging. But British hesitancy should not be underestimated. Former West German Chancellor Helmut Schmidt, in humble self-depreciation, admits that "there is only one man in Europe: Margaret Thatcher." Unfortunately, adds Schmidt, "She is not interested in Europe." The face-off between the EC and its lone dissenter may have solved itself with the crash of the Berlin Wall and the liberation of Eastern Europe. Britain's reluctance to enhance the EC is partially motivated by its desire to be a European co-power with West Germany. A common currency and central bank is viewed by Thatcher as a gift to West German influence and power. Both issues are likely to revolve around the strength of the Deutschmark. What the United Kingdom did not count on, prior to 1992, was the unification of Germany. The resulting economic reconstruction of Eastern Europe will favor the new Germany, just in terms of pure geography. Germany shares borders with more countries than does the Soviet Union and sits right in the center of Western Europe and the former communist empire of Eastern Europe and the USSR. If Britain were successful in convincing the EC to remain aloof of a common currency and central bank (which is favored by West Germany), then Germany may bypass the EC altogether and form their own alliances in Eastern Europe. Either way, West Germany will have the edge.

Common currency and central banking will probably not take effect until the mid-1990s. However, the agendas structuring the decisions leading to both realities will be formulated and discussed in 1990.

Also in 1990, all the makers and breakers in the neighborhood face scores of critical choices. These may not make the international front page. But the three just mentioned are indicators, serving advance warning that the trade war for triad power has begun.

A FAREWELL TO ARMS

Ending a book is not usually a trying task. However, in a world environment where the events of a single day can make 100 books obsolete, authors are a bit more reluctant. While we have indulged in the playful speculation that swords will be beaten into calculators, and trade war will be the first line of defense, there are political policymakers and consortia executives sincerely trying to lay the best plans for the future. To help in the quest for sound global strategy, we have tried to provide clues that nestle midway between the trivia of fast food and the trauma of toppled governments. We do not aspire or pretend to have exhaustive documentation. There are talented academics in the quest for the holy grail of tenure who can fill in the gaps of information. This can then be digested by legions of political staff and consortia administrative types before it migrates to the peak of the decision pyramid. But where the decisions are actually made, direction, not detail, is paramount. The right direction linked with even misleading information can be adjusted with time—much like making the wrong turn in the right neighborhood. In contrast, making the right turn in the wrong neighborhood can result in circling aimlessly for years, seeking the right street, in a region where that particular street does not even exist.

Author George Orwell in 1984 warned that technology would be the warden in a world deprived of freedom. Orwell was wrong. Technology and the information it processes has become a messiah, providing oppressed societies with a glimpse of global possibilities and the desire to join the game. We add our small contribution to the explosion of information that will soon compete for the mind and attention of those people who risk their careers, corporations, and countries on making sense of the new neighborhood. We also add a tribute in recognition of those who bear the mantle of decision:

"Those who can, do. Those who can't, write books."

Author Unknown

BIBLIOGRAPHY

Books That Have Influenced
Our Thinking and Writing

Aganbegyan, Abel. *Inside Perestroika*. New York: Harper & Row Publishers, 1989.

Bloom, Allan. *The Closing of the American Mind*. New York: Simon and Schuster, 1987.

Brown, Lester R. *State of the World*. New York: W.W. Norton & Company, 1988.

Brzezinski, Zbrigniew. *The Grand Failure*. New York: Charles Scribner's Sons, 1989.

Butterfield, Fox. *China*. New York: Bantam Books, 1983.

Cappo, Joe. *Future Scope*. Chicago: Longman Financial Services Publishing, 1990.

Cetron, Marvin and Owen Davies. *American Renaissance*. New York: St Martin's Press, 1989.

Drucker, Peter. *The New Realities*. New York: Harper & Row Publishers, 1989.

Dynes, Michael and Richard Owen. *The Times Guide to 1992*. London: Times Books, 1989.

Emmott, Bill. *The Sun Also Sets*. New York: Random House, 1989.

Fallows, James. *More Like Us*. Boston: Houghton Mifflin Company, 1989.

Gorbachev, Mikhail. *Perestroika.* New York: Harper & Row Publishers, 1987.

Halberstam, David. *The Reckoning.* New York: William Morrow and Company, Inc., 1986.

Johnson, Paul. *Modern Times.* New York: Harper & Row, 1983.

Kennedy, Paul. *The Rise and Fall of the Great Powers.* New York: Random House, 1987.

Kiplinger, Austin H. and Knight A. Kiplinger. *America in the Global '90s.* Washington, DC: Kiplinger Books, 1989.

Kishimoto, Yoriki and Joel Kotkin. *The Third Century.* New York: Crown Publishers, Inc., 1988.

Levin, Doron. *Irreconcilable Differences.* Boston: Little, Brown and Company, 1989.

Malabre, Alfred, Jr. *Beyond Our Means.* New York: Random House, 1987.

McKenna, Regis. *Who's Afraid of Big Blue?* New York: Addison-Wesley Publishing Company, Inc., 1989.

McKinsey & Company. *Japan Business.* New York: John Wiley & Sons, 1983.

Mitsubishi Corporation. *Tatemae and Honne.* New York: The Free Press, 1988.

Ohmae, Kenichi. *Beyond National Borders.* Homewood, Illinois: Dow Jones-Irwin, 1987.

Pauli, Gunter A. and Richard W. Wright. *The Second Wave.* New York: St. Martin's Press, 1987.

Roscow, Jerome. *The Global Market Place.* New York: Facts On File, 1988.

Schlesinger, Arthur M., Jr. *The Cycles of American History.* Boston: Houghton Mifflin Company, 1986.

World Almanac. *The World Almanac 1990.* New York: Pharos Books, 1990.

Wurman, Richard Saul. *Information Anxiety.* New York: Doubleday, 1989.

INDEX

Taxes: value added (VAT), 17–18, 133–35

Technology, 227–45; advances in, 23–24; integrated, 24–25; and culture, 25–26; and design, 26–27; military, 27; growth of, 31, 115–17, 233–42; and the Soviet Union, 41–42; and China, 42; rate and range of change, 66; and Japan, 66; and the United States, 67; and Europe, 67; change and communism, 84; and computers, 232–33; and military spending, 234–35; and space exploration, 235–37; consumer, 238–39; and consortia, 239–41; and expanding markets, 241–42; and maintenance of trade advantages, 242–45

Thatcher, Margaret, 18, 19, 95, 102, 108, 142–43, 215, 289; views on German unification, 251. *See also* United Kingdom

Tiananmen Square, 3, 256, 274

Tigers, Asian (South Korea, Singapore, Taiwan, Hong Kong), 27–28, 36, 81, 118, 265, 273, 275, 286, 289

Toffler, Alvin and Heidi, 230

Tonegawa, Susumu, 197–98

Trade: international, 36–39; reciprocity, 46–50, 64; United States and Japanese fear of restricted, 109–11; the EC and global, 136–46; between the West and Japan, 176–78; use of technology to maintain advantages in, 242–45; wars, 247–81; wars, 253–64; and triad economics, 267–68

Trade Bill 301, 288

Treaty of Rome, 130

Trevi Process, 128–29

Triad economics. *See* Economics, triad

Triad spheres. *See* Spheres, triad

Triad strategy. *See* Strategy, triad

Unification (of Europe): spirit of, 1; tariffs and, 16–17; value added taxes and, 17–18; currency and, 18–20; languages and, 20, 21–22; work habits and, 20; effects of World War II on, 20–21, 126–27; mechanics of, 31; and consumption, 51–52; differences from historical precedent, 101–2; as a populist revolution, 102–6; and population, 104; as an organic revolution, 106–8; effects on different countries, 106; American and Japanese fears of, 109–11; changes in spheres of influence affecting, 117–20; inevitability of, 121; outcomes of, 123–27; and foreign policy, 146–48; military, 148–50; Japanese fear of, 153–54

Unification (of Germany), 250–51, 269, 289

United Kingdom, 47, 67, 70, 103, 129, 131, 141, 218, 221–22, 223, 237, 270, 289–90; television in, 11; value added tax in, 18; con-